TOWARDS BELONGING

Tavistock Clinic Series

Margot Waddell (Series Editor)

Recent titles in the Tavistock Clinic Series
(for a full listing, please visit www.karnacbooks.com)

TOWARDS BELONGING

Negotiating New Relationships
for Adopted Children
and Those in Care

Edited by

Andrew Briggs

Foreword by

John Simmonds

KARNAC

First published in 2015 by
Karnac Books
118 Finchley Road
London NW3 5HT

British Library Cataloguing in Publication Data

A C.I.P. for this book is available from the British Library

ISBN: 978–1–78220–324–7

Edited, designed, and produced by Communication Crafts

Printed in Great Britain

www.karnacbooks.com

CONTENTS

SERIES EDITOR'S PREFACE

Margot Waddell

Since it was founded in 1920, the Tavistock Clinic has developed a wide range of developmental approaches to mental health which have been strongly influenced by the ideas of psychoanalysis. It has also adopted systemic family therapy as a theoretical model and a clinical approach to family problems. The Clinic is now the largest training institution in Britain for mental health, providing postgraduate and qualifying courses in social work, psychology, psychiatry, and child, adolescent, and adult psychotherapy, as well as in nursing and primary care. It trains about 1,700 students each year in over 60 courses.

The Clinic's philosophy aims at promoting therapeutic methods in mental health. Its work is based on the clinical expertise that is also the basis of its consultancy and research activities. The aim of this Series is to make available to the reading public the clinical, theoretical, and research work that is most influential at the Tavistock Clinic. The Series sets out new approaches in the understanding and treatment of psychological disturbance in children, adolescents, and adults, both as individuals and in families.

It has been a particular joy to work with Andrew Briggs, the editor of this latest volume in our long-standing Tavistock Clinic

Series. That is, a joy for many reasons for me to be Series Editor, but, perhaps especially, for the depth of thought, expertise, and experience that all the chosen contributors bring to what Briggs quite rightly calls "this deep and troubling field"—that of working with fostered and adopted children. The authors are from a range of background disciplines, and all draw on many years of working as professionals in a variety of settings with such inevitably vulnerable children and adolescents. All share something of fundamental importance: awareness of and insight into the poignant and elusive nature of what is called here, subtly and rightly, "a sense of belonging" and the impact of the presence or absence of that sense on the nature of a child's hopes, fears, and aspirations for the future.

The sense of belonging is a very potent concept in itself, one that is beautifully and extensively explored in this volume. The line-up of contributors is, indeed, impressive—impressive especially for the length and depth of their involvement in and commitment to this area of work. The chapter titles speak for themselves, perhaps particularly and unusually a chapter on "The Smell of Belonging": this is a truly original contribution to the field. Yet each of the other chapters also has a particularly deep and innovative perspective to offer: for example, "The Journey from Fear and Shame to Love and Belonging"; "From Owning to Belonging"; "Belonging Inside: A Child in Search of Herself".

Such chapter titles attest to the impressive depth that all the contributing authors have not so much "plumbed"—for this is an ongoing process from which we are learning all the time—as engaged with in so vivid, moving, and innovative a way. This is an area of work with disturbed children and adolescents that badly needs to be more widely understood. *Towards Belonging*—painful, moving, and deeply informed as it is—goes a very long way towards realizing the shared learning of all involved to make available something of the professional and personal experience that is owed to all such children.

The Tavistock Clinic has been involved for some years in work with, and writing about, this neglected area of plight—a plight that affects not just fostered and adopted young people and those in care. The efforts of the late Hamish Canham, who was a significant inspiration in this area, focused on the nature and massive dimensions of the plight for all involved: foster parents, adoptive parents, schools, communities, police, social workers, therapists. We read accounts daily in the newspapers of the failures of the system. This book, embracing as it does both therapy and social care, is impressive in its balance, range, and courage in trying to carry so essential a tradition further forward.

ACKNOWLEDGEMENTS

Clinicians have long recognized that patients' emotional well-being and mental health are largely dependent upon their sense of belonging. Nevertheless, this obviously very important observation has received little attention in the academic or clinical literature. There has therefore been very little exploration of the concept and reality of belonging. For this reason, this book has a deliberately wide disciplinary focus. This is to ensure that what is a deep and troubling field is at least covered by enough thought, so as to bring out salient issues in the relationship between emotional well-being, mental health, and belonging for these children.

The authors all bring to the field many years of experience working with these children in individual psychotherapy, systemic psychotherapy, residential care, and social work. In addition, the reader will find examples of consultation to organizations providing care to these children. For each author, the aim is to assess whether it is possible for children and young people so uprooted from their biological origins to develop a sense of belonging to their new environments. If so, how do they do this, and how much is it part of their success in their new lives? If not, why not, and how much does this lack of a sense of belonging contribute to the way their lives develop?

All of us working in children's mental health are aware that each child or young person we see leaves us with a great deal to think about. The children in care or adopted that I have seen over the last twenty five years shaped my determination to one day put together a book that attempts to give them a voice for one vital aspect of their struggle to develop. Along with the colleagues and my clinical supervisors who have given me so much, this book would not have been possible without these children and young people. I continue to learn copiously through working with them, and for this they have my gratitude. I would also like to thank all the contributors to the book. They faced with collaborative determination my editing their drafts, as they all wanted to get across their ideas in the interests of raising the profile of belonging for these children. Finally, I would like to thank Margot Waddell who, as Series Editor, has provided enormous good feeling and encouragement for this book.

ABOUT THE EDITOR AND CONTRIBUTORS

Sara Barratt is a consultant systemic psychotherapist and team manager of the fostering, adoption, and kinship care team at the Tavistock and Portman NHS Trust, where she also teaches on the Masters qualifying training and the systemic supervision course. She has worked for most of her career both as a social worker and a systemic psychotherapist with looked after and adopted children, those in kinship care, and their families, She also works as a psychotherapist in general practice and consults to social service teams and individual practitioners. Her publications include: *Positions and Polarities in Contemporary Systemic Practice: The Legacy of David Campbell* (2012), co-edited with C. Burck and E. Kavner; "Adopted Children and Education: The Experiences of a Specialist CAMHS Team" (*Journal of Clinical Child Psychology and Psychiatry*, 2012); and "Kinship Care: Family Stories, Loyalties and Binds" (in *Creating New Families*, ed. J. Kenrick, C. Lindsey, & L. Tollemache, 2006), co-written with J. Granville.

Andrew Briggs is a consultant child and adolescent psychotherapist and an organizational consultant with many years' experience working with senior managers and teams within public sector and not-for-profit organizations delivering services to adopted children and children in care. He is Head of Child and Adolescent Psychotherapy at the Sussex Partnership NHS Foundation Trust and a visiting lecturer at the Tavistock and Portman NHS Foundation Trust for courses on public sector leadership and management. He was previously a Teaching Fellow in the Centre for Psychoanalytic Studies at the University of Essex and Honorary Senior Lecturer in the Kent Institute for Medical and Health Studies, University of Kent. He has published several papers on aspects of child and adolescent psychotherapy and is the editor of two books in the Tavistock Clinic Series: *Surviving Space: Papers on Infant Observation* (2002) and *Waiting to Be Found: Papers on Children in Care* (2012).

John Diamond is CEO of the Mulberry Bush Organisation. His working career has been in residential therapeutic work with children and young people. He has published papers and has lectured in the UK and internationally on this work. He is chair of the National Association of Special Schools, on the editorial board of the *International Journal of Therapeutic Communities*, and a member of the Therapeutic Communities Accreditation Panel at the Royal College of Psychiatrists. He has trained in group work at the Institute of Group Analysis and the Tavistock Clinic and with OPUS and has an MA in therapeutic child care and in psychoanalytic approaches to consultation and the organization.

John Hills qualified as a family therapist at the Tavistock Clinic in 1984 and was tutor and lecturer on the Diploma in Applied Systemic Theory there from 1989 until 2008. He was previously a social worker probation officer in Kent. He co-founded and edited *Context*, the therapy publication of the Association for Family Therapy (AFT), from 1989 to 2007. From 1981 to 2013 he was a member of the AFT board and executive, including a time serving as a Vice-Chair. He has worked part-time for the NHS as a systemic psychotherapist in CAMHS and in adult psychotherapy. From 1990 to the present he has provided systemic psychotherapy consultation to an independent child care service. He has written numerous articles and papers on systemic thought, existential psychotherapy, and mental illness and has led experiential workshops on these themes. His most recent publication is *An Introduction to Systemic and Family Therapy: A Users Guide* (2013). He edited *Rescripting Family Experiences: The Therapeutic Influence of John Byng-Hall* (2002), a tribute work about the systemic psychotherapy training at the Tavistock Clinic. He is a member of the Society for Existential Analysis and a practicing Quaker.

Lesley Maroni trained as a child and adolescent psychotherapist at the Tavistock Clinic. She worked for many years in the Families Unit at the Cassel Hospital, carrying out parenting assessments for the courts and appearing as an expert witness. Currently she is Principal Child and Adolescent Psychotherapist at North Buckinghamshire CAMHS. She has lectured and written widely, especially on the emotional impact on a child when a parent does not have the capacity to care for the child. She is author of *Understanding 4–5-Year-Olds* (2007), which is part of the Tavistock Clinic's Understanding Your Child Series.

Richard Rollinson is Director of The Planned Environment Therapy Trust and an independent consultant in the fields of therapeutic child care, education, and mental health across the voluntary, statutory, and private sectors. He qualified as a social worker with an MSc from Oxford University in 1983, following the then Part 1 Training in Child Psychotherapy at the Tavistock Centre. In 2005 he completed the Ashridge MA and training in Organisational Consulting. He has been Chairman of the Charterhouse Group of Therapeutic Communities and is the Chairman of the Care Leavers' Foundation. Recently he became Chair of Trustees at the Mulberry Bush. He has a long association with residential therapeutic communities, having worked at the Mulberry Bush for over 20 years, including being its Director from 1991 to 2001. He was also Director at the Peper Harow Foundation from 2001 to 2005. In recent years, he has been working with the Department of Social Welfare in Portugal to support the development of therapeutic high-support residential communities across the country. He has published numerous articles and continues to lecture widely across the UK and Europe. His more recent publications include: "Society and the Antisocial Tendency: 'Physician, Heal Thyself'" (in *Broken*

Bounds: Contemporary Reflections on the Antisocial Tendency, ed. C. Reeves, 2012); "Failing Better in Our Work with Children and Their Families" (*Journal of the Portuguese Association of Child and Adolescent Psychiatrists*, 2009); and *Group Supervision: The Route to the Heart of the Matter in Residential* (National Children Bureau, 2006).

Jenny Sprince trained as a child and adolescent psychotherapist and psychodynamic organizational consultant at the Tavistock Clinic. She has worked in a variety of settings with children and their carers, including CAMHS teams, social services departments, special schools, fostering agencies, children's homes, and therapeutic communities. She is Clinical Director of Placement Support, a small company offering therapeutic interventions for looked after and adopted children, their families and their carers, and the professional networks that surround them. She contributed as expert witness on consultancy to the LAC NICE Committee in drawing up guidelines for the care of looked after children. She has published numerous papers on child psychotherapy and organizational work, including: "Joining Families: The Adopted Child, the Internal Group, and the Process of Assimilation" (*Funzione Gamma*, 2013); "Working with Complex Cases" (*NICE Public Health Guideline 28*, 2011); and "Developing Containment: Psychoanalytic Consultancy to a Therapeutic Community for Traumatised Children" (*Journal of Child Psychotherapy*, 2002)

Jim Walker is a psychoanalytic psychotherapist and retired social worker. He has many years' experience in child protection work and a particular interest in attachment theory. His publications include: "The Child as a Transference Object" (*Journal of Social Work Practice*, 1992); "Unresolved Loss and Trauma in Parents and the Implications in terms of Child Protection" (*Journal of Social Work Practice*, 2007); and "The Relevance of the Concept of Dissociation in Child Protection" (*Journal of Social Work Practice*, 2009).

Becky Wylde is a senior child and adolescent psychotherapist who trained at the Birmingham Trust for Psychoanalytic Psychotherapy (BTPP). She worked for several years in a specialist mental health service for looked after children. Along with colleagues there, she developed an early intervention service for infants coming into care and their carers. She teaches Infant Observation for the West Midlands Institute of Psychotherapy for adult psychotherapy trainees and has taught young child observation in Birmingham for the BTPP. She is also the clinical lead at NorPIP, a charity offering parent–infant psychotherapy as an early intervention treatment.

PREFACE

However we think about emotional well-being and mental health, whichever clinical and theoretical perspective we use to understand our observations of ourselves and others, it is unlikely that we can escape the realization that these states are dependent on a person's sense of belonging. Emotional well-being and mental health—core aspects of the way we function as individuals—are both dependent on and determine our sense of belonging to our society, community, peer group, family, and more intimate relationships. It is therefore surprising that so very little has been written about belonging, which is such a central component of human emotional and psycho-social being.

This book, however, is inspired not so much by the need to fill this lacuna as it is by the need to bring to an interested readership's attention the difficult situation of children who are in care or have been adopted.[1] These children are some of the most vulnerable in societies across the world, and not simply because they have been removed from their biological parents as a consequence of various abuses and neglect, along with other profound indications of the inability of their parents to care for and keep them safe. For some children, these experiences are part of their sense of belonging to the world from which they were removed by the State. For others, these traumas leave them unable to feel belonged to *by* their new environments, despite the carers in this environment wanting to feel that these children can have some sense of belonging to them. For yet others, they simply cannot feel that they can allow themselves to belong to it. This book is an examination of this very difficult situation both for those who are removed from a world they belong to and for those who have never felt they belonged to the world of their biological parents. It takes in the child's and young person's view,[2] and also that of their new adoptive or fostering families.

Exploring a sense of belonging brings into focus a number of crucial key aspects of the emotional life of children, whether in care or adopted. Recognized by mental health professionals as fundamental to both the maintenance of an individual's mental health and the recovery from mental ill health, understanding the components of their sense of belonging helps us to then understand the state of these children's mental health. For all children, a sound sense of belonging is a prerequisite for their psycho-social development. Mental health is one outcome of this and is seen as fundamental to educational success and, thus, to the acquisition of competitive life-chances. This was made clear for children in care by a government policy document, *Care Matters* (DfES, 2006, 2007). In this, a relationship was shown to exist between low educational attainment, placement instability, and poor emotional well-being and mental health for the child.

This book's overall task is to explore what a sense of belonging—its components and state—means for these children and therefore to contribute to our understanding of their emotional well-being, mental health, and potential for success in life through education and beyond.

As a sense of belonging is so important for mental health, it is imperative that we understand how such a sense can be achieved by these children. However, because of the complexity of their damaging experiences before coming into the care system, it is apparent that no clear answer exists to questions such as, do these children feel a sense of belonging to their new parents and families, or do they not? The chapters in this book all demonstrate that the child's complex past presenting through his or her current behaviour and thinking results in clinicians and others finding it very difficult to assess for and answer either question. What the contributors to this book present us with is a range of ways children attempt to keep themselves emotionally safe in the circumstances after being removed from their biological families. For some, there is an attempt to attach to their new settings as helpful; for others, there is not. Within this latter group there are those who seem to find a sense of belonging only to themselves. For all, belonging is best understood as an achievement arrived at through a process towards which the sense of belonging is either reached or not.

Despite mental health practitioners and others long recognizing the fundamental importance of a sense of belonging to individual development, it is under-utilized in empirical research for both adult and child populations. As a theoretical concept, belonging has yet to attain the same usage as other similarly relationship-based concepts such as attachment. Perhaps because so little has been written about its conceptualization and clinical application, belonging has not been used as an explicit concept around which to organize training for psychotherapists or the continued professional development of other disciplines. It is hoped that the chapters in this book might stimulate interest in the various complex issues associated with a sense of belonging and lead to research on this very important concept in our way of understanding adopted children and those in care.

These children have been removed from their biological parents and families because these parents were not able to meet the children's emotional, physical, and/or psycho-social needs. The act of removal invariably adds to their existing catalogue of trauma, as separation from those they are biologically related and attached to represents a severe and primitive loss. Often this loss is felt by children as a terrible tearing through their very being, leaving them feeling profoundly and painfully severed from those they were until then growing up with. At the moment of entering the care system, the only significant adults so many of these children have are the social worker who removed them and their nursery or school teachers. In the next instant, they meet their foster carers, with whom they are expected to live as part of the family. Whether they are able to recognize this or not, given all that is so rapidly occurring in their emotional lives, at this moment they have the complement of adults tasked with their care.

These adults, some so new and unknown to them, are each tasked with being their parent. Although each has a different role with the child, each is part of the collective parent. So, within a very short space of time (usually only hours), the child moves from being with a parent or two parents he knows to a collective of at least four adults whom he knows either partially or not at all.[3] While this transition from known to mainly unknown parenting is very complicated to successfully achieve for all involved, for the child this process is compounded by the construction and size of the new parent system. Furthermore, whether from a single-parent household or not, suddenly the child is confronted by the moment of feeling that the expectation is to belong to a collective parent while he still feels he belongs to the biological real parent(s). This collective parent is enshrined in law as the corporate parent.

The corporate parent was created as part of the driver for improving the life-chance outcomes for children in care. In *Care Matters*, the key component for this parent's approach to its task is that when a child is taken into State care, all those working for the State "should demand no less for each child in care than they would for their own children" (DfES, 2006, p. 31). The idea that decisions about children should be made together by members of the corporate parent, and in a joined-up way of thinking about the needs of the particular child, came about as a response to the poor life chances of children in care. In order to improve the link between low educational attainment, low school attendance, and unstable foster placements, the corporate-parent approach aims at reducing placement instability and thus the frequency and number of placement breakdowns for children. That this has proved effective can be in little doubt if we consider education-outcome statistics. In 1997, the DfES reported that only 25% of care leavers had any academic qualification, with 50% unemployed. Between 1997 and 2004, placement stability was promoted through a prototype of corporate parenting. In 2005, the DfES reported an improvement. In 1999, 34% of care leavers had qualifications, and by 2005 this had risen to 50%.

With such improvement predicated upon placement stability, it seems that a book about belonging may make a timely contribution to understanding the emotional lives of children and the relationship of this to improved life chances. In order to make such a contribution, this book bases its perspective on the experiences of children whether in foster or residential home care or adopted. It attempts to examine and understand what makes up a sense of belonging for these children, how much they can be expected to feel this sense, and how it is influenced by their experiences both of being taken into care and of what they receive from the corporate parent. In this way, the book overall seeks to identify what more might be done to help children achieve better life-chances outcomes through our better understanding how meaningful belonging is to them and in our explaining their emotional well-being and mental health.

Many adopted children and those in care are referred to child and adolescent mental health services because their behaviour suggests to the referrer that they are not attaching to the foster parent(s). Some referrals arrive in these services with elaborate descriptions of observed behaviour and the unwritten hope that some form of attachment therapy focusing solely on the behaviour will settle the child, and thus not put the child's placement at risk of breaking down. Between the lines of these referrals one can also see the referrer's merging together attachment and belonging. Hence, by hoping for attachment, the referrer is hoping for behaviour that makes the corporate parent feel that the child feels he belongs to it. In the opinion of the contributors to this book, this focus on the child's behaviour without contextualizing it within the processes and structures that the child is within is mis-focusing, and for two basic and related reasons. The first is that the structure of the corporate parent makes it a rather remote entity to attach to, even if the transitioning child were in the right frame of mind so to do. The second is the focus on behaviour alone. Without trying to understand the emotional world of the child in the context of removal and being suddenly presented with the expectation of attachment/ belonging to a stranger, one risks overlooking the implications for the child and the behaviour of the corporate parent as a systemic entity with its own specific remit.

As understood by the contributors to this book, a sense of belonging is an experience gained from being in a relationship. For the children concerned here, belonging to a corporate parent may be a difficult thing to get a sense of and from. Similarly, it may be very difficult for any one member of that parent, or the collective itself, to feel a sense of belonging to the child, and belonged to by the child. If this is the case, then it is a very appropriate thought to wonder whether mental health is compromised for both the child and the member(s) of the corporate parent. This question is also pertinent because, as mentioned earlier, the previous government saw stable foster placements as central to its aim of increasing the life chances of children in care, and the current (April 2014) government recognizes that the relationship between carer(s) and child is fundamental to adoptions not breaking down. In both cases, stability of placement (or adoption) is seen to rest upon the emotional well-being or mental health of the child. For most practitioners in the adoption and fostering fields, a placement's instability—and thus its stability—is seen as determined by relationships within it.

If for a moment we say that belonging is about feeling included in something one wants to be included by, then we can begin to see that from the children's point of view the experience of removal, and then placement with strangers, does not suggest a good start to their journey through the care system. Indeed, it might well be described as a fault line that needs to be crossed over by each child in order to become part of the new family and parenting arrangement. This fault line is as much internal as it is represented by the structuring of the process of transition, starting with removal and almost immediately being in the home of strangers. For many removed children, the fault line between biological family life and placement family is internally felt as an exclusionary experience: they are now simultaneously prevented from being in a parenting relationship with their biological families and have no history of being parented by the carers they are placed with. This sense of exclusion, profoundly felt by so many, is not made easier by the corporate parent's expectation for these children.

If we take as a basic principle of attachment that the infant seeks the satisfaction of her basic survival needs through attaching to one parent (the primary caregiver), then the assumption of attachment to anyone other than this person seems counterintuitive. In the case of children in care or who are adopted, however, the assumption is that they will attach to a second parent, one who is outside their biological family. However, the structural disconnection with the biological family is more extended. The child is expected to attach to an unrelated person corporately allocated as her replacement primary caregiver. It would be very difficult to imagine that in the first instance this stranger is not compared unfavourably with the original parent, regardless of whether that parent was abusive, neglectful, or otherwise unable to meet the child's needs. As it stands, whether one is focusing upon attachment or has in mind the idea of an attachment/belonging merger, the aspiration for placement stability may be seriously compromised while the psycho-social focus is not widened to include the construction and practice of the corporate parent around the child.

Among many other things, child psychotherapists are trained to discover the feelings and wishes of children. This is only possible if one enters a relationship with a child in which the child can achieve a level of trust sufficient to feel able to let the psychotherapist know what he is feeling and wishing for. The chapters in this book, although not all written by child psychotherapists, give us some insight into how children feel about themselves and others, and what they want from the system of adults around them. What we learn from the contributors is that a sense of belonging to those outside themselves—such a central part of a sense of self—is very difficult to achieve for so many children who are adopted or remain in the care system. What we see in all the chapters is evidence of just how important a sense of belonging is, and how it is struggled with by these children for reasons to do with them and to do with the parenting system in which they find themselves.

Note

1. In order to limit the task of attempting to understand the complexity of a sense of belonging for these children, the book will not include particular discussions of children in kinship care or special guardianship, as these children are placed within their own families. There are different basic issues between adopted children and those in care. Most obviously, children in care do not usually enter foster families with the expectation of permanence that adopted children may have been encouraged to hold.

2. The terms children or child will be used as shorthand to include young people of all ages from birth to 18 years.

3. Throughout, where the discussion applies to children in general, either masculine or feminine pronouns may be used.

FOREWORD

John Simmonds

For any individual, the experience of belonging is profound in its meaning and consequences. It provides a sense of security, identity, connectedness, and continuity. It is commonly associated with relationships, the people we are connected to. "To belong" for many people will mean "family", in the way that family builds, supports, sustains, and resources its members. Indeed, without the commitment and determination of parental figures to draw a newly born baby into the family from day one, the baby would not survive. The baby's dependency on the parent(s) and usually the wider family is absolute, and over time that creates that powerful sense of "being a part of" and "being connected to"—the fundamental dynamic for the child's sense of belonging. But the personal and the familial are not the end of the story. Culture, religion, language, and tradition; ideas, beliefs, and objects; art, music, sport, and ceremony—all these play an important part in the experience of belonging as well. They *symbolize* the meaning in our lives

John Simmonds is Director for Policy Research and Development at the British Association for Adoption & Fostering (BAAF). He was recently awarded the Order of the British Empire (OBE) for services to children and families.

and our connection to others. They allow us to rejoice, to celebrate, to be in awe, and to be humble.

On the other side, it is important to acknowledge that we will defend ourselves as individuals and as a family if we feel that we are being threatened. Our skills and knowledge in doing this well will be a part of our survival strategy. We will also defend our culture, religion, language, and tradition if we sense that they are being threatened, in the same way that we will defend family. Our membership of and sense of belonging in groups will play a significant part of this, whether these groups are societal or familial, large or small. Groups need to be as equally skilful and knowledgeable as parents and families are in the way that they do this. But we cannot underestimate the degree to which the human species has harnessed aggression and the capacity to fight in order to defend. There is a dark side to belonging, and we cannot underestimate how powerful and destructive that can be—for the individual as well as for the group. It is important to promote both the significance and our understanding of the formation, experience, and sustainability of belonging for the individual and the group. This includes the conditions that promote it and re-build it when it goes wrong. But we must not be naïve in the way we approach this—there are powerful forces at work on both sides.

The care system encapsulates both sides of belonging. Through its significant responsibilities to protect children from harm and promote their welfare and development, it has the power to intervene in family life. That may mean providing services to re-build the family, or it may mean removing children and building a new family elsewhere. These are interventions with "protection" as their justification, but they are also interventions that are likely to be experienced as disruptive by the family—disruptive to relationships, to the sense of connection, and most particularly to any sense of belonging. It is likely from the local authority's point of view that connectedness and belonging mean quite the opposite of what they mean to the family when the family organizes itself around drug and alcohol use, the consequences of serious mental illness, criminal activity, or aggression and violence. Belonging may be a very precarious affair in such circumstances—for the adults and for any children.

Removing children causes a profound disruption in their existing pattern of parenting and family relationships, even if it is justified because of the negative impact and consequences on their safety and development. They may have belonged to troubling, disturbing, and harsh systems of relating and relationships. We know that if they have experienced any threat in those relationships, they will have tried to protect themselves—physiologically, emotionally, and in the way that they relate. This will have had an impact on the intimate processes by which they have come "to know themselves and others". It is highly likely that this will have been significantly distorted through their experience of threat. Wanting and needing to belong, to feel safe and protected, to rejoice and celebrate may be at the core of the child, but experience to date may not have enabled this to the degree to which it is needed.

Creating a new environment for the child to address the consequences of this could not be more important. For many children in care, this means creating a new family life, but one where the shadows of the past are long and persistent. For the new carers—adopters, foster carers, special guardians—that shadow will be cast over them as well. To acknowledge the impact of the past on the present in the creation, disruption, and re-working of a sense of belonging could not be more important. Past and present need to be integrated as best they can. It requires acts of kindness, humility, and resolve to do so—but this is something that the human spirit is uniquely capable of doing.

What this book and the authors have done is explore this in its many dimensions and through its many experiences. There is a belief throughout in the significance of this both for carers and, most particularly, for the child. Each chapter could not be more important in its quest, and the book could not have been more successful in achieving its aims.

TOWARDS BELONGING

Introduction

The task this book sets itself is both enigmatic and complex. Starting from the widely accepted premise that a person's sense of belonging is a critical determinant in the state of his or her emotional well-being and thus mental health, it aims to explore how this premise appears when thinking about children in care or adopted. Mindful that there are legal differences in the status of belonging between these two categories of child, nevertheless they are included together in the book because both share not living with their biological parents. Within children in care there are distinctions to be made between, for example, those in kinship care and those with special guardianship orders and there are cases where children are in care but not removed from their parent(s). This book, however, is concerned with those children who no longer live with their biological parents or extended family and are extremely unlikely to be returned to them.

Many of these children will have suffered various abuses and neglect, and some will also have been living with parents incapacitated in their parenting function through substance abuse and or mental illness. Decisions to remove them will have been guided overall by the Children Act 1989 stipulation that the interests of the child are paramount in decision making about the child. Adults making decisions will have had before them sufficient evidence to think that either a crime has been committed against the child and/or the child's continued living with their parents will result in a crime or, at the very least, a failure to develop and thrive as other children. From my own clinical experience, as well as that of many other clinicians within child and adult mental health services (CAMHS), invariably children see their best interests being served by remaining at home with those who gave birth to them, and with whom they feel they belong. Many of our referrals of children in care or adopted, from social workers and others, mention the child's difficulties in attaching to the new carers or (in the case of adopted children) parents. This book came about through my experience of meeting such referrals to CAMHS and the subsequent conversations I have had over twenty-five years with many similarly concerned multi-disciplinary colleagues. While in no way wishing to negate the importance of positive attachment as a driver for good mental health, the line taken throughout the book is that attachment alone does not sufficiently explain how children who are in care or have been adopted enter and negotiate new relationships with substitute caregivers.

Focus

The concern about attachment to new families has several strands each underpinned by the problem of focus. Children are removed from where they feel they belong and are placed with people (foster carers or adopting parents) who are essentially strangers. The children arrive in new places and with the expectation from all adults involved that they will see them as home. The adults recognize that there needs to be a settling-in period for the child, in which he adjusts to his new life and setting. After a while, if things go well, the adults feel that the child is attached securely to the new carers/parents. However, if instead the child becomes withdrawn or explosive (and of concern along the spectrum between these possibilities), adults tend to believe a "honeymoon period" to have ended and that the child needs professional help for difficulties in attaching to them. The focus tends to be immediate and present, with a fear that in the short term the adoption or placement may be in jeopardy without this help.

The problem as presented to CAMHS is a question of attachment: how do we get this child to attach? This question is joined by: irrespective of their history, how do we get the child to attach now? This is a second problem of focus, as more often than not the attention is only on the child's immediately presenting difficulties. They are seen as the sole element in the problem, and thus the sole element in its solution. What is missing is the context, the system, within which the child is now placed or adopted. Widening the focus from the child to the system, one brings into view the carers, the wider corporate parent,[1] and the child's history with his biological parents as integral to his present experience and solution to the difficulties seen by the adults. In widening the focus, one inevitably recognizes that the child's attachment to carers is determined by how they, and others in the corporate parent, are seen by the child (external world) and that how they are seen is majorly shaped by what the child makes of his previous experiences with those charged with his care (internal world).

Attachment

The two problems of focus ask us to wonder how the term attachment is being used in so many of the referrals to CAMHS. In this, attachment seems to be a substitute for attachment theory. If this is so, then one next wonders whether attachment theory is being understood sufficiently.

Most CAMHS and allied professionals are familiar with the term attachment as a shorthand for what John Bowlby (1958, 1960, 1969) developed and then termed attachment theory. As is well known, in part Bowlby developed his theory as his response to what he saw as the limitations in Freud's development of psychoanalysis. Freud took psychoanalysis in the direction of the analysis of the inner world as the exclusive key to understanding human emotional and mental difficulties. Although Bowlby trained as a

psychoanalyst (his analyst was Joan Riviere and he was in supervision with Melanie Klein), he was uncomfortable with the lack
of focus on the importance of the external world. He saw human
development as being always in relation to the external, as we are
innately determined to survive and thrive in relationships—first
with our primary caregivers and then with the other people in
the world about us. So many of the referrals to CAMHS that cite
attachment as the concern do not appear cognisant of the fuller
meaning of attachment theory as laid down by Bowlby. While so
many referrals do not recognize the emotional history of the child,
they also seem to overlook the role of the external world in facilitating the nurturing relationship seen as pivotal to a damaged child's
recovery and development. In many ways this is not surprising,
given that Bowlby said very little about the actual nature of the
world external to the child other than it is something the child
attaches to in one of several ways in order to develop. The child's
inner world, so important to achieving a nurturing attachment is
also not focused upon in any detail. Bowlby and his followers speak
about the child's sense of shame following humiliation when her
attachments are poor, fractured, or broken. They do not recognize
that the inner world is more complicated and that, for example, a
child's unconscious phantasy life is real, and that it is real in its
consequences for attachment and development. This again is not
surprising when one considers one of Bowlby's last statements on
the difference between attachment theory and psychoanalysis:

> Psychoanalysis is Freud's discovery of what goes on in the
> imagination . . . it has no concern with anything else, is not
> concerned with the real world . . . it is concerned simply and
> solely with the imaginings of the childish mind. [quoted in
> Rayner, 1992, p. 22]

This book attempts to explore a focus on children that encompasses
their relationship to the system they are in, as either placed or
adopted children. This focus includes understanding their histories
and therefore that they have been removed from homes in which
they may have felt a sense of belonging to their biological parents.
This is not a focus that attempts to critique attachment theory, but
it is one that suggests this theory may benefit from an examination
of belonging as underpinning the capacity to attach.

The care system has been a concern to practitioners, policy makers, and interested observers for many years. More recently, adoption has returned to the political agenda as concern has again been heightened by the number of adoptions that are failing. The life chances of both sets of children are significantly increased if their placements or adoptions are stable. This is an important outcome to achieve. However, attention on improving stability has tended to be on the child, and on support for carers or adopters, in such a way that bypasses seeing them as in a relationship in which both need to struggle with what it means to be in such a relationship. It is here that belonging becomes both complex and enigmatic.

Belonging

Belonging is complex because of the various realities that come into the new relationship, including:

> the child's sense of belonging to biological parents (regardless of whether the child appears to or actually loves, hates, or is indifferent to them)

> the overcoming of the fact that both parties are strangers to one another and are not biologically related

> the problem of a good-enough character and personality match between both parties

> the question of the predisposition of both parties to want to belong to anybody

> what the child brings to the new relationship as transference of past experiences at the hands of parents and other caregivers.

This complexity gives belonging its enigmatic quality since any one of the factors just mentioned results in a basic difficulty in forming a relationship that might lead to a sense of belonging to that relationship and/or the persons in it. This is why the title of this book is *Towards Belonging*, as the aim in putting it together has been to assess what is possible in terms of a sense of belonging for thus constituted new families. The two central questions that run through the book are the ones that I asked the contributors to consider: is a sense of belonging possible, and, if so, how is it?

Dictionary definitions of belong include to be somebody's property; to be in a proper situation; to be attached by birth, allegiance, or membership; to be an attribute or function of a person or thing; to be owned by, be the property of, be part of, be a member of, be associated with, relate to, go with. The mental health literature on belonging is unfortunately rather sparse, and non-existent as far as thinking about a child's sense of this. In chapter 1, I propose in more detail what makes up a sense of belonging. For the time being, my overall synopsis of this literature produces the crude definition of a sense of belonging as the person's experience of feeling accepted, needed, and valued. Included with this is that the person feels his or her personality or character traits complement or directly fit with other people's in his or her systemic environment. One can immediately see that this fit, based on a sense of acceptance, of being needed and valued, is complex as in turn these rely on the successful outcome of the coming together of the personality and character traits of those involved. Understanding the sense of belonging, or whether this is possible, for the children who are the subject of this book is even more complex. Along with the vagaries and vicissitudes of being any individual and being in any relationship, these children come to their new ones having had their primary relationships disturbed and fractured by being removed from them. How then do we begin to understand what concept of belonging they may either have or might be helped to achieve?

Psychodynamic and systemic thinking

I asked the contributors to the book to consider the complex inner worlds of these children and to wonder, in the light of this, whether a sense of belonging is possible for them. The question of this achievement being possible needs to be addressed systemically for a number of reasons. First, as already mentioned, belonging is not only defined as achieved through a relationship, or relationships; being true to the evidence of clinical experience ensures this focus.

Second, being a concept and empirical reality of relationships, a sense of belonging for the child relies upon the carer/parent's ability, capacity, and wish to be belonged to. Without this there is no sense for the child of being accepted, needed, or valued. Third, so many of these children and young people arrive in the care system, or for adoption, in highly traumatized emotional and mental states. Clinically, they are seen to have fragmented minds and huge difficulties in containing themselves, and thus they powerfully project their internal states into the adult world around them.

Evidence from my work with these children and the network of care system adults around them confirms my previous observations (Briggs, 2004) and those of other clinicians (e.g., Britton, 1981; Sprince, 2002) that these projections are so powerful as to disturb the clear-thinking capacity of these adults. Such disturbance is, of course, extremely valuable in the putting-together of a picture of the child's inner world. However, until the adult network recognizes the importance of such an approach to the care of these children and young people, very often the disturbance is acted out in ways that are not helpful to the overall relationship with the child. So, the importance of a psychodynamic view of the system here is in understanding the adults' countertransference as part of the child's projected inner world. Overall, unless the child's projections are understood as a communication of his otherwise unbearable (to him and often then to the receiving adult) states of feeling and mind, and then the meaning of these is understood as part of the child's overall sense of self, any potential for developing a sense of belonging is very seriously compromised. This compromising is twofold. First, projection of the inner world is an unconscious attempt to make a link with a mind outside and thus to one other than one's own. If the receiving adult is unaware that his or her altered states of feeling or mind are the result of this form of communication from the child, then the child is left with an unsuccessful attempt at making a link. From the point of view of belonging, this represents a moment in which there is no connection of the two protagonists in the relationship. Second, unless adults recognize that they have been projected into in this way, they are not likely to feel the deeper sense of being in relationship with the child. This is particularly important because without this recognition adults are not available to children at the only level at which most of them initially are able to make a link and thus, potentially, make the early overtures towards developing a sense of belonging to their adoptive or foster parents.

The corporate parent

For children in care and their carers the potential to develop a sense of belonging is confounded further by the nature of the parental relationship. The previous government prescribed this for professionals working with children in care through its policy document *Care Matters* (DfES, 2006, 2007). These professionals are to see themselves as the child's *corporate parent*. A number of concerns were intended to be alleviated through the conceptualization of this parent. Previously there had been concern that placement instability and breakdown were partly the result of professionals around the child not linking up and thinking together in the child's best interests. The corporate parent was therefore designed to ensure that such integration in the system was achieved and thus to maximize the potential for placement stability.

The guiding principle behind the corporate parent is that when a child is taken into State care, all those working for the State "should demand no less for each child in care than they would for their own children" (DfES, 2006, p. 31). Children are taken into care either with the agreement of their parents or because of court processes. The State then is responsible to care for them through fulfilling the parenting task.[2] Fundamental to the fulfilment of this duty of care is the task of providing the secure attachment seen by the policy as essential:

> Secure attachment is essential to the healthy development of children. Babies and children need a secure emotional relationship with one or two main carers, usually a parent, in order to develop physically, emotionally and intellectually. They need to feel safe, protected and nurtured by carers who respond appropriately to them so that they can gradually make sense of the world around them. This secure relationship, or "attach-

ment", with consistent carers is essential to their development and to learning to trust their carers to meet their needs. [DfES, 2007, pp. 17–18]

Leaving to one side for the time being a discussion (begun above) about attachment and belonging, the idea of a corporate parent is somewhat difficult to imagine in terms of a child relating to it. Children not in care know that decisions about them are taken solely by the person or people they live with on a daily basis: the parents they have built trust in. In some instances, members of their extended family may take an active role in their daily care and thus have a contribution to decisions made. For children in care, this is very different. Decisions about their lives, even some of the most mundane and routine, are only taken by their carers in correspondence with other professionals in the network identified as the corporate parent. Big decisions, such as what secondary school to apply for or whether the child should have access to a mobile phone, are made collectively. Quite often one hears from children in care that this approach to parenting them feels top-heavy, remote, and alienating. Despite individual adults' more personable ways of being with these children, they do not feel part of the corporate parent: they feel that they do not belong to it and that it does not belong to them.

A matrix for belonging

Any attempt to understand the adopted or fostered child's sense of belonging (or potential for) is therefore immediately beset by the complexity of his psycho-social situations. Furthermore, any attempt to understand how the child's life-chances might be improved only through enabling placement or adoption stability is difficult without factoring in elements that comprise the potential for a sense of belonging. However, it is clear that without recognizing the child in his social—that is, systemic—context and employing an understanding of how the unconscious of the child and of the adults around them impacts on the relationships they are all in together, placement stability will either be in jeopardy or, at best, not understood. In order to begin this process of understanding, the book has in mind a matrix based on four ostensibly simple questions that go towards understanding whether belonging is an experience for an adopted child or one in placement: Can I allow myself to belong to you? Can you allow yourself to let me belong to you? Can I allow myself to let you belong to me? Can you allow yourself to let yourself belong to me? These four questions go to the heart of the problem of placement stability in that they ask about the crucial nature and quality of contact between those involved. It is a complex matrix that relies on each question being answered positively in order for a sense of belonging to be achieved by all concerned, especially the child.[3] If all are positive then the risks to emotional well-being and mental health are minimized. Indeed, the existence of a positive relationship may lead to amelioration of poor emotional well-being and mental health.

In summary

The belonging matrix indicates the highly complex nature of the individuals who enter it. Its positive outcome relies upon the reconciliation of a number of similarly complex emotional and psychological issues. Children come into the care system only after suffering various levels and repetitions of traumatic experiences. Coming into the care system is itself traumatic as they are taken away from their biological families and placed with people who more often than not until then are strangers to them. These strangers and their families also meet a stranger in that the child is often not known to them before placement. The child's experience is of losing his link and existence with the family of his biological origin and instantly being required to respond to the foster family as the provider of family life. There is a similar requirement on foster families and those adopting a child to think of the child as their own. There is an obvious difference here between being adopted and fostered. The legal situation created for adoption means that parents and children are not part of the care system. Nevertheless, if we are saying that a sense of belonging is fundamental to emotional well-being, and subsequently mental health, then the belonging matrix is as relevant to them as it is to children in care. The questions it poses help us to see what is possible for these children and those responsible for them, whether or not their new experiences and situations clearly answer them or not.

The chapters in this book

Collectively the contributions to this book cover a wide territory for the sense of belonging, and each of them touches on an aspect of the belonging matrix just outlined. There are chapters by child and adolescent psychotherapists that explore both the way such highly traumatized children survive emotionally and mentally as they enter and stay in care or adoption, and the importance of understanding the adult care network as part of more fully understanding the child. Chapters contributed by systemic practitioners demonstrate work with children in the context of the network of care around them, whether this be a specialist service for children in care or a residential setting. There is one chapter by an experienced organizational practitioner that looks at the importance of a sense of belonging for these children and the wider implications for society.

After an opening chapter in which I explore the matrix and some of the conceptual and empirical complexities of belonging, Richard Rollinson (chapter 2) writes with great passion about the difficulty for our society and for many professionals in understanding the needs of children in care or adopted. The basic need he identifies is to have recognition that the "enduring chasm" brought through separation from their biological parents is one that runs the course of their lives. He draws our attention to the difficulty professionals charged with their care have in genuinely accepting the essential need for these children to belong, "and to feel that they do". In part, this lack of grip on the issue of belonging has much to do with the everyday nature of the growing sense of belonging for children not subject to such overwhelming separation experiences. This brings about a taken-for-granted attitude that blunts sensitivity to the plight of those who are removed from their parents. Through an eclectic mix of literature, poetry, and religion along with material from his conversations with children, Rollinson arrives at his anti-dote for the hurt felt by the chasm. This is what he terms a frame-work for hope. In explaining this, he draws upon his experience of residential settings in which he saw "therapeutic parenting" as the "essential" ingredient in "recovery and belonging". Some children who are taken into care will have had a good-enough experience of reciprocal ownership to make use of the ordinary good parenting of long-term foster carers and adoptive parents; they may be suf-ficiently integrated to be able to describe what they have gone through and to know something about their own feelings. They may have been given sufficient emotional attention by their birth parents to have the courage to feel their own feelings, think their own thoughts, and express these honestly and spontaneously. They may have a capacity for insight into their own feelings and for sym-pathetic understanding for the feelings of other people. However, this is not usually the case.

John Diamond (chapter 3) begins his chapter by reminding us of the terrible consequences for society when there is a lack of a sense of belonging for children to parents, carers, or institutions. He brings back to our attention the boys who brutally attacked other boys on wasteland in Edlington, and he also points to some of the problems in the way Cafcass operates that appear to work against a concept and experience of belonging for the families and children involved. This is a very poignant backdrop to the chapter, which discusses in detail the role of specialist therapeutic residential child care in the facilitation of emotional growth and a subsequent sense of "belonging" for some of the most emotionally damaged children in our society. Diamond is the Chief Executive Officer of the Mulberry Bush School and thus is well versed and practiced in its therapeutic methodology, based upon the work of Donald Winnicott and of Barbara Dockar-Drysdale. In demonstrating how this enables a sense of belonging for children and young people, Diamond presents very moving accounts of work with some of those who have been helped by the Mulberry Bush.

Jim Walker (chapter 4) starts by reminding us of the protective function of attachment. From birth the infant needs the mother's protection. She is critical to the infant's emotional, mental, and physical survival and development. If she is a safe figure, her

infant will gradually feel able to explore the world nearby, leading to explorations further afield as the infant develops. So many
children in care do not have this security from birth. Attachment
theorists focus on the debilitating consequence of shame for children when something goes wrong in their relationship with either
parent. Walker focuses on the fear and shame that accompanies
children removed from their biological parents. With an eye to how
children might be helped to feel a sense of belonging, he argues
for the reparative function of safe, warm, and loving relationships.
Through these, children are able to restore their sense of identity
and establish relationships with carers and others, which allows
them to engage their minds with the world and develop through
life.

Jenny Sprince (chapter 5) explores the need for a more quali-
tative relationship between adopters or carers and the children
placed with them. The need for this comes from the well-known
belief among clinicians, practitioners, researchers, and policy
makers that if these children are to achieve a mature concept of
belonging, then foster and adoptive parents are likely to need
expert help that goes beyond behavioural regulation. Perhaps for
reasons associated with the economy of running the care system,
there has been an emphasis on support to bring about behavioural
regulation at the expense of support to help make sense of their
children's behaviours in the light of their histories. Sprince draws
on her work as a child psychotherapist and organizational consultant to demonstrate how for any family (birth, adoptive, or foster),
the mutual exploration and benevolent understanding of fantasy
life—either through conscious explication or intuitive empathy—is
the basis for feeling comfortably at home with one another. This
idea of fit comes from the concept of belonging that she uses: "The
concept of 'belonging' can be used in two distinct but related ways:
to signify ownership and the rights of property, and to express the
feeling of fitting in comfortably somewhere, being understood and
accepted. It is the task of parents to help children to move from
the first kind of belonging into the second." To illustrate this task,
Sprince begins with a baby's experience of birth and subsequent
few days, in which the baby (now out of the womb) has the "terrifying realization" that he is no longer totally owned by someone

else. In order to cope with these terrifying moments, babies need to feel they are safely claimed as the property of their parents. For many months, they need to feel still part of their mother and that they are part of them. Feeling comfortably at home with one another, Sprince says, "is an essential requirement if the adults who care for them are to lay the foundations that will prepare [the children] to feel at home with themselves, with their new families, and ultimately within the adult world". Through this, these children stand a better chance of engaging successfully with the adult world throughout their lives.

Becky Wylde (chapter 6) starts by making the important point that very few children in care (and I would add adopted) receive the opportunity for psychotherapeutic help. Her work with Laura, the focus of her chapter, demonstrates just how important this approach is for these children whose traumatizing abusive and separation experiences before care so often leave them confused, fragmented, lost within themselves, and consequently without a sense of identity or belonging. We learn that while Laura relied upon an adhesive or intrusive identification, she was unable to form a sense of belonging through developing a proper relationship either with an external object or with herself. The work Laura did with Wylde allowed her to begin experiencing herself and others as separate from each other, enabling her to develop a self to belong to. This shift was from searching outside herself for an identity and sense of belonging, towards being able to know who she is from the inside. It is described by Wylde as Laura's move from using adhesive identification to the outside world to something more resembling introjective identification. We see how this shift is possible, through her beginning to recognize her determination to control others (often through intrusion), and in this way not face the awfulness of her history, to being able to think about herself with an emerging sense of who she is as shaped by her history. Through this, we see Laura located inside herself, belonging to herself, with hopes for own future.

Lesley Maroni (chapter 7) explores the role that smell—the scent of the other—plays in helping children make a new attachment or hindering them from doing so. Central to this is how children removed from their birth family develop a sense of belonging when the smell of the caregiver is foreign and unfamiliar. Maroni moves

between mother–infant research and practice, neuroscience, literature, psychoanalysis, and everyday observations to assess how
olfactory memories developed between birth mother and infant are
taken into the relationship with adopters or carers and are crucial
to understanding the prospects of attachment. One implication of
her discussions relates to the stability of adoption or placement.
She draws our attention to the need for very subtle observation and
thinking when working with adopted children and those in care.

Sara Barratt (chapter 8) discusses a range of ideas and observations she has made over many years of working in a specialist
multi-disciplinary team within a CAMHS providing therapeutic
services for children who are "looked after", adopted. Her focus
is work with foster families and the complex emotions that arise
through developing a sense of belonging both for the families
that re-configure to include, as is often the case, a non-biologically
related member and for that child who is thus included. She
describes the approach the team takes, drawing on a range of different therapeutic modalities in order to provide a service that fits for
the children referred and their caregivers. Children and their carers
are worked with together and separately, but there is a different
underpinning to the approach depending on whether the child is
adopted or fostered. For adoptive families, the team uses step-by-
step work to help the family develop a sense of belonging together
as a family. For foster carers and children, the work can be complex
in that the child's future care may still be undecided. Overall,
Barratt considers the dilemmas for foster parents and children in
investing and believing in the future of a relationship and sense of
belonging that, through the fact of State involvement, is determined
by others. Of the many rich observations she makes through the
journey of her chapter, the one about belonging and educational
achievement rings through the rest and draws our attention back to
the overall problem the care system faces for improving outcomes.
As she says, "I have been concerned that children who give up on
education are feeling that ambition for themselves would take them
too far away from birth families and that it is safer to be loyal to
their tradition." One place in which this observation rings a bell is
in the moment that we hear or see children struggling to believe
that they have a permanent placement (or that adoption is permanent). Often, as Barratt notes, beneath this apprehensive struggle is

a feeling that the only sense of belonging they can rely upon is that with birth families, as they have a shared culture and experience.

John Hills (chapter 9) looks at the experience of belonging as a basic existential yearning. His chapter comes from the position that a sense of love and care, a secure identity, and self-confidence are the results of attached belonging. He sees this belonging as what all looked after children are looking for, and it is on this basis that he develops his discussion of systemic psychotherapy with them. Hills makes the important point that the systemic perspective allows a view of their lived experience from the variety of situational standpoints, including reasons for, and the provision for, their need for a sense of relational continuity, predictability, and certainty of attachment. He notes that their experiences of these are likely to be fragmented as they have meagre direct control over the living arrangements that surround them. Furthermore, so often the decision-takers are not part of the family kinship. The chapter has three main features. The first examines how systemic-based thinking takes into its framework both personal and interpersonal domains; the changes, gains and losses, and adaptation requirements that existence imposes on human beings; and the different levels of social power that exist in what we term society and have to be negotiated on behalf of looked after children. The second gives us an insight into the systemic way of approaching the problem of fragmentation for children in care. Here we see how a systemic approach helps us to see that connectivity and unity may be found to be elusive when we understand the meaning of the relational drama of family life. The third is a detailed clinical application of his thinking, illustrated by his work with Calvin, who has disrupted cultural roots and competing attachment dilemmas. Hills describes these in the context of Calvin's future prospects in a society whose orientation is not towards providing continuing life opportunities and social support and an awareness of the importance of helping establish a sense of secure identity.

The offer to readers is therefore both wide and varied. It is hoped that what is covered can lead to readers recognizing their own experiences and thinking. In this, the chapters may help them with their existing—or help stimulate new and different—approaches to working with children for whom belonging seems to be elusive.

Notes

1. As discussed later in this Introduction, the corporate parent is a bureaucratically conceived body of education, foster care, mental health and social care professionals associated with the child's life and tasked with the child's ongoing care.

2. This requirement has proved to be very difficult to achieve in many cases as it is part of the overall remit for the corporate parent, Because of its size and different professional roles with the child, the corporate parent appears as distant and procedural for many children, and thus it is difficult to feel a sense of belonging by either party. Nevertheless, a great many referrals to CAMHS of children in care identify the child's inability to attach to foster carers as the presenting difficulty in need of treatment.

3. For children in care, this matrix includes parenting by the corporate parent. Each individual who is part of the corporate parent is tasked with making decisions, or otherwise thinking about the child, as if the child were his or her own. Foster carers are part of the corporate parent and thus are charged with thinking about the child in concert with the other professionals. So, the child looking to belong to a foster parent is faced with that parent being just one element in parenting and thus with the question of the extent to which he allows himself (and/or to whom) to belong to the corporate parent.

CHAPTER ONE

Towards belonging: conceptual definitions

Andrew Briggs

M ental health practitioners recognize that a sense of belonging is, as discussed in the Introduction, critical to humans attaining and maintaining a sense of emotional well-being and good mental health (Anant, 1966). The title of this book—*Towards Belonging*—is intended to convey belonging as a state of being that is achieved through the development of a relationship. The ideas and questions raised in this chapter derive from the referrals of children in care or adopted whom I have seen for psychotherapy when working in CAMHS. The common experience for most of these children and young people is removal from their birth parents and placement with families who are strangers. This stark fact of movement has a huge emotional consequence, as the child is separated from the family he belongs to biologically and is placed with people for whom this link will never exist. Theoretically, this dramatic transition raises many important issues as far as a child's development is concerned. For attachment theorists, and especially those with a focus on neuroscience, the broken link with the primary caregiver represents an opportunity for a very serious disruption in neuro-developmental terms, leading to difficulties with attachment to new caregivers. For some, however, due to the primary caregiver's own difficulties, the link was already broken

before the child's removal. For psychoanalytic thinkers, one consequence of this broken link is the opportunity for the development
of severely unwell states of mind. This is due to the breaking of
the container–contained relationship. For some children, a prior
breakdown in this relationship does not bode well for this containment by a new relationship.

"Towards" implies a journey. Two questions that this chapter
address concern expectation: How far along this journey can we
expect these children to travel, given that they are taken from a
place where they belong to a place where they may not feel they
do? Does the proximity of children to the goal of belonging indicate
their state of emotional well-being and mental health?

Attachment and belonging

The majority of referrals to modern CAMHS of these children
mention difficulties attaching to their new families, with the
referrer's hope that an intervention from a mental health service
will enable the children to attach better to these families. Initial
exploration with referrers usually reveals that they use the term
"attachment" to convey a far deeper sense of involvement in a
relationship for the child than the term implies. While both foster
carers and adoptive parents recognize the need for the child to
use them as a stable resource for emotionally and psycho-socially
developing himself, often they speak about the child becoming a
member of their families, "like one of us" or "one of our own children". Clarifying this as their meaning of attachment leads to our
being able to establish that actually what is being requested is an
intervention that helps the child to feel that he belongs to the new
family—"I want him to feel he belongs to us." Although held on
to passionately as their goal for treatment, their conceptualization
of belonging is invariably quite unclear. However, for most new
parents/carers it includes an idea about sharing family life as the
basis of a common identity with the child, which they hope will
make the child feel he is part of them. Identity and seeing aspects
of this as being in common with other people requires a child to

perceive and think in more sophisticated ways than most children in care and adopted (and who are referred to mental health services) are able to do. This is largely because of the breakdown in the containing relationship, which brings a diminished capacity to think about experiences.

Almost always, new parents/carers overlook the stark fact that they and the child are not biologically related. One consequence of this fact is that they have different emotional and psycho-social histories that may accentuate the biological difference. Any potential for attachment and/or belonging will therefore need to be resilient to these major facts brought to the relationship by both the child and the new parents/carers. But these facts are galvanized by the legal structure within which adults and children are held. As mentioned in the Introduction, the government White Papers *Care Matters* (DfES, 2006, 2007) introduced the corporate parent. This parent includes all professionals with an interest in the child. It therefore includes carers, adoptive parents (at least during the initial period of adoption), social workers, and teachers. They are all tasked with making decisions about the child in the child's best interests, as if the child were their own. This directive was intended to facilitate a stronger sense of responsibility in the minds of the professionals. However, from my experience, it has often allowed for a denial of the stark biological fact of the difference between the child and this collection of adults. The question here is: Does the concept of the corporate parent serve to help or hinder the development of emotional well-being and good mental health for these children?

Belonging: a matrix

Children experience being removed from their parents as both complicated and traumatic. The emotional and psycho-social care of them is therefore a hugely complex task. Fundamentally the task is about the formation of a relationship that helps the child develop emotionally and socially. Whether the relationship can be established therefore rests upon the sufficient containment of the complexity of both the child and the task. In order to remain on track, through what often feels like chaos when working to help children and those tasked with their care, I have found the matrix outlined in the Introduction a trusty sextant.

The matrix

The following four questions help clarify the potential for a sense of belonging through identifying four basic points of contact between child and carer/adoptive parent. These are:

1. Can I allow myself to belong to you?
2. Can you allow yourself to let me belong to you?
3. Can I allow myself to let you belong to me?
4. Can you allow yourself to let yourself belong to me?

Each of these questions can be asked by both child and adult. However, it is more likely that these questions will become easier to formulate during the course of therapeutic work with them. The clarity of each question as it appears above has relied upon my working it out from many hours of contact with children and adults who comprise the corporate parent. Such clarification often reveals that there is a discrepancy between child and carer/parent. For example, my work with one child arrived at him being able to see that his aggressive behaviour towards his carers masked feelings of shame at being in care. While he knew his carers wanted him to belong to them, he answered "no" to Questions 1 and 3 above. I once worked with two foster parents who began with Question 2: Can you allow yourself to let me belong to you? Seeing the child's behaviour at home as intrusive, they were determined that it was driven by her wrestling with whether her carers could allow themselves to belong to her. As our work progressed, we were able to establish that, despite these carers' obvious wish to care for her, they were seeing in her their own ambivalence about caring. In this case belonging was hoped for, but there was clearly a serious chasm between carers and child while this ambivalence went unresolved.

While such a deep chasm exists between carers/parents and child, there also exists the opportunity for little or no development of a sense of belonging and of good mental health. This is a very serious problem, and the questions above help to clarify where attempts at amelioration may start. However, such attempts need to be mindful of the structure within which the child and the new family exist.

Corporate parent

As I mentioned in the Introduction, the basic idea driving the activities of the corporate parent is that when a child is taken into State care, all those working for the State should enter the caring relationship (including decision making) as if caring for their own child (*Care Matters*; DfES, 2006, p. 31). The task is written in *Care Matters* in such a way that we cannot but think of Bowlby's work on attachment theory. A secure attachment, which is both the input and product of a secure emotional relationship, is "essential to the healthy development of children" (DfES, 2007, p. 17). Babies and children need this security "with one or two main carers, usually a parent, in order to develop physically, emotionally and intel-lectually" (p. 18). As we also saw in the Introduction, this secure relationship is fundamental to feeling safe, protected, and nurtured by carers. Carers responding consistently appropriately to a child enable him to trust his carers and their provision of care and gradu-ally make sense of the world around him (DfES, 2007).

Attachment as mis-defined

This secure relationship and its products, referred to in *Care Matters* as "attachment", places the guidance for the task of the corporate parent firmly within attachment theory as developed by Bowlby and his followers. However, while attachment is so often stated as the hoped-for outcome from a mental health service intervention, my experience is that belonging is the tacitly expected outcome by referrers and carers. In reality, attachment then becomes difficult to achieve because it has been mis-defined as belonging, and a sense of belonging is very difficult to achieve for carers and children.

The provision of a secure attachment is a highly skilled accom-plishment dependent upon a great many factors, including the emotional well-being and mental health of the child and the abilities and capacities of the foster carer(s) to provide for invariably severely damaged children. Both the child's state and the carer(s)' abilities and capacities need to be understood by the carer(s) and the wider professional network—the corporate parent. Thus, secure attachment and understanding by the corporate parent each rely on there being a relationship between professionals and between them and the child, and on each recognizing the importance of being in a relationship with the other. However, relationships are complex, made more so when one or both parties have in mind the achievement of a sense of belonging as their definition of attachment.

A problem of structure

Whether we try to assess attachment or belonging within the child–new family relationship, the potential for a clear sight of the difficulties involved will remain small unless we begin by understanding how the relationship is structured. The child and new family are biologically different. The family and others, but not the child, are tasked with treating the child as if he is their own. "Their own" equates with saying their biological child. If they are supposed to treat the child as if he is their biological child, this is to deny the reality that he is not such a child. It also places on the new families an unreality, as they are expected to treat as their own a child they did not give birth to. Furthermore, the child has no such expectations on them. He is not required to think of the new family as if it is his biological family. So, from the start there is a chasm produced by the way the task for the corporate parent is conceived and the protagonists thus structured in relation to one another.

Towards the end of my work with an older adolescent, adopted at a very early age by caring parents, he said: "However much I may love them. However much I feel the same as them in outlook and interests, I am not them and they are not me. It is very powerful. It is raw and neat as a feeling. I am me and not them." He was referring to his feeling of being biologically different to his adoptive parents, despite having a sense of deeply belonging to them through sharing outlook and interests. This psycho-social similarity, bringing strong feelings of belonging, is common when adoption and foster placements allow for the factual differences between child and new family. However, if there are difficulties in accepting the fact of biological difference, and the fact that this significantly contributes to the child's sense of identity, then the wish for a sense of belonging by either party, and about either party, seriously runs the risk of being unfulfilled.

Biological influence

In terms of the four questions posed by the belonging matrix, we can see that neither party is likely to be able to answer them to convey a deep sense of belonging while there is the basic issue of their biological difference to contend with, which, although concrete and primitive, nevertheless has consequences on various levels of existence. A child's biological link includes emotional, neuro-developmental, and psycho-social links, which are severed by being removed from the birth family, but it also conveys something that transcends the experience of all these. I recognized this when working with Carrie, an 8-year-old girl who wanted a baby.

Carrie

Carrie was referred because her social worker and carers were concerned by what they termed her obsession with having a baby. The carers also felt that this got in the way of Carrie being able to attach to them, and to appreciate what they had on offer for her through providing a lovely home and understanding. They were, however, deeply upset by her wish to have a baby at such a young age and felt they were in competition with the baby that was always referred to by Carrie. Leaving to one side the work done to help the carers understand the projection of competition, envy, not being good enough, and concern that was fundamental to stabilizing what had become a threatened placement, the work with Carrie brought to light her attempt to keep alive her link with her biological family. The following is a fragment from a session towards the end of the work:

> Carrie sits by the dolls' house. She is in a world of her own stroking the hair of the little dolls' house doll. She says "Lovely baby. My baby. Carrie's darling." And then suddenly "Mmmmhhh!!! You smell so good. You smell like me and Mummy. You smell like my face. You look like me and Mummy (rocking the baby doll). You sound like me and your voice is like Mummy speaks."

Carrie was taken into care aged 18 months because of her mother's inability to care for her and her sisters. In the session here, she is clearly trying to connect with a memory about her mother's smell and voice. This suggested to me that she was trying to retain a sense of identity with her mother through identifying with her role and linking with something concrete (smell and voice). While her doll baby (and the wish for a real one) originated from the wish to conjure up herself as a baby aware of her senses, it also suggested the need for establishing her biological lineage while being in foster care. In terms of her sense of belonging, in her psychotherapy sessions it was clear that she felt she belonged to her mother rather than to her carers. In this, she demonstrated the difficulties in expecting such children to have a sense of belonging to the new family, when primitive linking and the need for memories made concrete have such a hold over the processes involved in identity formation.

However, links with the biological family are not always so easy to see. Some children and young people have been so severely damaged by their pre-removal experiences that it is extremely difficult to see the link to their biological parents. These children often present in such ways as to attract diagnoses from consultant child and adolescent psychiatrists. Chris is a case in point.

Chris

Aged 12 years, Chris was referred to me because his schoolteacher felt she could not get to know him. This was strongly echoed by his carers. He had been on medication for two years and had diagnoses of attention deficit hyperkinetic disorder (ADHD), conduct disorder, and depression. He was medicated so that he could both sleep at night and also be calm during the day. His depression went unmedicated. The referral mentioned his obsessional behaviour, but this was not thought to warrant another diagnosis. This behaviour is what first interested me about him. He was very tidy about the consulting room, making sure that anything he no longer needed ended up in the bin. He had a routine whereby he would always walk to the room on a particular side of the corridor, and at a measured distance from me. Once at the door, he would always wait to one side of me in exactly the same spot each week. When I let us into the room, he would always go in, look at the ceiling, walk to the window, go to the table, open his box, run his hands over the walls, and then sit down by his box. Watching this, I felt as if he were making a very noticeable boundary between him and me. The action taken to make this boundary left me feeling sleepy, as if drugged. I knew that his ADHD and other diagnoses followed his referral for being unable to concentrate at home and also being unable to respond to instructions without lashing out at his carers. His depression was diagnosed because sometimes he cried without being able to say why, and because he seemed flat when assessed.

Chris's early history was one of neglect, physical abuse, and being with a mother whose mental health difficulties prevented her from adequately caring and helping him thrive. Because of this, he was taken into care aged 9 and had many placements, which broke down because carers were unable to help him settle. He was violent towards some carers, damaged property, and threatened family members. This behaviour told me something about why he had been diagnosed and medicated, and why adults felt there was something to know about him despite his seeming to live behind a well-constructed boundary. Nevertheless, his carers and others did not see the link between his past, his being medicated, and his not being able to be known. Because of his behaviour, they began to feel very persecuted by him—got at for wanting to make him one of theirs. While they could be helped to see how their wish obscured their being able to see who he was behind his boundary, it took considerable work with a colleague before they could see how difficult it was for Chris to avail himself to them, let alone feel he belonged to them. Chris belonged to himself and to all the feelings he had that were now dampened by medication.

A child's sense of not belonging, and not wanting to belong, that is picked up by new families often upsets them extremely. Carers refer to these children as being in a world of their own and oblivious to the feelings of others. Such presentations concern them, and they seek help for the child. One such case was 9-year-old Kim. Like Chris, she presented a boundary to the world as her contact point with it. Unlike Chris, she had presented like this since before being taken into care.

Kim

Kim's carers were worried that they could not engage with her and "find the real girl". They described her as polite, tidy, obliging, diligent, and lovable. At school, she was consistently near the top of her class in all her subjects, and she was good at sports. At home, she read a great deal, played with her dolls, but kept herself to herself. She was on good terms with her carers and their wider family; she also had friends she saw whom she had met at the stables where her carers took her to ride. She could smile at things others initiated and found funny, but she did not initiate anything humorous herself. However, she did not hold on to friends for long, and several complained of feeling uncomfortable with her. She once was inconsolable for hours after failing a spelling test. She had been taken into care aged 2 years because of severe neglect due mainly to her mother's mental health difficulties. During her first two years she had been noted by health visitors to be very quiet and delayed in speech and walking and was being kept in nappies longer than necessary. It was understood that her mother spent a great deal of time under the influence of alcohol and drugs, and there were seemingly constant visits by social workers to find Kim alone in her cot late in the day, looking at the ceiling while her mother recovered from her recent episode of substance abuse.

From quite early in our work, I noticed a strange feeling of something being torn off my side once I returned Kim to the waiting room at the end of sessions. Gradually I observed this to be Kim's experience of separating from me at the end of sessions. Shortly after this, I recognized how she seemed to stick to me throughout them. Seemingly getting on with her drawings or playing with the doll's house, she nevertheless was very aware of my presence. Her responses to my interventions were always polite, quietly spoken, and had a very soothing effect on me. She was so calm and collected that sometimes I wondered to myself why she needed to be in treatment. However, I was concerned about the charm effect of her soothing me into being very passive and still being brought out of this state by the feeling of having something torn off me. Over the following months of work, I searched to find the "the real girl" but concluded that I probably had already through the clue of the tearing-off. Kim had very little inside her because nothing much of value had been put there through the relationship with her mother. What she had inside were experiences received through being in care with such attentive carers. However, her carers and I were unable to see this because her energy was directed at keeping herself from falling apart inside. I had read social workers' reports of her as a silent baby alone in her cot endlessly looking at the ceiling and of her non-responsiveness and obsession with the corner of her blanket, which she constantly held in her mouth without sucking it. She was not taking anything in further than her lips, holding on to the blanket at this boundary with her body and self. In this way, she had held control over things coming into her and from feeling she could fall apart whether they came in or not. It was her way of containing herself in the absence of a reliable primary caregiver.[1] This and the quiet way she now presented suggested her actively covering taking in anything she could in order to protect herself from falling apart. In this sense, I was like the riding at the stables, the school successes, and the friends. Despite her outward calmness, she was sticking to me vigorously for her protection. Like the friends, I could also feel uncomfortable in my relationship with her. However, her desperateness was seen in the failed spelling test. This was felt to her like a laceration as she was ripped away from feeling on top of her process of creating school success as part of the carapace under which she lived. With this as the function of her way of being in the world, it is hardly surprising that her carers felt they did not know her. The work with them was therefore aimed at helping them see how the new experiences they provided were taken in by Kim without a sufficient emotional and mental capacity to allow herself or them to recognize how they enriched her.

* * *

Not all children and young people presenting similarly to Kim and Chris are referred to child psychotherapists, as so often they do not seem of concern. A diagnosis and medication might help adults to feel that all that can be done has now been done, as the child settles and behaviour can be explained in terms of the diagnosis alone. A diagnosis also allows the child's difficulties to be seen as just his and thus not related to the context of being expected to settle within a new family. For other children, such as those like Kim, their success is a missed opportunity to help them. Often very quiet at school, diligent in the classroom and on the playing field, they are seen as model students and receive encouragement and support to carry on achieving. Often with placements that are stable, there is reluctance on behalf of professionals to raise concerns about emotional well-being, in case this leads to interventions that disturb this equilibrium.[2] For some of these children, their similar emptiness as found in Kim is protected by a carapace that is far more brittle than hers. It is this brittleness that is often shied away from by concerned adults wary of disturbing a child who is otherwise demonstrating that she can function in the world. But what does all this say about the sense of belonging?

Like Carrie, Kim and Chris also belong more to their pasts than to their presents. Carrie kept the link alive through her wish for a baby and what this brought in terms of feeling that she was with her mother. Chris's dampened feelings, sense of being overlooked, and experiences of neglect kept him in a relationship with the past and not the present. His boundary created through his apparently obsessional behaviour further prevented a sense of belonging in all the ways described by the matrix. These children appear to keep the world at bay while they desperately try to keep themselves together in the only ways they can develop. Other children and young people pull the world towards them.

However, the ways that many do this leave me unsure that they feel a sense of belonging.

Pulling in and pushing out the world

It is at last becoming commonplace among those working with children in care and adopted that their behaviour provides a key to understanding what preoccupies them. Within their behaviour there are clues to their preoccupations and their states of mind and feeling. This derives from Winnicott's (1956, 1970) idea of the "antisocial tendency", which he developed through his work with children in care.[3] For such children, their behaviour is aimed at disturbing the environment (care workers and other professionals) in order to get it to respond to their needs. This places an expectation on the environment. It is required not only to be receptive, but also to understand and respond appropriately to the need within the emotional content of the projection, often concealed within disruptive or apparently meaningless behaviour (the antisocial tendency). The environment can be a single carer or the entire corporate parent. If receptive, both will receive the unconscious communications within the child's behaviour and other forms of presentation. For some children, the message is for the adults to contain unbearable feelings for them. For others, it is for adults to act upon these feelings in ways that demonstrate them. The question of how a sense of belonging might develop is a moot point.

Children in care or adopted whose behaviour indicates the need for containment may have various motives for using this form of projective identification. For some, the need to communicate their states of feeling and mind is sufficient so long as the container responds appropriately. For others, there is a wish to damage the object projected into. This is similar to Bion's (1959) suggestion of two types of projective identification, normal and pathological, the distinction resting on the degree of violence in each act of forced location of parts of the ego. Both types are characterized by two different aims. The first is to evacuate a painful state of mind through which one enters the object in order to control it. The second is to communicate a state of mind to the object so that it becomes aware of one's mental state. This second aim is featured in the containing relationship of mother and infant, with the mother transforming the projection and attending appropriately to her baby's needs. The first aim tends to push the world away from the child, while the second pulls it towards him.

Entering and controlling

One of the hallmarks of entering and controlling the object through projective identification is individual professionals in the network around the child—the corporate parent—in dispute with one another over almost any aspect of the child's life. Often one sees a particular professional over-identified with the child's history and feeling he or she knows the child better than any other professional. Another may be vehemently opposed to anything anyone says in network meetings. These and other developments were at issue in network meetings I convened to support the work of another child psychotherapist with a 12-year-old boy, Ross.

Ross

Ross had been in care for most of his life but only moved from his home borough at the age of 10 years. Until then he had been in numerous placements near his family home. His parents were convicted drug dealers, and their home was a crack den. Ross spent time there when he absconded (frequently) from placements. He was known to have been gang raped and beaten badly by older boys and adults. Numerous foster carers reported that he terrified their children and was very sexualized. He entered psychotherapy aged 11 and had been in a year's treatment when the network around him began to collapse.

Ross's social worker felt especially close to him. She saw him as almost cherub-like, an image she gave to a meeting to convey her impression of his innocence. Ross's female carer saw him as "evil" because she thought he was deliberately trying split up her marriage. Ross's teacher saw him as "a ring leader" because he was able to bring about trouble in the classroom. His psychotherapist reported that he seemed to be identified with a very vicious gang-boss figure that terrorized and destroyed things. This insight might have been sufficient to contain the network and begin a thinking process about the meaning of his behaviour as experienced by the other professionals. However, in fact it served to harden their positions.

Hearing about Ross in such detail seemed to enliven within these professionals the feelings that he had left with them. The meeting became very fraught as each professional became more forceful and strident in his or her views on Ross. His foster-carer began attacking what she saw as the naivety of the social worker. When the social worker argued her case, the foster carer sought an alliance with the psychotherapist and teacher. Soon each professional appeared to take on the position of the other. For example, the social worker protested that she, too, could see how Ross was evil, which forced the foster carer to say that she felt the social worker was demonizing Ross. The teacher then said he could see a way forward if only everyone could stop arguing. This good sense soon turned into him being the ringleader for another shift in positions. He said that perhaps he had over-stated Ross's power in the classroom, which lead to the others in network attacking him for seeing Ross as innocent. In protesting against this, the teacher soon began to sound like a ruthless gang leader as he threatened to shut everyone up "somehow".

There are very good ways of understanding this meeting from a group relations perspective, one informed by Bion's (1961) thinking on work groups and defences against these. For the purposes of this chapter, the way this meeting developed is illustrative of Ross getting inside the minds of each professional and, through the powerfulness of what he projected, their acting it out. The quite fluid nature of these projections, the way in which they quickly take residence in and move on from any of the professionals involved, makes them dangerous not only through their content but also because they are not resident for long enough for one person to think about them before acting on them. Overall, the network at this point of its existence in the work around Ross's psychotherapy was in the grip of the internal object that Ross both identified with and wanted to rid himself of. He entered the minds of two professionals with aspects of this violent gang leader, the evil splitter and the ringleader, and they went on to act these out in such a way that the rest of the professional group itself ended up with someone threatening to shut it up.

The overall effect of such a set of dynamics between Ross and the network was to push the network away from him. Their links were based upon projective identification of the sort that aims to invade and control the object, not feel closer to it through having needs for understanding met. Ross and the network would not have been able to answer the four questions of the matrix positively.

Containment and belonging

Containment is fundamental to human emotional and mental development. Bion (1962b) described containment in detail as the basis of development and of the capacity to think. Through her reverie, the infant's mother contains and transforms the infant's projected fears into something that helps him to manage his anxiety. This can be seen most clearly when mothers correctly interpret the cries of their infants. For example, in their reverie they may differentiate the cry for feeding from that emitted due to another painful experience. For Bion (1962b), the mother in this example would be using her reverie as an alpha function: to transform the beta elements conveyed through crying into the alpha element that she deciphered from the crying. The mother's mind as a transforming process is introjected by the infant to form the basis of his function of thinking. If the mother is unable to use her reverie, then the infant is left alone with his fears and his needs not being addressed. Bion (1962b) sees the infant's only alternative as to increase his attempts at projecting into his mother, and these might be violent. If a mother is consistently unable to contain her infant's projections, she becomes for him a "projective-identification-rejecting object". She is experienced as a wilfully misunderstanding object with which he inevitably identifies. As his fears and frustrations continue to go uncontained and made comprehensible, the infant feels they are deliberately denuded of meaning by his mother, which leaves him with a feeling of "nameless dread".

Looking back through this chapter at the experiences of the children discussed, we can see that containment helps to explain a great many of their difficulties in gaining a sense of belonging. Several things stand out. The first is the connectivity between child and new parent. For so many, the experiences of their mothers have been of "projective-identification-rejecting objects". Entering the care system, they have no expectation of being connected with, and so do not expect to feel contained by, a substitute mother. Identified with this sort of rejecting mother, they are unable to think about their feelings or those of others. Often they present as suspicious of overtures towards them intending to be helpful, as a helpful object is an unfamiliar object. These children are more comfortable either dissociating themselves from their experiences and their own minds, or continuing to increase their methods of projective identification—not so much with the hope that they will be connected to, more because this is a trusted way of evacuating their fears and discomforts. A sense of belonging, should it exist, is more likely to be experienced in relation to the self as rejected and subject to wilful misunderstanding than to a containing adult or system of adults.

Containment and identity

As Bion demonstrated, containment is fundamental to developing the capacity to think. Damage to the container–contained relation-ship therefore impedes the development of this capacity in the infant. This helps us begin to understand why so many children in care and adopted do not develop a sense of belonging as defined by—that is, recognizable to—researchers and others interested in it. The literature search I did for this chapter revealed few texts on belonging and only two that referred to children. This is surprising given that Maslow (1954) places belongingness one higher than physiological and safety needs in his famous hierarchy. What exists in the literature is psycho-social in emphasis and does not detail the emotionality or psychodynamics of such a sense. Its basic position is that a sense of belonging is achieved when a person feels there is a fit between him/herself and some person or group in his or her external worlds with which he or she wants to fit. Concepts of identity and self are key here, as the sense of belonging is both attained by and maintains a sense of identity and self-worth. This is immediately too sophisticated a concept to describe the children discussed in this chapter and what is achievable for them. Their damage leaves them with very limited capacities for thinking about themselves and about the world around them.

Identity

Hagerty, Lynch-Sauer, Patusky, Bouwsema, and Collier (1992) make the important point that a sense of belonging relies upon a fit through the person and his or her external or social worlds having shared and complementary characteristics. For this to happen, there have to be active antecedents. They define these as "energy and involvement . . . potential and desire for meaningful involvement, and . . . potential for shared or complimentary characteristics" (p. 174). This definition rules out the children I have discussed from gaining a sense of belonging since their energies are directed solely at keeping their psyches intact and therefore have limited capacity to consider meaningful involvement with anyone else. Triseliotis (1984) remarks that identity is the result of an "integrated and unified self . . . that gives a feeling of separateness from others while enabling participation in social interactions and relationships" (p. 151) and, in a later publication: "Identity is basically about what we feel about ourselves and how we think other people see us" (Triseliotis, 2000, p. 89). This gives identity a feeling state to go with the perception we have of ourselves. The children of this chapter have not developed integrated and unified selves. Ryburn (1995) mentions that "Messages that conflict with our self-concept challenge our self-esteem and make the achievement of a satisfying personal identity difficult" (p. 41). Grotevant (1997) has perhaps the best summation in the available literature: "The construct of identity stands at the interface of individual personality, social relationships, subjective awareness, and external context. Identity is thus a psychosocial construct" (p. 5). Removed from their families, and assuming that they have an intact sense of themselves that sufficiently constitutes a self-concept, they have ample opportunity to receive messages that conflict with their sense of self. For example, for those who are riddled with abusive experiences, the experience of not being abused (by the new families) represents messages that may challenge their concept of themselves as members of abusive families. For some who are sufficiently in touch with their very early experiences of a maternal object (and for whom this may have been a frightening or otherwise unsatisfactory experience), care and containment provided by the new family may act as messages that exacerbate the feelings of shame that are so often a feature of children whose maternal object has let them down so badly.[4] Overwhelming shame can flood the self so as to prevent the child understanding the benign nature of the messages brought in the various acts of care and ordinary containment by the new family. Shame is a very debilitating emotion, the minimizing of which for children settling into new families is behind the thinking by policy makers that contact with birth families should be encouraged.

Identity and biology

With a paper nearer the experiences of the children of this chapter, Triseliotis (1984) makes clear that identity is the outcome of the integration of the self. This integration is based on knowing one's background and history and on being considered worthwhile to the adults caring for you. A sense of belonging, therefore, relies on knowing one's biological history and integrating this within the self in its current context. Macaskill (2002) goes further and argues that, "Children need to be connected to their biological and historical past if they are going to grow up with a positive self-image and identity" (p. 4). Harris and Lindsey (2002) report professionals being convinced that "physical contact with birth relatives ensured a sense of completeness of the self, which . . . could not be compensated for through further identity development in a new relationship. . . . Loss of connection with (the family of origin) was equal to a loss of identity" (p. 152). These comments point to just how important the connection to their biological parents is to the identity and self-image, and thus to the sense of belonging of fostered or adopted children. However, as mental health and social services practitioners know so well, contact with biological families is not always indicated as beneficial. Unreliable attendance by parents, being overly intrusive or distanced when they attend, are just some well-established difficulties with contact that go with the dangers of evoking and stimulating unwanted memories in the child's mind.[5]

In summary

In this chapter I have tried to cover some of the issues and questions that are raised as soon as we wonder about the development of a sense of belonging in children who are fostered or adopted. While there are many examples of children who do have a sense of belonging to their new families, based upon the four questions of the matrix being answered positively by them and their families, there are significant numbers known to mental health and social services who have no real chance of developing such a sense without considerable help. These children with broken relationships with primary caregivers—often with consequent damage to their neuroreceptors and neurotransmitters, and nearly always with a damaged capacity to contain themselves—are seriously hampered if belonging means to find a fit with something or someone outside oneself. With a seriously impaired capacity to think, it seems unlikely that such children would be able to identify sufficiently with the beliefs, thinking, and cultural activities of the new families, let alone those of others outside the home environment. Indeed, what we have seen is that children with these difficulties in forming a conventional sense of identity do so because they are so desperately holding on to their inner worlds, their pasts, and thus their hope to continue existing in the face of damage caused by the traumas of their existence. A sense of belonging to themselves may be all we can expect. Similarly, their consequent state of emotional well-being and mental health may be all they can achieve. We may need to lower our expectations that these damaged children can travel further along the journey to a more universal sense of belonging. This does not mean we abandon any aspiration or hope for them achieving satisfying emotional and socioeconomic lives. It is, however, a comment on the need for mental health and social services to take the time to understand what these children struggle with in order to remain accessible to our attempts to help.

Notes

1. See Bick (1968, 1986) for a discussion of this form of behaviour as indicative of the infant holding himself together in the absence of taking in the mother as what Bion (1959, 1961, 1962b, 1970) discussed as the container.

2. One motive for the establishment of the corporate-parent approach is the link between poor socioeconomic outcomes for children in care and their unstable careers in the care system. The stabilization of these careers through reducing the number of placements that children have was seen by the then government to be achievable through better linking together all those with a duty of care to the child. However, this focus often overlooks the fact that children who appear to be on track to succeed socioeconomically may be doing so at the expense of healthier emotional lives. Thus children who disturb their classrooms and placements should not necessarily be more of a concern than those who do not.

3. Winnicott was not aware of the terms "children in care" or "looked after children" as they were coined many years after his death. However, his writing on children in care homes is particularly insightful as it makes clear the link between difficult-to-understand behaviour by children and their emotional states. This behaviour was seen by Winnicott as an expression, usually the only medium, through which children convey what they hope from the environment made up of adults with a duty of care to them.

4. Gill Hinshelwood (1999) discusses shame as the gatekeeper to other emotions or emotional states, which often acts to prevent the rest being accessible in psychotherapy. I have worked with children and young people who carry the shame for the mother who has either neglected them or been active in their sexual abuse through allowing perpetrators to act or through being active with them.

5. This contentious issue is the focus of debate in the literature on contact. For adopted children, the question of contact and identity had brought about two main camps. Both agree that the child has two families—birth and adoptive—which represent two sources for identity formation. Adams (2012)

sees little difficulty in contact as it is part of developing "a coherent narrative of the self" (p. 12). On the other hand, Neil and Howe (2004b, p. 242) suggest that children may manage identity and loss through talking freely with their new parents about their backgrounds. Brodzinsky (2005, pp. 149–151) suggests that such openness should include dialogue between the birth parents and the adoptive parents to achieve a "healthy psychological adjustment for the child" (p. 151).

CHAPTER TWO

Some reflections on "towards belonging" for children in care: guided journey or "wandering lost"?

Richard Rollinson

"Give sorrow words: the grief that does not speak
Whispers the o'er-fraught heart, and bids it break."

Macbeth, IV.iii.209–210

Fundamentally, however much each person is an individual, with skills, abilities, interests, passions even, we all define and know ourselves, and are known by others, as part of a live, complex network of "belonging"—at all levels, in all aspects of our lives, and across all distances, whether these be geographic or relating to time. This living and belonging permeates our existences and binds together not only our network of "belonging" itself, but the individual experience of our "self" as a whole and wholesome person. And this "me" or "I am" is part of something bigger, which in its dynamic action and interactions recognizes and affirms the individual as belonging.

Few dispute that we all need this belonging, its reality in living, and the sense we have and make of it. Out of the early experiences of our lives, many of us will have it reliably enough; however, a few do not, especially within the particular population that is our focus here—a small but significant number of those who are or have been in State care. Of course, over recent years all

41

government communications about the status of these children in its care declare emphatically that each child without exception is everybody's child. Given that "the State" is the corporate "body" that is the expression of society, which itself is the aggregate of us individual citizens, in theory each child in care is indeed and remains thereafter the child of us all, of "everybody". The reality, however, is that too often the child will belong to nobody at all, be "stateless". Declared one Care Leaver recently,

> "When we grow in our mothers' womb, we are given a heart, a mind, limbs and belonging. Children in care are not given belonging [in some actual or equivalent way]; at best we must earn it. And that's what renders us invisible, a minority who, while others are free to seek success and wealth, seek belonging which can blind us from all else. It is everything, but we have nothing and are nobody."

For this population there is a deep and potentially enduring chasm on the path of their journey through life—and between themselves and many others—that is hard to bridge/cross over effectively. Something is missing, lost somewhere along the way, or perhaps never really experienced—and this loss or lack is felt powerfully, for some continually and for others at critical times in their lives. For them, there is the absence of a presence that would and should bind them closely together with significant others. As a consequence, for too many the presence of that absence, like a cavernous gap or black hole with a force of "attraction" or distraction, sucks them away from any release and forever towards its "everything" grasp.

All of these individuals have their very own story of what brought them into State care and what happened when in that care and thereafter. What is common to them all is that their families and the ties that in ordinary "good-enough" living bind their members together could not and did not hold enough for them to continue to feel a connection that kept them linked intimately and reliably. So for most if not all of them, there was, and often remains, loss, sadness, distress, grief, and "upset" in their lives—from the point of that separation and movement into State care, and not infrequently before then. As will become clear, that which many of us can regard as unconditional as a provision becomes for a significant number of those in State care conditional and withheld—a difficulty for anyone needing reliable nurturing experiences and environments. It also represents a particular challenge for those children in care needing special help to counter the often numerous negative beliefs, especially about themselves, that they can bring with them and hold on to resolutely for long periods.

Facts and analysis

While it is the case that the population of looked after children is not enormous, it is growing again after some years of reducing, and the life experiences of these children continue to place them in great need of high-quality care, education, and treatment. The key statistics and details have been widely circulated (DfE, 2012). While these need not be repeated here, many continue to highlight stark contrasts with the experiences of those not in State care. Nevertheless, while many of these statistics give cause for concern, they need not sow alarm and despair. That is because beneath and not captured by the surface data there are causes for hope. It is not the case that all, or even the vast majority, of those in or having left care struggle to live with themselves and with others in schools, colleges, and their communities as responsible children and young adults. We know from their own reports that an impressive number not only survive adequately in care or living independently; they also thrive, in themselves and in the valuable contributions they make in their education and to life in their alternative families and to the social life of their communities (Access All Areas, 2012). They know they belong as part of a live network whose relationships with them are unconditional. Indeed, it is this experience and their enduring sense of belonging that gives them great heart and often continuing support.

The key here is that those who do well, or well enough to experience the wonders of common, ordinary living, do not do it on their own. While in care and thereafter, they are enjoying reliable, close relationships with caring and concerned individuals and substitute families, relationships formed and sustained during their periods into, through, and out of State care. This is an achievement to celebrate. Yet it also casts a light directly on the different experience that makes still too many others in and after care struggle in the absence of the same or equivalent enduring support. This is the gap—the absence of a real belonging, on top of the original gaps.

The difficulties obscured within the experiences of ordinary living

The difficulty for our society and for many professionals in understanding and truly accepting the essential need for this troubled population to belong, and to feel that they do, lies in the very ordinary manner in which such a thing usually develops. This growth of belonging, on its own and as it is happening, does not often catch the eye as significant. It just happens, even while giving security, safety, and pleasure to those involved. It is a living reality and is not in the first instance, if ever, an idea or an Ideal. It is the absence of its living presence that prompts the noticing, sometimes by those missing it and expressing that absence through the "upset" they feel and not infrequently as well through putting it into others who may be trying to care but not quite "getting it". Occasionally through words some can say so, more often succinctly only after they have left care, as our Care Leaver has also said: "Without belonging we are lost, without direction, without a platform. It's like being lost in space"—an unrelenting painful realization of separation, often barely thinkable or speakable.

For most of us, thankfully, our sense of reliable belonging arises from that extraordinarily ordinary good-enough experience of living and growing. For example, consider the child not yet 3 years old, at a picnic with his family in a park alongside a river, a summer gathering place much visited in pre–air-conditioning times because it had lots of trees where small breezes and the shade might relieve the hot, humid days where they lived. The family that day was part of a large group of the father's friends. Somehow the toddler wandered off and became lost. One of the group, a motorcycle policeman, was there on his big Harley. Looking at the child, he said, "Sonny, with a freckly face like that you can only belong to one family." He lifted the child up on his bike and took him to where the family was. They gathered him in, with great thanks to their friend. Sixty years later, this tale can be related with much detail because the then child and now adult has always had a vivid picture of it—not because he remembers anything but the slightest fragment himself. No, this tale was told so often in and by the family when he and his siblings were growing up that the telling fixed it in his mind. He imagined all the bits—the facts, the feelings, the tiny details—into a visual narrative strand. For the family and relations it was a tale of belonging, being lost but then found and reunited safely and forever. It is a happy-ever-after tale effectively containing the confusion and fear felt by child and family while he was wandering lost. Of course, for the other family members it was the child who had wandered off and been lost, but the child himself knew differently. At the level of the lived experience, they had lost him. It was therefore their responsibility to find and recover him. For a child who "belongs", no amount of rational explanation will alter the living reality of "who is responsible for me?" And such a memorable experience of building will have been reinforced, for him as for us all, by many hundreds of common daily living experiences.

The contrast in living and in language

For that population of those in or having left care, such equivalent extraordinary and ordinary experiences that embed a sense of connectedness will often have been missing—experiences that were supported by efforts beyond the child to connect him up and join him to a belonging more fundamental, deep, and wide than any one experience or relationship. Even the word "belonging" itself highlights the potential risk and damage for those not enabled to have not just what Winnicott called a "continuity of being . . . without which doing and being done to have no significance" (Winnicott, 1949) but a continuity of belonging as well. And without distortion to Winnicott's thinking, it can be added in relation to belonging that "doing with and together has no significance either" in the absence of that experience of continuity of being and belonging. By way of confirmation our Care Leaver observes, "I belong in the town I live and to my friends, but I don't belong to any individuals . . . I don't feel loved." Clearly those more surface "belongings" just do not hold that deep significance that would make all other belongings feel safe and truly life- and self-affirming.

As Winnicott identified in his brief paper, "Anxiety Associated with Insecurity" (1952), for him the "centre of gravity" of a healthy person does not start in the individual. Rather, it exists in the "total set up". The caring as part of the being together—really, for Winnicott, being one—prevents feelings of disintegration. Without this experience to a good-enough degree, or with its subsequent severely traumatic breakdown, the child (and then adult) is not grounded by a "centre of gravity". Instead, the person is "lost in space", with no platform to launch him/herself confidently and competently into other secure orbits of connectedness—never a connected body (celestial or otherwise); at best, not even a useful satellite but a "rogue" and out-of-control one, always at risk of crashing to earth or spinning out ever farther into deep, cold space, especially if this predicament is not recognized and efforts made to ameliorate it with and for the child.

Moving from Winnicott's creative thinking to linguistics, the very word "belonging" highlights the respective routes to health and to damage when we construct and deconstruct it. Notice that when the word is separated into its apparent two roots—being and longing—you find that the explanation of the word "be" before its many definitions classifies it "a defective, incomplete word".[1] Considering how often we use it, it is interesting that "be" is probably the most irregular, slippery word in our language, constantly changing form, sometimes with little discernible pattern. It has no function on its own; it can only operate usefully with a subject, "I am", or verb (and implied subject and/or object—e.g., "Being John Malkovitch or "Knowing me, knowing you"). Meanwhile "longing" is defined as "a seeking, increasingly desperate, for something or someone, usually unattainable". Indeed, it continues that if something/someone persists in being unattainable, then the state of longing becomes first yearning and then pining, "a consuming . . . wasting away of a person, especially from an intense grief".

Then, most interestingly for our purposes, only when the two words are fused together does a word emerge with a meaning entirely different from either of the roots if they had remained separate. As one of its many definitions clarifies, belonging can be "a state of feeling at home". Therefore, it seems that, as often in chemistry and physics, when two very different elements are fused together—in this case, being and longing into belonging—the emergent word/element is bound together by a powerful force that in ordinary conditions is greatly resistant to dismemberment and destruction. However, as in chemistry and physics too, when/if the fusion of those elements of belonging is somehow broken, usually by the focused application of very powerful external forces, then equal or greater powerful, uncontained, and often long-term and highly toxic energy is released—as in the breaking of fused atomic elements in the natural world (fission). When destroyed actually or potentially, the human condition and the relationships that constitute "belonging" will suffer similar uncontrolled, destructive impacts, especially in the emotional dimension of people's lives and in their prospects of going "towards belonging", unless there is a dramatic intervention to contain the unleashed toxicity and "re-fuse" (not refuse) being and longing. Given the power when the bonds break, in both physical and emotional worlds, it is little surprise that those suffering such ruptures and losses of connectedness are not just alone but lonely as well. They can feel not just unwanted but unwantable, toxic material that can damage or destroy when or if they even try to get close, causing on some occasions considerable "collateral damage" to others alongside expressing their own damage. Again, our insightful Care Leaver observes, "When I am gone, I will be missed [if I belong]. But still I am lonely." Whether we consider it via Winnicott or the natural sciences, belonging holds together not just people in networks, but also individual people in their internal worlds and in their minds.

Subject and/or object

The philosopher Isaiah Berlin once wrote, "I wish my life and decisions to depend upon myself. . . . I wish to be a subject not an object" (Berlin, 1969). There is a certain Winnicottian paradox contained in that statement. To be the "I Am" subject he seeks to be, he must first be an object, or perhaps more accurately a "subject as object", both simultaneously. Those who have attended one of the Queen's Garden Parties at Buckingham Palace have the opportunity to understand this paradox. Gathered together in their hundreds, they have a good amount of time to mingle, munch, and drink tea or something stronger. Then, without any special signal, a hush begins to fall. People are gently ushered about to form a lengthy human corridor. The Queen and her attendants have appeared. As she commences her progress along this human avenue, equerries going ahead bring forward the occasional person to be greeted directly by the Queen. It is, however, the rest of the many people gathered, and the Queen's apparent interaction with them, that is especially interesting in respect of being and belonging. Throughout her progress, her eyes move left to right just ahead of her. They seem briefly to catch each person's eye with a nod of recognition. It must take great practice, and a willing audience, to create that interactional illusion, but it is very effective. And it is indeed a creative illusion, because for a moment each person feels that he or she is the object of her attention and a subject, her subject, someone who belongs to and with her. And by that experience of "subject as object [of her attention]" each person can feel, as Berlin sought to be, an "I Am" subject.

The entire royal progress through the Garden revisits and affirms on a grand scale the earliest human experiences of finding the self through having that self recognized by our intimate carer(s) and mirrored back to us in and through their caring responses of words and actions. Of course, the Garden Party experience is momentary. Soon everyone is heading back out into the city and home. Our early experiences, on the other hand, are far longer lasting, laying down as they do the foundations ultimately for everyone, like Berlin, to have the life of a subject, living and deciding for themselves. That is, they can be Subject if those early experiences are reliably enough available for and experienced by a person either early on or through later careful (or care-full), thoughtful compensatory ones.

Nobody really needs to attend the Queen's Garden Party to have a sense of belonging in their life. In ordinary living beyond the palace walls, however, everyone needs a significant "good-enough" experience and an enduring sense of belonging that can be taken for granted and enable us to feel healthily object and subject simultaneously—in relation to and with significant others. Here, then, beyond the palace walls, lie the challenge, the problems and dilemmas, and the opportunities in moving towards belonging for those who come into State care, for those involved directly in providing the services that will "deliver" that care, and for those who actually provide the care on a daily, 24-hour basis and not just 9 to 5 Monday through Friday.

The State becomes parent

Since the first Children Act, in 1948, the State has taken on an ever-increasing role and responsibility for parenting children who cannot live safely with their birth parents. This has created a unique and enduring relationship between the child and the "State as parent" that is not replicated anywhere else in the many relationships that exist between citizens and their government (Care Leavers' Foundation, 2012a; Reeves, 2012a). The State has conferred upon itself a duty that must not be held intermittently, discharged casually, or set aside thoughtlessly. Indeed, throughout all the subsequent time from 1948 until today, the intent and sentiment of the State has been undeniably positive and determined to act responsibly in its role and duty of "optimizing the life chances" of the children in its care. Similarly, the language of successive government initiatives in this area has been ever more eloquent and promising. However, as we know, the language of intent and sentiment is always "with the angels"; the devil lurks in the detail from the point when words and their often slippery meanings meet State systems and structures. From there, it is the detail of the actions and their consequences, whether intended or unintended, that will determine the nature of the movement towards belonging for the child in care or who has left care.

In the transition and translation from words to structures and actions, something happens that too often prevents the State from being a "good-enough parent" (Reeves, 2012a). With the best of intentions the State invariably adopts a service focus towards the child at risk and in need, most notably in recent years by the regular reconfiguration of services. It is undeniable that these service initiatives reflect a genuine concern about the safety and welfare of vulnerable children, and in that respect they affirm the State's legal duty of care. What often gets missed in this approach is the duty to care for this population through attending to the way we actually provide care for these children. Real care requires continuity, sustained involvement, and commitment. Certainly every parent knows, as do most of those being parented, that they are engaged in a living process and a "work in continual progress" and constant negotiation. It does not lend itself readily to fixed command-and-control approaches. When these are applied, and it is often the experience of children that they are (Morgan & Lindsay, 2012), it too easily becomes an exercise in routinized rigidity, not personalized flexibility.

Corporate systems often behave in this "controlling" way. When applied to the care system, the individual child and the reality of each child's predicament are obscured within the operations of the entire system, which will almost always dwarf an individual. It might not be as hard as if one tried to identify our own Sun from the extraordinary composite photograph created by astronomers of the myriad stars that make up our own galaxy. But it is still not easy to keep sight of the individual in the care system as it exists today. Moreover, there is a secondary gain for the system operating in this corporate way to "look after" children. That is, it protects those in the command-and-control positions at many levels, even at the "front line" of delivery, from facing directly and feeling the impact of the hurt, pain, and despair of each child and the actual circumstances that brought them into the care of the "corporate parent". Hence the corporate system of delivering services and the avoidance of pain combine to keep this "parent" at a distance.

Yet our State system of care is not simply a large monolith that resolutely maintains a great corporate distance from "its children". In fact, through its local agents—the professionals and other staff in social care departments and in all the other departments in local government—it often quite paradoxically manages simultaneously to be close in. However, this closeness is often experienced as impingement by the child in care and even by those providing the day-to-day care. This is because the nature of that proximity and the responsibilities the system exercises are both determined in important ways by the remote corporate "uber-parent". This effectively ensures that much intervention is at best periodic and relates to cycles of contact determined by bureaucratic imperatives such as reviews or statutory visits, assessments, examinations, and reports. Because of this, some of the key features of reliable, good-quality care for those in care is effectively undermined (Morgan & Lindsay, 2012; Voice for the Child in Care, 1998). Consistency and unconditionality in the experience of care, which do much to endow a healthy sense of belonging at the immediate level of daily living, must give way to an inconsistency and conditionality that sow uncertainty, doubt, or even despair—about the reliability and stability of a placement and of the relationships developed therein, now and going forward "towards belonging". How often is it reported that a child or young person is informed without warning that her placement with/in X is ending, but as yet it's not known where and when she will go. For some in care, this intervention not only destabilizes the present and future, it undoes much of what had been painstakingly built, sometimes over many years, by the child and her carers.

Recently one social worker was challenged following just such a communication to a child, delivered without any consultation with the carers about not only whether but when to give this message. Her reply was that she had to inform the child because the decision had been made by her department, and it was the child's human right to know—a human right undone by an inhumane righteousness. While an extreme example itself, even if not uncommon, it does nevertheless underline the tension between a corporate parenting that constructs a system with the child as just one factor and one that more organically holds a child in the centre of a caring mind. Too often in the current system, the tension is less a creative one and more one that strains and constrains healthy human living and belonging. The problem for our care system, and hence for those in care having a true sense of belonging, is that it often lacks a flexibility of foresight and thoughtful response. Too much leaks or pours out on or away from the child without adequate thought being applied. Belonging for children in care is embedded in trust, as it is for everyone—a trust in others and their reliability and predictability, and in the children's belief, born out of learning through living together, that they really do belong. It is not a sham, a surface phenomenon. Such a trust, as Reeves observes (2012b), "is best secured by foresight and prevention rather than pity and reparation", and certainly not by organizational neglect or thoughtless, distracted disregard. An organizational capacity for finely tuned behavioural modulation and flexible emotional distance regulation, sometimes moving closer in and sometimes giving some space, is a rare phenomenon in our current care system. Yet it is a capacity essential in order to know the real child in care and meet his needs. Sadly it is more often noticeable by its absence than recognizable in its presence.

Interestingly, in ancient times the word "*therapes*", from which our word "therapist" is derived, did not mean a trained therapist. It was simply a person who served by standing alongside and helping to do what was requested—a reliable, supportive presence and service, a servant in the fullest sense of the word. Those notions of public service and public servant, or at least the reality of serving, have rather faded from our social discourse, particularly over the last 25 years. It is bound to be difficult to really be a caring corporate parent when driven by directives to achieve targets and perform within budgets, alongside resource and time constraints. Perhaps the resolution of this amalgam of social paradox, organizational dilemma, and persistently ineffective care experience for too many lies in releasing corporate potential in another way. Rather than require the State to be parent, perhaps it can be expected and encouraged to occupy the role of a grandparent—someone who loves unconditionally but, when not indulging the grandchild on occasions, supports those doing the parenting and parenting function in whatever setting—whether home, Home, or elsewhere. It will be helping and expecting them to make caring and wise decisions for and with the child, and it can let go of the tendency to "micro-manage" from too far within or without. While there will always be a few decisions and actions that are downright wrong, many, many others are simply different ways to get to the same goal—the care and support of a child on his journey towards living and belonging healthily in a social world, towards an independence that is a mature interdependence with others, not an isolation and loneliness on the margins of our communities. It is terrible for the child when the strong tendency of the State to default to control swamps or denies entirely a daily living experience adapted not to control but to life. And it does not really help society very much either, certainly not in the long term.

A life through metaphors

Until such a transformation to organized non-interference occurs, the experience of those children who have had too little exposure to the opportunity to feel they genuinely belong will continue to be hugely difficult for them and problematic for those trying to ensure a better quality of State care for them. For these children, a particular challenge, even if they themselves can only occasionally articulate it as such, lies in managing to cope with the feeling of living in and through a filter of metaphors rather than simply living life directly. In these circumstances, children can feel not so much a total rigid barrier between them and ordinary living but a kind of opaque screen that, like a cataract, acts as a constant shadow or fog between them and their seeing and experiencing the full light of living with self and with others in the same world. Things are rarely clear. Some may suggest that this experience is only a difference in degree rather than kind when compared to the experience of ordinarily developing children who themselves sometime cannot completely fathom and understand the world they inhabit and those relations they live with. If so, then it is a difference of a massive degree for a good number of the care population. In fact, the difference in degree can be so great that it effectively constitutes a difference in kind, when the very different life experiences of the two populations are factored in.

In this respect, it is the case that there can be very poor relations between those in or now out of care and those professionals responsible in law for them and sometimes even those directly providing their care in foster placements and residential homes. In these circumstances, the road "towards belonging" is missing or heavily overgrown and hard to pass along. It is less that this population is entirely cut off and ignored, more a case like that presented in many films. Typically in such films, large extended families do not completely deny any recognition to some of their members they may regard as "poor relations", usually for a complicated variety of family, social, and economic reasons. Instead, their desire and effort in more or less conscious ways is devoted towards minimizing any contact in terms of meaningful closeness, frequency, and duration. During any times of contact that simply cannot be avoided (and do remember one of the most frequent complaints of those when in care and later is that their social worker rarely visits and often cannot be contacted; Stein, 2012), there is an undercurrent of unease or worse never far below the surface of what can appear to be civil or even "relaxed" association. The relief is therefore palpable when, sooner rather than later, these professionals and carers (again, not all by any means, but still far too many) can re-establish a greater physical and emotional distance so they are no longer close in and face to face with the child and the child's need to feel true connectedness and belonging. The formula quickly kicks in—"out of sight, out of mind"—at least as a person, if not as a "case", until they next cannot be avoided.

Those in care who experience these conditions can feel they inhabit an unrelenting and rather bleak, grey hinterland, even when geographically they are located in the midst of local neighbourhoods and perhaps attending local schools. Nevertheless they sense that, at the levels that really count for belonging, they are still disconnected from others and from themselves. Any lingering feeling of belonging drains steadily from them—or, at certain times of distress, haemorrhages away. As "poor relations", they often suffer from a chronic form of "relative isolation" in all levels of their lives, sometimes effectively invisible to sight, other times mute to the ear and conscience. Too dramatic and persistently bleak a metaphor? Not according to the many testimonies of those who have experienced State care (www.thecareleaversfoundation.org). Exceptions notwithstanding, this "Poor Relations" metaphor captures a significant part of the experience of those in care. Nor can all the problem be laid at the door of professional and government departments. A particularly problematic obstacle to belonging, and not simply an occasional event for a not small proportion in foster care, is the practice of the child having to move to another placement for "respite" while his "host family" has a break, not infrequently going off on a "family holiday". The child is left behind rather than just going along or extra resources being put in to enable his continuing presence. The question is thus twofold: whose "respite" is it, and how can you feel you truly belong when your presence is conditional in such powerful ways—and when those doing the "care planning" do not notice the powerful impact of what it means to the child. It may not come down to "All or nothing at all", but it sows that seed of doubt—about the real nature of these children's desire or claim to belong and about the true feelings held by others about them.

This uncertainty about how significant others really feel about them leads to another of the metaphors too many children in care carry with them, as if they were wearing a type of cutting-edge "Google Glasses". However, these "glasses" do nothing except cast a set of metaphors in front of their eyes as they move along in life. In this case, the dominant metaphor viewed and felt is, "damaged goods". The doubt about being good, or even "good enough", sown by a range of care (and pre-care) experiences, can transform into a feeling of being damaged, probably beyond repair. In many super-markets there is a shelf or a deep wire bin, usually in a less visited rear corner of the large store. in which are placed, or thrown, a mix of products that have no connection with each other than that they are all damaged. Over a few weeks, some of these now discounted products are claimed quickly. Others remain in the bin or on the shelf week after week, not only unclaimed but also further dam-aged by careless handling by passing, vaguely interested shoppers or by other items being dumped in and damaging them further. After several weeks, these even more damaged items are no longer there. Perhaps, just perhaps, they have been claimed and taken home. But the likelihood is that, having suffered damage upon damage compounded by lack of interest and neglect, they have been deemed "unwanted", removed from the "last-chance bin", and dropped into the skip for carting away as landfill. In the case of children in care suffering this fate, not only are their possessions still regularly carried in bin bags, but they themselves are "binned".

In fact, it is worse for these children, who, unlike a damaged packet of cornflour, are conscious, have a conscience, and often even have a capacity for concern for others, if it is but noticed. They come to regard themselves not merely as unwanted "damaged goods", but as "damaging, not good" who are "spoiled", unwantable, and even toxic when in contact with people. Given the many negative beliefs about themselves from their earlier pre-care childhoods that those in care can superimpose on these children's current experi-ences, it is not surprising that they can continue to attribute falsely to themselves a negative active agency and responsibility whenever things in their lives go wrong or do not seem to "add up"—"I'm not good enough; it must be my fault; that good life, out there, is for others, not for me", and so on. In these circumstances, their road is one less travelled, not towards belonging as a fully engaged and engaging citizen but towards a lonely life as a denizen of the margins of society.

There is no opportunity to feel a subject as Berlin sought to be. For those struggling to feel they belong, there is, while in care, only the experience of being subjected to and subjugated by thoughtless, uncaring systems and the people in them, who could not or would not understand the nature of their needs and the sometimes troubled and troublesome behaviours and attitudes they present (Care Leavers' Foundation, 2012; Stein, 2012). Through the filtering screen of metaphors, and without serious efforts at redirection, the journey for them—from "poor relations" through "damaged and damaging goods"—is likely to continue in a direction very different from that they desperately hoped for. Nor are they travelling slowly: they are moving fast along a superhighway—towards becoming end-of-the-road "wastage". While usually a word used in relation to goods inadvertently damaged or stolen from commercial companies and organizations, "wastage" can be felt by those in care as another telling metaphor for their lives where goodness has been withheld, trampled upon, or stolen from them and often not recognized in them.

Enveloped by their metaphors, it is understandable that for many in care so much in their lives can feel a puzzle, and they themselves in turn become "puzzled"—not about completing a two-dimensional wooden jigsaw but about how the pieces of their lives fit together to form a coherent narrative and have an overall meaning. It is a quite common experience even in ordinary life that, when fitting together the pieces of a puzzle, there often will be one piece that is either lost or does not seem to fit properly or anywhere. The piece is very much needed to make a whole (and, in life, a wholesome) picture, and in itself it "needs" to be put into and to be part of that larger whole, both connecting others and being connected. Then the puzzle piece can belong, as the puzzled child in care also needs to be and needs to feel. The not uncommon experience, however, suggests that too many do not or did not have that experience and role of linking and being linked to in order that everyone and everything necessary belongs together. And often the child could not figure out what kept her from fitting together and feeling this belonging. In fact, for many, that failure of "fitness" was located in the reality that the State as parent, even when somehow physically present through its various agents, was rarely emotionally available and attuned to the child. The relationship and activity was largely formulaic and, on the surface, happening at a pace driven by the organization, when it was not being neglected almost entirely. Depth or substance were rarely present.

To relate, or not to relate

Relationships, then, are that *sine qua non* for healthy belonging. Without them there will be nothing, or little good enough and lasting. They lie at the heart of all belonging, making it a living reality, not just an inert idea. Therefore, relationships should be the primary focus of efforts by the corporate parent of the State to support its children. After all, we do not derive our sense of "who we belong to" from an intuitive sense of "who we are"; we determine who we are from our sense of "rootedness" in our living relationships and only then in our name and habitat and so forth. From this position, we can identify who belongs to us too, allowing a sense of mutual "ownership" to exist in place of a crude possessiveness. Those in care can be casualties of this sense of belonging, having lacked or lost the stability and security of relationships within which they can feel that sense of "being owned" and then come to "own" others and eventually themselves. They need a special and stable figure or figures whom they can call and think of as their own.

Yet in their struggles to achieve and maintain this belonging, too often with very little support and in the shadow of earlier failures, they can still be misunderstood in the present. Instead of being recognized as one of life's casualties, in need of concerned attention, they are constructed as "causalities", intentionally controlling all they say and do, however contrary to their own best interests and needs are their words and deeds. When reflecting on his experiences of being blamed and rejected before, during, and after his life in care, our Care Leaver declared "It's a Curse. So many people may like me, but I don't feel loved. I'd give away all I have achieved to feel loved." Despite his many scars from life's vicissitudes, not for him Harry Potter's iconic scar that affirms love. In *Harry Potter and the Philosopher's Stone* (Rowling, 1997), following his adventures the young wizard asks Dumbledore why Voldemort had not been able to kill him. Dumbledore replies that Harry had been deeply loved by his mother, who had given up her own life to protect him. That degree of love and the object of it could never be destroyed by anything, not even evil hatred. Harry was inoculated by love in a way that as yet our Care Leaver and many others in care have not. They remain vulnerable to continuing hurt and harm, even if they are unlikely to encounter an evil wizard. The curse of leading an ordinary life without feeling loved is serious challenge and risk enough.

One positive and helping function of a loving or at least genuinely caring relationship is that a person need not feel "unheld" emotionally (Winnicott, 1960b). In particular, within a relationship that affirms belonging the child feels held in a healthy mind. For two related reasons touching on mental health, this is much more important than it might seem in the saying. First, of that minority of very troubled children fortunate enough to be referred to a variety of specialist services, many arrive with a professional's "health warning": "I'm not sure why you want to see her first. We're referring her to you because she can't seem to say anything sensible about herself or what she keeps doing." When, after gently insisting about the need to meet and speak, the child is brought before you, quite often either directly or indirectly she declares to you a major dilemma and source of distress she carries almost continuously. Through words and actions she says she does not feel held reliably in the mind of a caring, consistent, and responsible (to her) adult. And when not feeling this emotional holding, she gets anxious, which anxiety then drives her to follow the formula that "if I am not held *in* anyone's mind, I shall try at least to be *on* their mind". Of course, she also knows instinctively that the best way reliably to be on the mind of others is to produce an unrelenting flow of difficult, demanding, and even dangerous behaviours—"that always gets their attention!" It might not gain attachment. In fact, it often secures mainly criticism, frustration, and punishment by sanction or further chastisement. Nevertheless, in the circumstances, for the child this is preferable to being neither on nor in the mind of an adult who is supposed to be there to care.

The second reason flows directly from this readiness to accept only attention by being on people's minds. This is because if they feel they are neither in nor on the mind of the adults charged to care, they feel not only entirely out of the mind of these others but also out of their own mind. Without delving too far into any theory of mind, it is known that each person realizes the capacity to have a mind of one's own by first being held in the healthy mind of a significant other. This is the source of Descartes' error (Damasio, 1994). Descartes declared "I think, therefore I am", whereas we now know it is more the case that "I am because I have come to know myself in and through being held in the mind of another. Therefore I think, I think." Moreover, when being only on the mind of others continues for too long, to avoid the further risk of falling "out of my mind" and to secure somehow the experience of being held in mind, the child in care can seek or not resist what can be called the delinquent and dangerous "Mind of the Streets and Shadows". Time and again those in care get ensnared in this predicament—from which it is always a painful and damaging struggle to escape or from which there can sometimes be no way back. There are regular, frequent even, reports of children lost to this unhealthy existence and a predatory "mind" bent on the exploitation of those already hurt and vulnerable and not sufficiently held in a healthy mind (Office of the Children's Commissioner, 2012). It is this latter point—not being held in mind—that is almost universally overlooked in all the commentaries about these situations and how to prevent or remedy them. Being held in a healthy, caring, and bounded mind creates a reliable space to explore and find one's self and to learn and grow into one's own healthy mind and a social world. Living in the unhealthy mind of the streets "commodifies" and devours the person, giving nothing of worth and taking many things, including sometimes life. But it does offer an alternative to the mindlessness of lonely isolation and madness. Just because it is a major challenge to provide the alternative of a healthy mind for those who struggle to inhabit and use it well does not mean society, the State, and its services need not try and try again to offer it.

An antidote for hurt and a framework for hope

For belonging to be realized, an antidote for these current conditions is needed, as is a fundamental culture change. If this happens, those still vulnerable in care may be able finally to secure a natural justice, one tempered by caring and mercy. Then they will not remain exposed too often to a formal or informal Justice, which one care leaver now resident in a secure unit called tellingly "Just-Ice", an untempered, judgemental mis-treatment of the hurt and vulnerable. Yet we need not despair at the scale of the task, although we might well still take a deep breath. Much exists already that, if implemented in the right spirit, will make an enormous difference. In fact, the recent *Charter for Care Leavers* (DfE and Care Leavers' Foundation, 2012) can make a very positive contribution much further upstream too—for those still in care. It commits government at national and local levels to ensure to care leavers (and now those in care too) that they will:

⯈ respect and honour the identity of all

⯈ believe in each person

⯈ listen to everyone

⯈ inform them

⯈ support them

⯈ find them (or help them to keep) a home

⯈ be a lifelong champion.

While back again in the area where the "devilish detail" will determine whether positive change will or will not occur, at least an explicitly "owned" set of principles and promises now exists to shape the attitudes and actions of the corporate parents of the State. They will make a difference, especially if they are married up with some other "strengtheners".

One such strengthener is "therapeutic parenting", most recently celebrated by Cameron and Maginn (2009). They identify key areas for careful attention in order to ensure good-quality care and improve outcomes for children in State care:

> ensuring the provision of primary care and protection
> promoting secure attachment
> helping to grow positive self-perception and emotional compe-
  tence
> supporting age-appropriate self-management skills
> promoting resilience and a sense of belonging.

Critically, Cameron and Maginn continually highlight the distinction between simply caring about a child in care and genuinely
caring for the child within a frame of "therapeutic parenting" that
is essential to recovery and belonging.

Conclusions

Any and all efforts to change a culture and to honour important
values require courage—for adult carers to do and for children to
face. However, acting within these well-intentioned frameworks
and wise guidance at least offers a chance. Previously, little enough
that offered hope and positive difference has been within the grasp
of the child in care and his corporate parent agents.

   While we struggle in the present day with these matters, the
reality is that a positive alternative has long been known. In the
early eighteenth century, the philosopher Wilhelm Leibniz summed
up succinctly the key message for our day as for his: he declared
, "If we can offer wise loving care [*caritas sapientis*], then we shall
not go far wrong" (quoted in Riley, 1999). His phrase in the Latin,
caritas sapientis, translates not as wise charity, as we often now
regard the word *caritas*, but as the word was originally meant: a
loving care. This is something that, when delivered with wisdom
and with a degree of humility and self-examination while offering
it to others, will keep us and those we care for on the right path
towards belonging.

   However, it must also be said—should we stray or stray too
far from that path and fail or, worse, let down these children in
our corporate care—that even if we escape censure today, we shall

certainly be judged harshly by a more enlightened and compassionate future generation. Then we shall have to fear that all of us culpable for this continuing failure of State care will face the *"contropasso"* or poetic justice punishments that Dante observed being suffered for eternity by some of the worst offenders in the pits of Hell, those in the last two circles, the eighth and ninth (James, 2013)

In the eighth circle are the hypocrites, who are forced to walk listlessly along wearing cloaks made heavy with lead linings. These represent their falsity that weighs them down now that the reality of their living actions and attitudes are exposed. We who will have been bystanders and onlookers, only voicing worthy words when committed actions are needed, will be wearing the modern equivalent of those heavy leaden cloaks if and when we are judged to have not acted to make a real difference, even though we could or did know the right path towards belonging. Meanwhile, in the ninth circle are the traitors. These are distinguished from the merely fraudulent because their acts involved betraying a special relationship of some kind. The special relationship with those in care that the State and its agents have, with their fingerprints all over it and them, qualifies many of us for this ultimate *contropasso*—to be encased at a great depth in the searingly cold ice of the lake in the lowest reaches of Hell.

The path towards belonging clearly follows the way of *caritas sapientis*. The road to perdition takes us to the Inferno. We must choose wisely, for the sake of those in State care and for ourselves!

Note

1. All definitions are from the *Oxford English Dictionary Based on Historical Principles*, 1978 edition.

CHAPTER THREE

Towards belonging:
the role of a residential setting

John Diamond

his chapter explores the role of specialist therapeutic residential child care and how it can facilitate emotional growth and
a subsequent sense of "belonging" for some of the most emotionally damaged children in our society. How such a provision can
decrease mental health problems for emotionally troubled children,
complement and support foster placements for these children, and
lead to a deeper sense of self and belonging is also explored. The
chapter begins with a brief discussion of the importance of belonging in the mental health of children and young people, goes on
to discuss the need for residential provision for some children in
the care system, and then focuses on how this is provided by the
Mulberry Bush School. Throughout, my concern is to demonstrate
the central importance of belonging for children and young people
and how, based largely upon Winnicott's concept of holding, it is
developed with them by the Mulberry Bush School.

Belonging

Little has been written in either the mental health or social care
literature on the nature and importance of belonging. However,

the need to belong is, according to Baumeister and Leary (1995), a "desire for interpersonal attachments as a fundamental human motivation", and they define two critical elements:

> Human beings have a pervasive drive to form and maintain at least a minimum quantity of lasting, positive, and significant interpersonal relationships. Satisfying this drive involves two criteria: First, there is a need for frequent, affectively pleasant interactions with a few other people, and, second, these interactions must take place in the context of a temporally stable and enduring framework of affective concern for each other's welfare. [p. 497]

Pearce and Pickard (2013) argue that a psychotherapeutic approach can ameliorate the negative effects of a lack of a sense of belonging:

> Decreased belongingness is associated with increases in stress and mental health problems, as well as somatic illness such as heart disease. . .; conversely, increases in belongingness lead to a decrease in health problems and an overall increase in happiness (for a review see Baumeister & Leary 1995). A psychotherapeutic approach that is able to promote belongingness is therefore likely to have a range of beneficial effects. [p. 638]

The mental health implications for a sense of belonging may be very familiar to clinicians and others with a duty of care to children and young people. Some of these implications are extremely serious, as the well-known case of the two brothers from Edlington chillingly illustrates.

Some serious consequences of a lack of belonging

On Saturday, 4 April 2009, an 11-year-old boy was found with critical head injuries near a brickpit in a rural area of Edlington. His 9-year-old brother was also found wandering nearby with knife wounds.

The following Tuesday, two brothers, aged 10 and 12, were each charged with the attempted murder and robbery of both of the injured boys. They appeared at Sheffield Crown Court, where a hearing revealed the extent of their actions: they had led the two boys to isolated wasteland; one was forced to strip naked and perform a sex act, and a metal ring was used to strangle the other. The brothers threw stones and bricks at the boys' heads. When alerted by the sound of passers-by, they covered the two boys with a sheet that they then set alight, causing burns to the victims. Dr Eileen Vizard, an expert witness, told the court that the younger brother was a "very high risk" to the community and at risk of becoming "a seriously disturbed psychopathic offender" unless he received appropriate treatment.

Through the subsequent court reports, it later came to light that the brothers were from a chaotic and abusive home environment. It would seem that in this terrifying and tragic case, both sets of brothers were far from "being in the right place". The environment was a disused semi-rural wasteland "out of the sight" of any concerned and protective adult. For the two protagonists, this place might be described as an external manifestation of their own inner worlds, worlds that had become this way through a lack of holding and thus of a sense of belonging to families. Therefore, we might also hypothesize that the violence that was meted out to the victims (brothers who "have" family) was because they had become the targets of an unrestrained envious and murderous assault by their attackers, who instinctively knew that they *did not belong to anyone or any family*.

At the request of Michael Gove, Secretary of State for Education, in 2012 the case was reviewed by Lord Carlile of Berriew. In the report, Lord Carlile identified a range of failures by the local authority which together failed to prevent the brothers "acting out" their innate tendency for violence:

> 125. . . . the decision was made to place [J1] and [J2] in the foster care of a well-meaning couple, but they were not a suitable placement in the circumstances—not least because they lived near the home of the father who had caused much of the difficulty . . . but whom they chose to be with if they could gain access to him. There seems to have been an assumption that the boys needed comfortable care, but insufficient attention paid to their escalating pattern of violence.
>
> 126. The foster care provided was for respite purposes. Given the nature of the boys' difficulties and behaviour, there should

have been a much more effective assessment of their individual
needs, and a long-term solution. [Carlile, 2012, p. 42]

Fortunately, such disturbing cases of child-on-child violence are not
that common. However, child neglect and abuse are regular occur-
rences. Each week in the UK, one or two children are killed at the
hands of adults and families, and annually up to 40,000 children
are subject to child protection plans, the highest categories of which
are for neglect and then emotional abuse.

Between April and August 2012, Cafcass, the courts advisory
service, received 4,489 new care applications, 8.5% higher than the
same period in 2011. There were 982 applications in May 2012 alone,
the highest ever recorded figure for a single month (Cafcass, 2012).

According to the Department for Education First Statistical
Release of 31 March 2012 (DfE, 2012.), there were 67,050 looked
after children and young people in England and Wales, of which
41,790 were originally taken into care under the category of abuse
or neglect. Of these:

1.   In homes and hostels subject to Children's Homes regulations
     there were: 2,640 inside Council boundaries, 2,250 placed out-
     side of Council boundaries, and 960 in residential schools.

2.   50,260 or 75% of all were in foster placements.

Foster care remains the preferred option for looked after children.
Government and local authority policy focuses on finding substitute families for those who, for whatever reason, cannot be with
their birth family. The logic goes: children who have been rejected
or displaced by their birth families need a stable placement and
loving parental figures. But what if many of those children find
the concept and intimacy of family life alien and intolerable? Many
children who due to early years' trauma have no basic trust in
adult or parental figures, and are driven to test the containment
provided by a family to destruction, still find themselves placed in
foster provision. The intention is clearly to *foster* a sense of belonging, but the outcome all too often is to increase the experience of
multiple placement breakdown and the child's sense of alienation
and social exclusion and internalization by the child of the feeling
that she cannot "belong" to anyone.

The nature of the problem

In such absence of the experience of belonging to a family, children and young people in the care system may become further dislocated from the possibility of meaningful integration into a family.

Clough, Bullock, and Ward (2006) propose a distinction between three groups of young people who find themselves in the care system:

- Children with relatively simple or straightforward needs who require either short-term or relatively "ordinary" substitute care
- Children or families with deep-rooted, complex or chronic needs with a long history of difficulty and disruption, including abuse or neglect requiring more than simply a substitute family
- Children with extensive, complex and enduring needs compounded by very difficult behaviour who require more specialized and intensive resources such as a therapeutic community, an adolescent mental health unit, a small "intensive care" residential setting or a secure unit. [pp. 2–3]

Many of the children in the first category are suitably placed in foster care; they will have enough of a coherent sense of self to be able to be discerning about how their needs might be best met, or, with support, they can be helped to identify which placement best meets their needs. Some children and young people prefer residential care as a positive option; in 2007, after consultation with young people in the care system, the *Care Matters* White Paper unequivocally identified that:

> Residential care will always be the placement of choice for some children and we know that some children say they do not want to be in foster care. We need these children to be able to enjoy a genuinely excellent care experience, drawing on the best of what homes in this country and elsewhere do now. [DfES, 2007, para. 4.49]

For some children, choosing residential care over foster care is an informed and conscious choice. Others—those in the second and third category, who are more unintegrated and traumatized (or are too young)—have less ability to act on their own sense of agency and make such decisions. For these children, the role of the professionals who have responsibility for them is to find a placement that will best increase their chances of belonging. However, all too often the "corporate parent" is made up of procedural systems, and if the child does not feel that these are "navigated" by empathic adults, she is at risk of feeling further "cast adrift".

This group of children have often suffered severe early trauma—deprivation, neglect, and abuse—leaving them with a profound sense of confusion and mistrust and without a coherent sense of self. Without a sense of agency, these children need the active involvement of social workers and other professionals acting in their best interests to make difficult and complex decisions about the type of placement that will in their case keep them and others safe, and to meet their needs in a placement that will provide the best possible outcome for them.

Residential care can offer a different experience from that of foster care. Thoughtfully delivered residential care can provide an ethos of professional neutrality, which allows children a safe environment and the conditions in which to explore relationships; if this is backed by a responsible financial commitment, they can do so in their own time. This requires the provision of a relational system that can provide appropriate "emotional distance regulation".

Unfortunately, in a time of economic uncertainty, there is a tendency for residential care and foster care to be constructed as in competition, rather than as having the potential to complement and support each other, and this can work against the development of a system of flexible provision. Also, in the current context of local authority cuts and the general ethos of national austerity, the costs associated with residential care do little to raise the profile of this important and valuable resource into public consciousness.

Towards belonging:
the role of specialist therapeutic residential care

Some children who have suffered severe and early complex trauma are placed in specialist residential services such as the Mulberry

Bush School, where the ethos aims to provide "attuned emotional holding" to meet the needs of the child. Such specialist provision as a "psychologically informed planned environment" is able to provide the conditions where such children can begin to start to grow emotionally. Our work with Lucy illustrates this point.

Case study 1: Lucy's story

At the age of 3 years, Lucy was taken into care by social services. She had been discovered living in a derelict house that was currently being used as a base for trading in drugs and sexual relations. As a result of living in this environment, Lucy had experienced severe emotional neglect as well as extreme physical and sexual abuse. Lucy's behaviour had become so disturbed that she was found to be eating off the floor with several dogs that were also inhabiting the house.

Prior to admission to the Mulberry Bush School, Lucy was placed with foster parents. In Week 1 at the foster home, her behaviour included wetting, smearing, self-harming, aggression, insomnia, inappropriate affection to strangers, extreme controlling behaviour, and cruelty to animals. Her insomnia resulted in one or other of her foster parents having to stay awake all night with her. Attempts at schooling failed, as her behaviours were so aggressive and uncontrollable; she was therefore also severely under-achieving.

As an early intervention to help her make sense of her chaotic life, Lucy started play-therapy sessions. Her therapist described her as being in complete emotional turmoil. During the sessions she was described as being highly aroused, tense, and exhibiting signs of the physical and sexual abuse she had experienced, and she showed no understanding of keeping herself safe. Her therapist commented that "she brings chaos and destruction into everything she does".

Because the foster placement was at serious risk of breakdown, at age 7 Lucy was placed at the Mulberry Bush School. She joined the intake household, living in a group with other children of primary age. A dedicated staff team lived alongside the children, creating a reliable daily routine. The structure of this routine included close supervision and support through all aspects of the day: meal-times, playtimes, bedtimes, transitions to school, and so forth. The team managed and resolved the frequent behavioural breakdowns, arguments, rivalries, and general antisocial behaviour of the group of children. With time, Lucy responded to this re-education in relationships and started to understand that she could be helped to engage with normal and respectful social living. Through this daily routine, the care staff gave Lucy opportunities to help her think and talk about her confused, betrayed, and angry feelings. She started to find alternative ways of interacting and, little by little, started to come to terms with the injustices in her life. She seemed to belong on her terms, which was a significant difference to her foster placement.

Educationally Lucy joined the foundation stage, where she was helped to enjoy learning again. Alongside an introduction to the National Curriculum, the children are encouraged to play with pre-school equipment, listen to stories, sing, dress up, and learn to work cooperatively. After a year, Lucy moved to the second-tier class, where expectations of behaviour, application, and learning are higher. She was still a noisy child, readily distracted, and eas-ily led into others' misbehaviour, but she made good progress and was able to move to the top class a year before she left the school. During this last year, she successfully participated in a weekly visit to a local mainstream primary school, supported by staff from the Mulberry Bush.

During this treatment process at the school, periods at home with her foster parents were still difficult, with Lucy exhibiting her previous testing and challenging behaviours. However, the school placement offered some respite for her exhausted foster carers, who were able to recharge their batteries during term time. With time, the foster carers also noticed an improvement in her behaviour; Lucy was becoming more articulate about her needs and started to display more loving and affectionate feelings. The carers began looking forward to a time when she could come and live with them full time and attend a local school with teaching assistance. After three years, Lucy was able to make this transition and return home to her foster parents. She is currently doing well, and the placement remains stable. She is successfully placed at a local school for chil-dren with moderate learning difficulties and, despite being quite demanding, is no longer unfosterable nor unacceptably disruptive in school or in other social situations.

The use of specialist residential provision enabled Lucy to explore and experiment with developing a sense of belonging. In turn, this enabled her to achieve better self-regulation of her traumatic states and improved emotional well-being and mental functioning.

Creating the foundations for belonging: the holding environment

As I have explained in the case of Lucy, the therapeutic milieu of the Mulberry Bush School is designed to facilitate a sense of belonging through providing consistent emotional holding for children. There are various components to this milieu.

Hannon, Wood, and Bazalgette (2010) argue that if children are to develop in a psychologically healthy way, in the holding environment they need to experience:

> - a secure attachment
> - "authoritative" parenting that provides a combination of responsiveness and demandingness (or warmth and consistent boundaries)
> - stability.

This of course applies equally to the foster family as it does to residential care. But group models of care offer groups as a therapeutic medium out of which individual needs are met.

Donald Winnicott identified the ethos of the holding environment:

> . . . it has as its aim not a directing of the individual's life or development, but an enabling of the tendencies that are at work within the individual, leading to a natural evolution based on growth. [Winnicott, 1965, p. 228]

The concept of the "holding environment" refers to the provision of a compassionate, understanding, and tolerant place that also has firm and robust boundaries. The holding environment also aims to facilitate "attunement" to verbal and symbolic forms of communication, in the same way as the mother is attuned to the infant's pre-verbal and instinctive needs, and the therapist is to the patient. As a therapeutic residential community, the Mulberry Bush uses relationships within the planned environment or milieu as the core therapeutic intervention and principle. It is from this experience of feeling emotionally held that the child can start to feel the stability, continuity, and safety of the "secure base", leading to the establishment of a sense of self and identity. The ultimate aim is to create the ability to form a foundation of meaningful relationships and internalized good experience, which enables the child to grow into mature, responsible, and productive adulthood.

Residential care as emotional holding

At the Mulberry Bush School, we consciously use the school community to develop a way of learning and living together. Our approach ensures that children have their individual needs met, but also that they are able to live and learn through the process of being together in their household and class groups. Our belief is that being part of a group is essential for children. It is only through a positive internalized experience of living together that we are able to prepare the children to return to live in families and attend mainstream schools.

Some historical and cultural precedents for belonging: the therapeutic milieu of the Mulberry Bush School

In the early days of the Mulberry Bush, Barbara Dockar-Drysdale and her young family shared the original farmhouse with a group of deprived children who had been placed in Oxfordshire during World War II as part of the national evacuation campaign. Via monthly clinical consultations with Winnicott and, later, a

Freudian psychoanalytic training, Barbara Dockar-Drysdale provided the children with one-to-one therapeutic sessions. Her husband, Stephen, recently demobbed after war service, supported the enterprise by providing robust boundary setting—a "live" authority for the group. We can imagine how this familial experience offered deprived children an experience of "oedipal" parental roles. In 1948, their work achieved School status, as a hybrid "special school and child guidance clinic", and from thereon they were able to employ a few staff and the school began to grow.

The therapeutic culture of the school continues to provide troubled children with good experiences of primary care within a nurturing and safe residential environment. Through staff support and training systems, we have continued to develop this supportive culture to enable staff to remain preoccupied with the daily experience of routines, behaviours, thoughts, feelings, projections, and relationships that exist between individual children and adults, their groups, and their teams, and with each other across the community. The therapeutic task supports children to grow emotionally so they can negotiate and make use of individual and social relationships.

Hermeneutic discipline

Essentially, psychotherapeutic work is a hermeneutic discipline: it concerns the creation of meaning through interpretation.

Our work is underpinned by a synthesis of the following disciplines:

1. Child psychoanalytic psychotherapy, as defined by Donald Winnicott (including Dockar-Drysdale's own distinct application of this work) and Melanie Klein.

2. Attachment theory, as defined by John Bowlby and Mary Ainsworth.

3. Ongoing neuro-scientific research and its relationship to attachment theory, as defined by researchers and practitioners such as Bruce Perry and Bessel Van Der Kolk.

4. The concepts of therapeutic community, planned environment, or milieu therapy, with three distinct features:

    › group care for its account of the overall context and mode of practice

    › psychodynamic thinking as an underpinning theory, with the concept of the "holding environment" as a specific model of practice

    › systems thinking as a way of holding the component parts together (Ward, 2003, p. 41).

Currently, our provision for children consists of three defined task areas:

1. *Group living,* in which the residential therapy is delivered as a "lived experience" by a dedicated staff team who live and work "close in" with the children in order to develop individual relationships and help them achieve a way of living together as a social group. This work is contained within robust and nurturing domestic routines, planned over each 24-hour period.

2. *Education,* which aims to provide and meet the child's entitlement to an age- and stage-appropriate educational experience. Access to the National Curriculum is delivered within a nurturing environment that pays equal attention to the child's social emotional needs. The curriculum is organized and delivered in practical and fun ways through which the children are most likely to learn. The education area is organized in three developmental stages: foundation stage, middle stage, and top class. Children move up and through these levels as they become more able and independent learners.

3. *The Therapies and Networks Team,* which comprises four therapists and three family network practitioners. The family practitioners aim to maintain and support close communication and partnership working between the parents and carers of the children placed at the school and the referring network. This work serves to strengthen the core residential task. The team "holds the child and family in mind" and can offer some limited therapeutic support to parents. The therapists provide

some individual, but mostly group-based, music and drama therapy for all the children. The two child psychotherapists are involved in the oversight of the clinical work of the treatment teams and consult to care teams. The drama and music therapists provide individual and small group therapeutic sessions. Group psychotherapeutic work supports the core task by supporting children to make a fuller and more meaningful use of the total residential experience, and consultation continues to enable staff to reflect on their team dynamics and on the impact of working with the children.

These component parts of the therapeutic milieu work together to provide an integrated and holistic environment that is organized to maximize the emotional growth of each child. The sum of the "emergent properties" of each department on the child is difficult to quantify. However, our observations of the emotional development of each child suggests that when we achieve good outcomes, a sense of belonging has been internalized by the child. We are currently engaged in a seven-year outcomes project, which will deepen our understanding of the effectiveness of our approach.

Some of the key historical developments of our therapeutic task are outlined below.

Treatment methodology

Out of this experience, Dockar-Drysdale developed the residential treatment methodology that she later named "the provision of primary experience" (1990). She conceptualized this work in a series of papers, which were later published in her books *Therapy in Child Care* (1968) and *Consultation in Child Care* (1973).

Christopher Reeves, a former principal of the school and consultant child psychotherapist, writes:

> Dockar-Drysdale's *primary experience* seems to be an amalgam of the Winnicott concepts of *"primary home experiences"* and *"primary maternal preoccupation"*. The term encapsulates what Dockar-Drysdale came to see as the essential element in therapy for children who had missed out on that early maternal

provision. . . . her view of primary provision could be summed up by saying that it was a matter of the caring adult having to feel and act like a mother with her new-born baby, and with the same preoccupation and sense of vulnerability. This is what the "frozen child" required as an absolute condition of change. [Reeves, 2002, p. 10]

Within this concept of "the provision of primary experience", Dockar-Drysdale carried out her most renowned work, defining different syndromes of deprivation and formulating treatment approaches to these syndromes. Maurice Bridgeland (1971) states:

Dockar-Drysdale has done her most important work in seeking to explain the nature and needs of the "frozen" or psychopathic child. The emotionally deprived child is seen as "pre-neurotic" since the child has to exist as an individual before neurotic defences can form. The extent to which there has been traumatic interruption of the "primary experience" decides the form of the disturbance. A child separated at this primitive stage is, therefore, in a perpetual state of defence against the hostile "outer world" into which he has been jettisoned inadequately prepared. [p. 274]

The early therapeutic milieu was managed by the staff, who provided "close-in" lived experiences of containing and nurturing routines, along with robust behaviour management, through which the "authentic" and chaotic child emerged. Attachment to (then "dependency on") an adult was supported, and in the case of the "frozen child" a localized regression to the "point of failure" was therapeutically managed. Often, a regular and reliable symbolic adaptation, termed a "special thing," was introduced within the relationship. This allowed the child an experience of primary adaptation to need and an experience of the "rhythm" of close bonding and "nursing" with a primary carer:

. . . it was this familial or social factor Dockar-Drysdale particularly attended to. It led her in due course to a greater appreciation of the therapeutic potential of "ordinary devoted carers" within a setting such as the Mulberry Bush. She seized on the fact that, even without specific training and qualification as therapists, carers could become the critical focus of a child's regression to dependency, provided that the requisite therapeutic support systems were in place. [Reeves, 2002, p. 14]

Therapeutic intervention

Most often this symbolic adaptation would take the form of the child's "focal therapist" providing a food chosen by the child, such as a boiled egg or a rusk with warm milk. The child's choice of food often had a significant primary connotation. As the use of the "special thing" became embedded in the work, staff began to use this as a way of meeting the needs of the child. They found that the provision improved the child's sense of security and reduced delinquency (stealing as self-provision to "fill up"), and the localized and protected time seemed to help children cope with their feelings of envy and jealousy when having to share the adult with other children in the group care setting.

In essence, this "attachment" model of meeting need, with special attention to symbolic communication, still underpins our work today. In Dockar-Drysdale's view, for chaotic "unintegrated" children the traditional "analytic hour" was not enough. They required a total environment in which therapeutic interactions could take place within the routines of child care; she did not place the primacy of therapy as being outside daily child-care routines, hence the development of the concept and methods now known as "therapeutic child care".

Today at the Mulberry Bush School, as in its formative years, it is through the experience of reliable and consistent relationships and routines within a containing and nurturing environment that children can start to internalize good experiences and a sense of belonging. These provide the foundations for mental health.

Creating opportunities for appropriate forms of belonging to develop

In an environment such as the Mulberry Bush School, when children initially arrive their regressive behaviours are often the primary emotional currency. Through the daily structured "lived experience", staff share their experiences of being "close in" and alongside the child and use their emotional experience and observation to help them to understand how the child relates to them and to other members of the groups in which they live. They share these observations and hypotheses within the multi-disciplinary treatment teams and use reflective spaces, supervision, and consultation both to reflect on the impact of working "close in" with highly disturbing children and to create hypotheses on how to treat them.

We support our therapeutic care workers, who are engaged in the day-to-day work with the children, to resist the demands of the child; our aim is to create the conditions within group living whereby the child will, instead, reach out to the adult. This requires the child to work on a conditional acceptance of care and respect from adults. Unconditional provision for the most unintegrated children is targeted within the assessment process and is aligned to the child's age and stage ability. Children are given as much responsibility as they can manage appropriately. They also learn over time that their anxieties will be increased by the emotional distance they create through negative and antisocial behaviour.

Distance and temperature

We require our staff to be "participant observers" with the child, to engage in the tasks of high-quality child care, and to use their colleagues within team meetings to help them think and develop ideas about the child's care and treatment. We require staff to be observant, creative, sensitive, and thoughtful in their interactions with children and to use the team as a reference point for their work.

This requires staff to maintain a neutral "boundary position" (non-judgemental participant observer) in which they both interact and observe in order to develop a hypothesis about what aspects of the child's functioning (or lack of functioning) needs to be supported. This emotional distance regulation does not mean the worker physically withdrawing from the child; rather, it means creating an appropriately bounded distance, in order to develop a thinking space and an emotional economy of relating.

Without a clear conceptual framework that can be translated into day-to day-practice, the idea of "deep relationships" can belie the risk of enmeshment with the child, eventually leading to feelings of alienation, demoralization, and acute anxiety for the worker. (This may also be one of the hidden pitfalls when foster parents take on a very troubled child.) Deep relating can be interpreted by the child as an "open season" on unbounded and pathological forms of relating. There are two risks in this way of working. First, it gives the child little responsibility for starting to think about how and why he relates in inappropriate ways; second, adults' own unresolved issues can be made available for the child to exploit or are projected onto the child. Ultimately, staff are there to meet the child's needs, not to have their own needs met via the relationship.

> The business of setting up the therapeutic system is, therefore, the business of setting up structures to reduce the effect of the staff unconscious on the staff/child relationship and to maximise the chance of detecting the effect of the child's inner world on the system. [Stokoe, 2003, p. 83]

Ongoing observation and discussion

Through this process of observation and discussion, the child's strengths and regressive tendencies can be identified. The team can then create a treatment plan that helps give the child a positive message that "we will support your strengths" (e.g., via schooling), but "we will not nurture your regressive behaviours, we will manage them for you" (the unintegrated child) "or help you manage them" (the recovering or fragilely integrated child). Within this framework, the professional delivery of the conscious therapeutic task is the worker knowing when to intervene, and intervening thoughtfully and decisively rather than getting lost or merged in the child's disturbance.

As the child usually arrives with a sense of some form of family, we require a commitment from the family to work with us. Along with the referring agency, they are "the stable third" of the network. Our Therapies and Networks Team work closely with the residential and education staff to ensure that the family is regarded as a key and critical partner and is kept in mind for the child. For some children, this involves keeping their connections with their birth or foster family alive through regular contact such as weekly phone calls; for others, it may be to help them modify or come to terms with the distorted or abusive sense of family they have internalized; for yet others, it will mean helping them engage with the concept of what a family might be like.

The provision of attuned, safe, and well-bounded relationships and a regular partnership working with the families of children further increases the sense that the child is being "held in mind" by a network of concerned adults. For the child, our aim is to increase her sense of belonging to a caring and integrated network of committed adults. Such partnership working increases the likelihood of good outcomes for the child and her family.

Unconscious material

How the child is worked with is identified within her integrated treatment plan. In one sense, the transference material that children project onto staff is too readily available. However, we also need to think about how the unconscious infantile needs of staff are reactivated within this work, and we try to reduce these being acted out in the workplace. This is achieved through the delivery of consistent and reliable supervision, consultation, training, and reflective support structures.

Our work with Anna illustrates extending belonging through integrated residential and extended community services.

Case study 2: Anna's story

Anna was born in November 2003. Her mother had experienced early neglect and abuse, and as a result of this she suffered bouts of severe depression. She regularly used drink and drugs during such times. Due to her illness, Anna experienced inconsistent care throughout her early years. She was often neglected and was unable to develop a healthy attachment to her mother. She developed severe emotional and behavioural difficulties: insomnia, enuresis and encopresis, damaging furniture, biting and hitting her mother, and refusing food. These behaviours increased during her mother's periods of depression.

Eventually, neighbours expressed concern about Anna's dishevelled appearance, and the family received an intervention from their social services department. At age 6 years, Anna was accommodated by the local authority and placed with foster carers. She started to attend a nearby school for children with emotional and behavioural difficulties. Her mother, however, received little support. But the foster carers found Anna's relentless destructive behaviours too difficult to manage, and the placement broke down. Anna was placed with new foster carers, but this placement quickly became unstable. During this time, her school was placed in "special measures", as it was unable to meet the diverse needs of its pupils.

At age 7, Anna was referred to the Mulberry Bush School. She joined our intake household, where a dedicated team of staff provided consistent routines and structures. The team worked closely with teachers from the "foundation stage" in our school and with our therapists and family support workers. Anna started to experience adults who could manage her behavioural difficulties, engage her in daily education, and provide her with caring and meaningful experiences. Over time she began to develop basic trust in adults who could understand and tolerate her chaotic behaviours and strong feelings.

Outreach services: supporting Anna's school. Through working in partnership with the referring local authority, the Mulberry Bush was also able to offer its expertise to Anna's failing school. Outreach staff from our "MBOX" (Mulberry Bush Oxfordshire) service were able to visit the school on a weekly basis. The project encouraged the teachers to reflect on their practice and the causes of emotional, social, and behavioural difficulties, using a collaborative problem-solving approach. The Head confirmed that the project had helped to develop a more cohesive atmosphere, with staff improving their ability to support each other. The provision and assessment of pupils who displayed challenging behaviour showed significantly high rates of improvement.

Working with Anna's mother. As a result of our initial assessment of Anna and her mother's needs, the Mulberry Bush Therapies and Networks Team identified that unless Anna's mother also experienced a meaningful relationship-based intervention, she would not be able to grow emotionally in order to support the potential future reintegration of Anna back with her. Her mother has accepted fortnightly support and counselling from a Mulberry Bush family support worker. She now regards this as a "lifeline" and is making gradual but good progress in managing her depression and lifestyle. She is looking forward to attending a residential weekend with other single mothers at the school, the aim being to help develop her parenting skills and her relationship to Anna, to develop a local support network, and ultimately to deepen their sense of belonging as a family.

Conclusion

I have explained how a sense of belonging is central to the emotional and mental health of children and young people. The examples and vignettes given demonstrate how a deficit of an internal sense of belonging can lead to poor mental health and dangerous and destructive behaviours.

For many children and young people a foster family placement is appropriate in meeting their needs and providing the foundation for a sense of belonging. But for the most traumatized and "unintegrated" children and young people in the care system, family life does not provide an experience of safety, nurture, and belonging; rather, these young people often regard the intimacy of family life as alien and intolerable, and they are often driven to test the home environment to destruction.

For these most emotionally troubled youngsters, a specialist therapeutic residential "holding environment" such as that of the Mulberry Bush School can provide a more emotionally neutral but attuned environment. In such environments, children can explore and make deep therapeutic relationships with highly trained staff through the medium of purposeful group living and educational experiences. I propose that, from such provision, an authentic experience of "belonging" and thus emotional health and well-being can emerge and be sustained for each child.

Note

Parts of this chapter are based on material previously published elsewhere (Diamond, 2003, 2013).

CHAPTER FOUR

Establishing a sense of belonging for looked after children: the journey from fear and shame to love and belonging

Jim Walker

This chapter explores the idea of belonging through the lens of attachment theory. I believe that attachment theory can offer many insights into belonging. When we are accepted and loved by others, we experience feelings of warmth and belonging. In contrast, rejection by others can cause feelings of fear, shame, and loneliness. Attachment theory would argue that the roots of belonging lie in the early years of life and in our relationships with our primary carers.

Having an autonomous state of mind enables a person to have a feeling of safety and a sense of belonging. The challenge is how to enable a child who has experienced significant loss or trauma to develop a secure attachment and ultimately an autonomous state of mind. This will include establishing a coherent narrative about himself and his life story. Mourning for past loss and trauma plays a vital role in this process. Unresolved grief can interfere with any sense of safety or belonging. Additionally, it can sabotage the development of a secure attachment between the looked after child and the substitute carers. Coming to terms with trauma and loss becomes a key requirement in developing a sense of belonging.

Attachment theory and a sense of belonging

In evolutionary terms, the function of attachment has been to protect the child from danger. The attachment figure—an older, stronger, wiser other—functions as a secure base and is a presence that obviates fear and engenders a feeling of safety. The greater the feeling of safety for the child, the wider will be the range of exploration and the more exuberant the exploratory drive. From this insight comes the fundamental tenet of attachment theory: security of attachment leads to an expanded range of exploration. Whereas fear constricts the range of exploration, safety expands it. In the absence of safety, the child has to contend with fear-inducing aloneness. The child will devote energy to conservative, safety-enhancing measures (defence mechanisms) to compensate for what is missing. The focus on maintaining safety and managing fear drains energy from learning and curiosity, stunts growth, and distorts personality development (Fosha, 2003).

Attachment theory speaks about organized and disorganized patterns of attachment. In secure attachment, the individual is confident that attachment figures are maximally available and responsive and will, when necessary, provide protection. Securely attached individuals feel safe enough in the world to be able to be creative, explorative, and curious. The securely attached child experiences her caregiver as being physically, emotionally, and mentally available to respond to her needs. This sense of safety allows securely attached individuals to feel authentic in themselves and to have a sense of belonging. Confidence in the availability of the carer reduces anxiety and liberates the infant to explore, play, and learn, only returning to the secure base if stressed or anxious. Hence an apparent paradox: the securely attached child is more confident in moving away from the secure base provided by the caregiver in order to explore the environment.

In contrast, in disorganized attachment the individual feels physically and psychologically unsafe, abandoned, and extremely vulnerable. Attachment theory argues that a child will turn to an attachment figure for comfort and reassurance when frightened or threatened. But if the attachment figure is itself a source of the threat, the child is presented with an insoluble problem, which leads to "fright without solution" (see Main & Hesse, 1990). On the one hand, the parent is the child's attachment figure and the potential sense of safety in a frightening world. On the other hand, the abusive parent is the stressor who can suddenly and unexpectedly threaten the child with physical or emotional violence. The child becomes placed in an irresolvable situation in which the safe haven and base to explore the world is at the same time the source of threat or terror. The child becomes afraid of the person who is also his source of protection. This situation becomes inherently disorganizing for the child. Disorganized attachment can develop as a result of this dilemma. I believe that disorganized attachment leads to a sense of homelessness and alienation.

The secure base refers to the caregiver whom the infant visibly seeks out when feeling frightened, ill, or distressed. In time, this sense of having a secure base can become internalized as a representation of security within the individual psyche. Thus, the secure base originates as an external figure but, when things go "well enough", becomes internalized as the capacity to self-soothe and nurture oneself. Securely attached children who have internalized a secure base are likely to feel a sense of confidence and belonging within the world. In contrast, individuals with a disorganized attachment pattern are likely to feel anxious, unsafe in the world, and without any sense of belonging.

However, on a more optimistic note, the Adult Attachment Interview (Main & Goldwyn, 1998) has a category called "earned secure". This refers to individuals who have had childhoods that involved significant loss or trauma but who have "come to terms" with their experiences. It suggests that attachment patterns are not fixed but can be changed through nurturing care and love. Attachment research is demonstrating the potential plasticity of the brain. Fosha (2003) comments on the way in which changes in the child's attachment status occur as attachment-focused interventions produce changes in the caregiver. Marvin, Cooper, Hoffman, and Powell (2002) have shown how changes in the attachment status of children from disorganized to secure have been obtained by means of a 20-session group intervention with their caregivers. Similarly, Solomon (2003) describes attachment research of adult couples: where one of the couple has a secure attachment, an insecurely attached partner may, in time, develop an earned secure attachment.

Unresolved loss and trauma

Being able to talk about one's life in a coherent, consistent, and understandable way is fundamental to having a sense of belonging in the world. Having a coherent narrative about one's life enables one to feel safe and authentic. "Coming to terms" with past trauma and developing a coherent life story enables the individual to establish the sense of a secure base within and feel a sense of belonging. In contrast, a lack of resolution of trauma in children has many consequences. Unresolved trauma separates and disconnects: it separates us from ourselves and it disconnects us from others. It can leave us isolated, alone, and without any sense of belonging. Thus, Siegel (1999) writes that children with unresolved traumas will have "a marked inability to regulate emotional responses and the flow of states of mind establishing a tendency towards dissociation, disruptive behaviours, impairments in attention and cognition, and compromised coping capacities, as well as a vulnerability towards posttraumatic stress disorder" (p. 111).

This points to the crucial role of grieving past traumas. Looked after children who have been separated from their birth family will need to grieve for their loss and establish a coherent narrative about themselves. They will only be able to form a secure attachment with their new carers when they have grieved for the losses in their life. For example, a woman I worked with in psychotherapy told me that she was removed from her mother's care and placed for adoption when she was nearly 4 years old. She had been removed because of her mother's long-term drug use and chaotic lifestyle. However, she reported that after being removed from her mother's care she subsequently idealized her birth mother. She in time formed a strong relationship with her adoptive father, but she never became close to her adoptive mother. She said that her adoptive mother could never compete with the idealized picture she had of her birth mother. Allowing herself to become attached to her adoptive mother would have felt like a betrayal of her birth mother. Her inability to grieve for her birth mother made it impossible for her to attach to her adoptive mother. She was unable to feel any sense of belonging with her adoptive mother, and, as a result, she had felt "homeless" and without a mother.

Dissociation

Dissociation sabotages any sense of belonging in the world. Schore (2003b) states that dissociation is a response to trauma in which the person disengages from stimulation in the external world and attends to an internal world. He likens dissociation to "playing dead", in which "the individual becomes inhibited and strives to avoid attention in order to become unseen" (p. 126). He comments that the child's dissociation in the midst of terror involves numbing, avoidance, compliance, and restricted affect. Traumatized infants are observed to be staring into space with a glazed look. Dissociation is thus an unconscious process in which thoughts, feelings, and memories that cause anxiety are cut off either from consciousness or from the associated affect. Dissociation involves the capacity to separate ourselves from an aspect of our experience, and it leads to a reduced ability to see reality as it is. It can lead to a sense of detachment from ourselves, leaving us without any sense of safety or belonging.

Shame

Another consequence of unresolved trauma is shame. The shame-filled child will feel unwelcome in the world. Shame sabotages any sense of safety or belonging. In order for a child to feel any sense of belonging, a reduction in her shame is necessary. The roots of shame lie in the early years of life and results from a chronic and catastrophic lack of attunement between the child and her primary carer. Shame can result from the experience of being cut off from the primary source of love. Having had this experience repeatedly as a child, the shame-filled person lives with the ongoing fear of being unloved and unlovable. The experience of feeling unloved by our primary carers becomes extended to a total feeling of being unlovable: "If you really knew the whole, unvarnished truth about me, you would know that I am unlovable" (Downs, 2012, p. xii). Shame can thus be thought of as being the fear of being unlovable.

Shame is also closely linked with trauma. Children who experience severe trauma are likely to develop a deep sense of shame about themselves. When someone has been exposed to prolonged interpersonal trauma, feelings of shame and guilt become intensified into a state of toxic shame (Mollon, 2002). From an attachment perspective, it is dangerous for the child to think of his parents as being "bad" or threatening. Because the infant or young child is totally dependent on his parents, acknowledging the reality and thinking of his parents as dangerous would create fear and anxiety. It is much safer for the child to protect the image of the parent and instead think of himself as being "bad". The child comes to internalize a sense of himself as being "bad" and consequently feels full of shame about himself . Unless the child gains some resolution of this, he will then grow up as an adult with a deep sense of shame. It follows that abuse from an attachment figure is likely to create a stronger sense of shame than abuse by a stranger. Furthermore, abuse by an attachment figure is likely to sabotage any sense of safety or belonging that the child has. Children who have been abused by an attachment figure are particularly vulnerable to feeling a lack of a sense of belonging.

Withdrawal

One response to feelings of shame is a withdrawal into oneself. Shame can lead to a freezing in which the individual feels alone, exposed, and terrified. The response can then be one of hiding and a covering up of oneself. Shame leads to the exposure of undesirable aspects of oneself. "It is as though something we were hiding from everyone is suddenly under a burning light in public view" (Izard, 1991, p. 332). Shame throws an exposing light that leads to a "compelling desire to disappear from view" (Friijda, 1988, p. 351). Similarly, Erikson (1950) speaks of the "impulse to bury one's face, or to sink, right then and there, into the ground" (p. 223). Tomkins (1963) says that "the humiliated one . . . feels himself naked, defeated, alienated, lacking in dignity or worth" (p. 118).

The effect can be that the person becomes silenced: "shame forbids communication with words" (Kaufman, 1985, p. 565). Someone who is vulnerable to shame lives in fear of being humiliated. To speak or express an opinion risks humiliation. As a result, many people who are vulnerable to shame spend their lives hiding from the world. This withdrawal can then lead to a sense of loneliness, alienation, and lack of belonging.

Shame and the false self

Winnicott distinguished between the true self and the false self (Winnicott, 1960a). The true self describes a sense of self based on spontaneous, authentic experience. In contrast, the false self is a defence to protect the true self by hiding and protecting it. However, the false self can become problematic as it can prevent the person from feeling spontaneous, alive, and real.

There is a strong link between shame and the development of the false self. Many people who experience deep shame develop a false self in an attempt to protect themselves from the full impact of their shame. The false self can give an illusion of competence, but it can mask a much more vulnerable, frightened, and shame-filled part of the self.

Children who are vulnerable to shame can develop a personality that is organized around the concealment of feelings of weakness, vulnerability, and neediness. A false self based on a display of strength, confidence, and arrogance may be developed as a defence against the underlying feelings of shame and inadequacy (Mollon, 2002). Thus, arrogance and the need to be in control may be part of a false-self system that is an unconscious attempt to hide the vulnerable, shame-filled part. The development of a false self can lead to an individual feeling emotionally cut off from himself. On a deep level, such a person will know that he has lost touch with the authentic part of himself, in this way becoming a stranger to himself. In this sense, belonging can be thought of as being a sense of being at home with oneself, something that the development of a false self destroys.

Shame and the adopted child

Mollon (2002) comments that "shame is where we fail. And the most fundamental failure is the failure to connect with other human beings—originally the mother" (p. xi). Similarly, Broucek (1982) notes that shame arises when "the mother becomes a stranger to her infant" (p. 370). Shame can also be thought of as being the consequence of being cut off from the primary source of love and protection. Mollon goes on to say that he believes that children who have been separated from their parents, and especially their birth mother, are particularly vulnerable to developing a deep shame about themselves (Mollon, 2002). Children who are placed for adoption have had their connection with their birth mother ruptured, often with no possibility of any repair. This can make them particularly vulnerable to feeling acute shame about themselves. Thus, Verrier (2009) says "that the severing of that connection between the adopted child and her birth mother causes a primal or narcissistic wound, which affects the adoptee's sense of Self and often manifests in a sense of loss, basic mistrust, anxiety and depression, emotional and/or behavioral problems and difficulties in relationships with significant others" (p. 16)—and, I would add, potentially evoking a deep sense of shame in the child.

In addition, many adopted children will also have experienced further neglect or trauma prior to coming into care. For many looked after children, shame becomes the default position at times of stress. The experience of being adopted can in itself feel shameful. Thus, Guidry (2012) writes: "I am adopted. I am shame".

As discussed earlier, underlying all shame lies the fundamental conviction of being unlovable. Thus, Downs (2012) writes that "shame is the internalized and deeply held belief that we are somehow unacceptable, unlovable, shameful" (p. 24). Love requires trust and the capacity to be open and vulnerable, things that shame sabotages. The shame-filled person will keep other people at a distance out of fear that anyone who gets to know him will discover his essential badness. Traumatized children can become highly skilled at making their carers feel useless, impotent, and rejected. In addition, traumatized children often unconsciously seek to recreate their own traumatic life story and lead "the interactive dance" with their carers (Dozier, 2005). In this way, their traumatic history becomes repeated within the substitute family. Specifically, the shame-filled child often experiences himself as unloved and unlovable. This experience becomes his core sense of self, and he becomes filled with shame.

Identity issues

Shame is also linked with the identity issues that many looked after children experience. Genealogical bewilderment is a term referring to potential identity problems that can be experienced by a child who has been separated from her birth parents. This bewilderment can include questions such as: "who am I?"; "who am I as an adopted person?"; "where do I belong?"; "am I essentially unlovable?"; and "why was I adopted?". Other feelings arising from genealogical bewilderment can include rage, fear, anxiety, mistrust, and loneliness. Thus, Rustin (2006) says that "children who cannot be brought up in their families of origin suffer a basic disruption in the sense of membership, of knowing where they belong" (p. 107).

In order for a child to establish a clearer sense of his identity, he will need to develop a sense of genealogical connectedness. This is defined as:

> the extent to which children identify with their natural parents'
> biological and social backgrounds . . . the degree to which
> children identify with their natural parents' background is
> dependent upon the amount and quality of information they
> possess about their parents . . . socio-genealogical knowledge is
> fundamental to our psychological integrity. It is essential to our
> sense of who we are, what we want to be, where we come from,
> and where we belong in the order of things. [Owusu-Bempah
> & Howitt, 1997, p. 201]

This highlights one of the dilemmas for children who have been separated from their birth parents: how can they achieve a sense of belonging both with their family of origin and with their substitute carers? How can they belong with their new carers while retaining an emotional connection with their birth family? I have known several adopted people who only began to explore details of their birth family after their adoptive parents had died: it had felt too difficult and contradictory for them to make this move while their adoptive parents were alive. The danger is that the looked after child feels that he does not belong either with his birth family or with his substitute carers.

This tension of belonging in two different families can potentially be helped by the birth parents. Ideally the birth parents will give "permission" to the child to become attached, happy, and settled with his adoptive parents. The birth parents would give the child the following message: "I love you but am not able to care for you at the moment. I want you to love your new carers and be happy with them." This is one of the potential benefits of contact with birth parents: the birth parents can give their ongoing blessing to the child to be happy with his adoptive parents.

Similarly, it is enormously helpful to the child if his substitute carers can think of him as belonging in two different families. This requires the carers to have sufficient confidence in themselves as carers to allow the thought that the child can belong in both families. Carers with an autonomous state of mind are much more likely to be able to carry out this function.

The role of substitute carers in helping the child to grieve

All children who have been separated from their birth families have experienced significant loss. As one adoptive father said: "there is no adoption without loss or pain. Adoption is . . . born from and a response to hurt, loss and sorrow" (Monroe, 2015).

Substitute carers play a crucial role in helping their child to grieve. Substitute carers need to have resolved, at least to some degree, any experiences of loss and trauma in their own lives in order to remain emotionally available to any child placed with them. Hughes (2003) makes this clear: "Adults who intend to provide a child with a sense of psychological safety that is sufficient to resolve and integrate experiences associated with trauma and loss, need to have resolved any similar experiences in their own attachment histories in order to remain present for the child affectively and cognitively whenever the memory of those experiences emerge" (Hughes, , p. 273). Research at the Anna Freud Centre also identifies that the resolution of loss and trauma issues in carers is an important indicator of the progress that the child will make in the placement (Steele, Kaniuk, Hodges, Haworth, & Huss, 2003).

The degree to which substitute carers have "come to terms"

with any traumas they have experienced will determine their capacity to help their child to grieve. Carers who are themselves unresolved will find it very hard to enable their child to grieve. This applies particularly if the carers are adopting because of their own infertility. If they have not been able to grieve for their own infertility, there is a danger that the adopted child could always be a disappointment in contrast to the idealized image they might have of their own imaginary child.

In order to help their child to grieve, carers will need to accept that their child is a member of two families. Carers who need to claim the child as exclusively their own will find this challenging. This is demonstrated by one substitute carer when discussing her child's contact with her birth family: "She's my daughter. Not her daughter . . . why should I have to tell her what she is up to and doing when she couldn't look after her . . . with all this contact, this one letter and whatever, you feel as though she is not yours. At all. And all you are doing is just looking after her for them" (Neil, 2004, p. 56). Thus, rather than being able to think of the girl as the daughter of both her and her birth mother, she thought of her as being exclusively her daughter. The result would have been that she would have been unable to help the girl to grieve for her birth mother.

In contrast, another substitute carer spoke movingly about how he sees his role as being alongside his child in his grief: "All we could offer him was our reassuring presence to help him run toward the loss and pain, not away from it. To help him own the grief that he feels and to own it redemptively" (Monroe, 2015).

As this second example illustrates, it is important to give "permission" to the child to grieve. Enabling the child to "run toward" the pain, rather than away from it, is an important part of allowing grieving. The sensitive carer will understand that some of the child's behaviours such as anger, rebellion, or fear may be connected with his grief.

Age-appropriate books about adoption can be used as a way of introducing the child to the idea that she is adopted. Ideally carers will give their child the message that it is ok for her to ask questions, to be curious about her life history and to want to have information about her birth family. As the child grows older she can be given an increasing amount of information about her life history. The adopted child will need to have an understanding of why she was adopted. As she grows older she should develop an increasingly subtle understanding of why her parents could not look after her. It is, at least in part, the responsibility of the adoptive parents to help their child gain such an understanding.

Open adoption

Open adoption can be defined as the planned act of contact or communication between adoptive parents, adopted children, and birth families. Open adoptions can help a child in terms of both mourning the birth family and developing a sense of genealogical connectedness.

There is an ongoing need for flexibility with contact with the birth family. The child's need for, and the frequency of, contact can change as the child grows older. Similarly, who the child has contact with—potentially, birth parents, grandparents, uncles and aunts, siblings and cousins—can change over time. The nature of contact can vary between face to face, letters, and increasingly now, especially as the child grows older, through social media.

Historically, adoptions in the UK have tended to be "closed" adoptions, in which contact with the birth parents was terminated. I suspect that this was partly based on a misunderstanding of attachment theory: believing that before a child can form an attachment to his new carers, any attachment he had with his birth parents had to be terminated. However, in recent years there has been more reflection on the idea of ongoing contact with the birth parents. In part, this has been due to an increased recognition of the problems that can be inherent in closed adoptions. As Barratt (2006) comments, "the traditional system of closed adoption leads to adopted children feeling that they have no access to a part of themselves" (p. 149). This absence in their lives can make it hard for them to have any sense of their own history or sense of belonging. It can intensify feelings of genealogical bewilderment. Finally, it can disrupt the process of mourning.

Thorburn (2004) discusses some of the advantages of ongoing contact:

the evidence . . . is that, when contact continues during and after placement, the new family may have a more "bumpy" ride. They have to deal from day one with issues around the reasons for the placement, the complexities of having two families and often the distress, confusion and anger of the children as the unreliability and other shortcomings of the birth parents becomes more obvious to them. However, the young adult usually emerges from such arrangements with a sense of belonging to the new family but still having a place (if they choose to take it up) in the extended first family . . . there is a higher likelihood that those who retain some direct contact with one or both birth parents will emerge with a better understanding of why they could not remain with their birth families. [pp. 196–197]

She goes on to say that, in contrast, families where the child has no contact with the birth family can have often a "smoother" ride in the early years of the placement, but issues around identity and belonging can then become much more of an issue for the adopted child during adolescence. Thus, while contact with the birth parents can be very challenging for all concerned, contact can keep the issues alive, enabling the possibility of grieving, rather than pushing the grief underground, which termination of contact can arguably do. Contact can also be hugely beneficial in giving the child a greater sense of genealogical connectedness and an increased feeling of belonging.

Another potential benefit of contact is that it can challenge the child's belief that she is unlovable. If the birth parents are able both to support their child's long-term placement and give her the ongoing message that they love her, this can be enormously beneficial for the child. In contrast, termination of contact runs the risk of intensifying the child's sense of being unloved and forgotten.

As children grow older, contact arrangements can become more flexible. Initially, contact tends to be supervised and held on neutral territory. However, I once worked with an adopted boy who as a teenager began staying some weekends with his maternal grandparents. This relationship became extremely important to him. His adoptive parents were secure enough in themselves to encourage this relationship, and, in time, they became good friends with the grandparents. The relationship with his grandparents enabled the boy to develop a sense of belonging in both families and gave him invaluable information about his family of origin.

However, it is also important to add a note of caution about contact: some birth parents will be too angry and hurt immediately following the removal of their child to be able to prioritize their child's needs and not attempt to sabotage the child's new placement. Birth parents may need a period of time to grieve for the loss of their child before any contact is in the child's interests.

Similarly, children who have been abused may be re-traumatized when they have contact with the maltreating parent (Howe & Steele, 2004). Traumatized children can quickly become re-traumatized through seemingly innocent triggers. This, in turn, can lead the child to feel unsafe with her new carers and interfere with her capacity to form a secure attachment with her new carers. I once worked with a child who had been removed from his birth family but continued having contact with them while in his foster placement. He subsequently disclosed that he had been sexually abused as a child and that this abuse had continued during contact with his birth family.

It is therefore vitally important to assess whether contact with the birth family is going to interfere with the child's need to feel safe and attach to his new carers. When the birth family are able to prioritize the child's needs, ongoing contact may significantly increase the child's sense of safety in the world and feeling of belonging. However, in other situations it may be necessary to terminate a child's contact with the birth family until such a time as the child has developed greater resilience and the birth family have become more able to prioritize his needs.

Letter-box contact

Letters can also be used both as a way of providing a child with information about their past and as a means of indirect contact, particularly if face-to-face contact is not possible. Some birth parents write "goodbye" letters to their child. This can be used as way of giving "permission" to their child to attach to their new carers and to be happy with them. Again, this will rely on the birth parents' capacity to prioritize their child's needs. Some birth parents may need a period of time to elapse before they can write such a letter to their child.

Other indirect contact involves the birth parents sending occasional letters to their child—for instance, at Christmas or birthdays. This can help the looked after child to feel loved and remembered. It can give him ongoing information about his birth family. However, in practice I have found that many birth parents find this a hard thing to do, often dropping out of writing letters, which in turn can increase their child's sense of rejection. I suspect that this is partly because writing a letter can re-evoke some of their grief about being unable to care for their child: it may feel less painful simply to cut the child out of their lives. Thus, some birth parents may need support, encouragement, and ongoing information about their child's progress for them to be able to maintain letter contact.

However, potentially letter-box contact can help looked after children to gain an increased understanding of their family history and a greater feeling of belonging.

Life story work

Social workers frequently use life story books in an attempt to help adopted and looked after children to have knowledge of their birth family and their history. This process can help the child to develop a coherent narrative of his history. Life story work can also be an important part of the child's process of grieving. However, Vaughan (2003) argues many life story books "tend to over-simplify and sanitize the child's past, leaving him with an incoherent and inauthentic story line" (p. 160). Burnell (2003) states that life story book work is often suspended if a child becomes distressed. The implication is that some social workers lack confidence in carrying out life story work.

In the past, life story work has often been thought of as a one-off, static process. The social worker would obtain photos of the child's birth family, gather some information about the family history, and put it all together in a book. I would argue that, in contrast, life story work should be an ongoing process that deepens as the child matures and becomes more able to process painful experiences. For the child to develop a coherent narrative about his life story, he will need gradually to have access to an honest, truthful account of his life experiences. A child who is given a sanitized account of his life will recognize on an unconscious level that it is inauthentic and alien to his subjective experience. It would only increase his sense of alienation and lack of belonging. It could also interfere with the process of grieving.

As with contact, life story books can be re-traumatizing for the child. For some children it may be appropriate to delay life story work until they feel safer and more settled within their new placement. It may also be necessary for life story work to be used in conjunction with skilled therapeutic work.

The role of substitute carers in establishing a secure base for the child

The first step in helping a looked after child to feel a sense of belonging is to provide him with a secure base. Neil and Howe (2004a) argue that the priority for looked after children is to help them establish a secure attachment with their new carers. They suggest that any decisions about the child should be determined by whether it would increase the likelihood of establishing a secure attachment with the new carers. This is likely to be particularly challenging, as emphasized by Schofield and Beek (2005). They say that "the challenges of providing a secure base availability for children whose experiences have taught them to see hostility and rejection are great . . . children simultaneously craved and resisted, needed and resented, demanded and rejected the care and concern of their foster parents" (p. 10). However, we know from attachment research that carers who have an autonomous state of mind and have come to terms with past trauma are more likely to be able to function as a secure base for their child.

A priority in caring for looked after children is to attempt to increase their sense of safety and reduce their fear. Only once their fear is reduced can they begin to form an attachment with their carers. We know that once a child has experienced repeated incidents of trauma, relatively little is required to trigger the same kind of responses that the initial trauma created (Perry, Pollard, Blakely, &

Vigilante, 1995). For instance, some carers I worked with reported that they were puzzled that their foster child became severely distressed whenever they asked him to wash his hands. Eventually it was learnt that he had been abused by his stepfather in the bathroom. The seemingly benign act of washing his hands became deeply re-traumatizing for him. It can, therefore, be very helpful for the carers to form an understanding of what things might act as a "trigger" for their child's distress.

Verrier (2009) argues that looked after children are particularly vulnerable to feelings of abandonment. She says that it is vital that substitute carers never threaten the child with abandonment. Similarly, Hughes (2006) says that traumatized children need to be kept close to their carers at times of distress. Thus, placing a child on her own on a "naughty step" may not be appropriate for looked after children. Keeping a child close at times of distress is an important aspect of providing a secure base for the child.

An important part of the development of a secure base is to give the child a sense of permanence. Long delays in planning a child's future can be harmful and increase a child's insecurity and lack of belonging. The use of the term "forever family" is a way of trying to give the child a sense of permanence, belonging, and an awareness of his carers' long-term commitment to him. One couple I know frequently call their 4-year-old adopted son "my boy"—"well done, Thomas, my boy"—as a way of emphasizing their commitment to him and his membership of their family. The use of rituals around birthdays and major religious festivals can also be an important way of establishing a sense of belonging within the family.

Dozier (2005) argues that children need carers who are strongly committed to them. She states that the more committed the carer, the greater the likelihood of the long-term stability of the placement. She challenges the notion of long-term foster care, arguing that children need above all else a sense of belonging and permanence within their substitute family.

Schofield and Beek (2005) suggest that an important element of establishing a secure base comes from the child developing a sense of family membership. If the child can feel a sense of belonging and being part of the family, this can have a stabilizing and reassuring effect. Celebrating an "adoption day" every year with presents can be a helpful way of emphasizing family membership, while also being explicit about the child's history.

Another important element for looked after children is their possessions: photos, cuddly toys, and presents they have been given can all act as transitional objects (Winnicott, 1971) and help to establish a sense of continuity for them. Possessions like this can also help in the establishment of a secure base for the child.

Ultimately, the most important factor in establishing a secure base will be the qualities that the carers have. As well as the resolution of past trauma and an autonomous state of mind, carers of looked after children need to have a capacity for reflective function, have resolved any feelings of shame, and be able to manage a wide range of feelings, both in themselves and in others.

Love

Love can play a crucial role in enabling the looked after child to develop a sense of safety and belonging. The capacity of substitute carers to be able both to give and receive love is crucial. This is linked with shame: if a shame-filled child is placed with a carer who is vulnerable to shame, it can create a toxic mix. Crucially, the adoptive parent who is vulnerable to shame is likely to experience the child's behaviour as a personal attack on him or her. Thus, rather than understanding the child's behaviour as a result of the child's traumatic history, the adoptive parent is more likely to think of it as a personal attack and as a confirmation of his or her own uselessness as a parent. Substitute carers need to be able to tolerate the child's potential attacks and rejections of them without retaliating or withdrawing. Carers needs to carry on loving the child despite the child's attempts to push them away and reject them.

The most effective remedy for the lack of a sense of belonging is the experience of being loved, nurtured, and understood by an empathic and attuned other. As shame and fear decrease, the child can begin to allow the possibility of being loved by another. The experience of being loved can, in time, become internalized into a sense of having a secure base within and a feeling of belonging. Love "greatly decreases activation of the fear systems . . . love is a relief from scanning the outer world for threat and our inner worlds for shame. Love turns off the alarm, cancels our insurance and frees us from worry" (Cozolino, 2006, p. 316). This idea that love can make us feel less fearful is said more simply in the Bible: "perfect love casts out fear" (1 John, 4.18).

The experience of feeling loved can enable the child to have sufficient safety in his life to be able to face the losses and traumas that he has experienced. In time, the sense of feeling loved and understood can help the child to develop a coherent narrative about himself and internalize a sense of a secure base within, leading, in turn, to a feeling of belonging in the world.

Conclusion

Neil and Howe (2004b) say that looked after children can achieve optimal levels of psychological development by:

> building a secure attachment with their new carers

> resolving feelings of separation, loss, and rejection

> forming a coherent sense of self and a clear identity by achieving autobiographical completeness and a sense of genealogical connectedness.

These three criteria also apply to developing a sense of belonging. Looked after children face particular challenges in establishing a sense of belonging. Their separation from their birth family leaves them vulnerable to unresolved trauma, potentially leading to dissociative processes, shame, a difficulty in giving and receiving love, and a sense of genealogical bewilderment. Grieving for the loss of the birth family is a crucial developmental task for looked after children, and substitute carers have a major role in helping this process. This process of grief, together with forming a secure attachment with their substitute carers and achieving autobiographical completeness, can in time enable looked after children to develop a sense of safety and a feeling of belonging in the world.

CHAPTER FIVE

From owning to belonging

Jenny Sprince

A ndrew Briggs, the editor of this book, poses a difficult question: how does a child taken away from his or her family of origin get to feel a sense of belonging elsewhere?

The concept of "belonging" can be used in two distinct but related ways: to signify ownership and the rights of property; to express the feeling of fitting in comfortably somewhere, being understood and accepted. It is the task of parents to help children to move from the first kind of belonging into the second.

As babies we all start off by being named, claimed, and owned by our parents. In order to feel that we "belong" in the second sense, we first have to feel that we exist as a separate self, rather than as someone else's possession. Beyond that, we have to understand that other people are also separate and complex selves, with their own wishes and needs, who can never be viewed as our property, any more than we are theirs. These are developmental tasks that take time and effort to achieve. We do not expect a child to begin to have a sense of her own identity until she is perhaps 2 or 4 years old. It takes the child longer still to begin to appreciate the complexities of other people's identities.

This chapter looks at this early process in more detail before exploring the problem of providing a sense of belonging for children in care. This is because so many of the children who are taken into care come from families where the conditions for the process of creating a sense of self may never have been adequately met in the first place. Others may have successfully acquired a rudimentary sense of self, but their further development may have been halted at a stage where their concept of belonging implies ownership and the exercise of control, rather than the kind of belonging that is about feeling understood, understanding others, and fitting comfortably in to a family group.

What happens in good-enough families

The origins of belonging

We start life as part of someone else's body. Birth precipitates us into a sudden physical separation, but psychological separation takes longer to achieve. The struggles of babyhood begin with the terrifying realization that we are no longer totally owned by someone else: that there are moments—even minutes and hours—when we have to go it alone. In order to cope with these terrifying moments, we need to feel that we are safely claimed as the property of our parents. For many months, we need to feel that we are still part of our mothers, and that our mothers are a part of ourselves. When a baby mirrors the expression on his mother's face, he expects a reciprocal response. And indeed, good mothers instinctively act as auxiliary aspects of their babies—performing the functions of doing and thinking that babies cannot manage for themselves.

Babies have to rely on their parents' empathy and intuitive understanding to make sense of their feelings, to name these feelings, and to respond appropriately and reassuringly. In this sense, their parents' minds and bodies are at their disposal: their parents belong to them at least as much as they belong to their parents.

Belonging to our babies

First-time parents are routinely shaken by the extent to which they find themselves forced to become their baby's possession and by the power of what they find themselves forced to experience on their baby's behalf.

It can be very hard work to soothe an unhappy or terrified baby, to work out what she may be feeling, and to put those feelings into words. But it is something parents do all the time, without even thinking about it. They may say things like: "It's alright, I know you got dumped in the cot very suddenly: Mummy heard the doorbell ring and had to run and see what was happening, but she's back now. It's horrid having to wait, isn't it, but it's not the end of the world!" The mother who says these kind of things to her baby is automatically attuning herself to a range of feelings in her baby and putting her own feeling self at her baby's disposal: she is providing a narrative thread, an understanding of the emotional consequences of everyday experiences, and an ability to moderate extremes of emotions.

Babies cannot link one fragment of emotional experience with another: the baby who is panicking does not feel the same to himself as the baby who is happy and contented. It is a mother's job to organize the baby's different states of feeling into one coherent sense of self, with a story that holds them together, that provides an understanding of the continuity of self, and that teaches the rudiments of a language to define and express both positive and negative emotions: "That was scary, wasn't it? You thought I'd never come back! Horrid Mummy, leaving you like that! But you like it when I pick you up and tickle you, don't you! That feels really nice!" She does this by allowing the baby to own and to occupy her feelings and her mind, and in return she gives the baby the beginnings of a sense of self and of the range of contrasting feeling states of which that self is capable. This includes giving the baby permission to be angry with her for the times when she does things that feel terrifying or infuriating, rather than blaming the baby for a terrified or furious response.

Installing a sense of self

When a child remains firmly rooted in a stable environment, the same adults who have experienced and moderated these early passionate feelings, and have installed a capacity to name them and make sense of them, will put together, on the child's behalf, memories of baby-hood, toddlerhood, and all the stages beyond, talk with him about his emotional responses to particular events, and gradually help him to understand and express his own feelings and to take responsibility for his actions, and for the feelings he passes on to others.

A little child's first sense of self is inextricably linked with the adults who have helped to organize the child's feelings and experiences into one coherent identity and narrative. At the same time, the child's emerging sense of a separate self demands that he start to differentiate between this separate self and the parental selves that continue to provide this organizing function. The typical toddler tantrums of the 2-year-old are driven by the child's need to test out his existence as a person in his own right—not just as an adjunct of mother. This need coincides with feelings of rage and jealousy at the discovery that mother also belongs to father—and to the other important adults in her life: she does not belong just to her child and is not totally under his control. It is the job of fathers and mothers to reconcile their children to the reality of this situation, by giving them a sense of the privileges of childhood and the advantages of not being expected to take on the same responsibilities of owner-ship that parents undertake for their babies and toddlers.

The importance of fantasy

One of the ways that children learn to tolerate the painful loss of total ownership is through stories and fantasy. When parents read fairy tales to their small children, or the children involve them in games of "let's pretend", they are playing out conscious and unconscious fan-tasies about the state of ownership that they are having to relinquish in a way that lessens the pain and gives hope of eventual reward. Parents are usually tolerant of a child's need to stay in a fantasy world as he becomes accustomed to the reality of feeling excluded by the adults—like Hansel and Gretel, chased out into the forest; or like Peter Pan and the Lost Boys, exiled to Neverland; or like Cinderella, ejected from a life of luxury to sit among the ashes in the kitchen. They allow for a child's compensatory need to pretend to be Super-man or the Fairy Queen. And they expect that there will be times, as a child learns to moderate the extremes of his jealousy and rage, when the child will momentarily confuse fantasy and reality and stay obstinately in the fantasy world that he has created for himself.

Most adults will not remember or understand the emotional meaning of these fantasies, but they will nevertheless resonate intuitively to their content and symbolism. We were all once children, preoccupied with similar fantasies ourselves. As we grow older, we learn to differentiate between reality and fantasy—and to dismiss, repress, or leave unexplored the "irrational" thoughts and ideas that interfere with acceptable adult functioning. Gradually, we leave such fantasies behind. However, in all of us, infantile beliefs persist at the level of unconscious fantasy—which psychoanalysis distinguishes from conscious fantasy by the use of a different spelling: "phantasy". Part of the pleasure of bringing up children is the permission it gives us to make vicarious and tenuous contact with these hidden parts of ourselves, through sharing the language of childhood play.

These games, stories, and fantasies are a part of what bind families together, and many a teenager has become furious with parents who insist on lovingly quoting the anecdotes that have accrued around these difficult times of transition that they have already shared, and which give some hope that the turbulence of adolescence may likewise arrive at a successful outcome.

Only after they have passed successfully through this stage are little children able to begin to feel that they belong in the second sense of the word: that they are understood and accepted by parents who can allow them to be fully themselves.

Installing insight and consideration for other people

As the child gets older, and starts the complicated process of making relationships with other children, parents in good-enough families will mediate and talk about how one person's actions may impact on another: "I'm not surprised she got angry, after you snatched her doll away without asking. Still, she shouldn't have hit you. So go on, both of you, say sorry to one another!"

They will model a process of insight, reflectiveness, collaboration, and the capacity to think about the ambiguities and complexities of feelings: their own and other people's. These are the tools and prerequisites for emotional resilience; they are passing on to their children the capacity to feel at home in the world, and to make other people feel comfortable and safe with them. This involves—at an unconscious level—a syllabus that includes:

- emotional availability
- thinking about emotional consequences
- moderating extremes of emotions
- continuity of care
- holding memories, telling stories
- modelling insight
- modelling collaboration
- resolving disagreements.

The benefits of belonging

In other words, children brought up in good-enough ordinary families will have achieved experiential learning of an unconscious emotional curriculum. You could describe it as providing the following outcomes:

- a coherent sense of self
- an ability to name and make sense of their own feelings
- an ability to create a narrative of events and of their emotional consequences
- a capacity for reflectiveness about themselves and others
- a capacity to collaborate.

It is impossible for children to reach the advanced stages of this curriculum if they have not first learned the basics. However, once the basics are achieved, children will—most of the time—be content to comply with the rules and boundaries that their parents create around them. And as they move through the primary-school years, they will be able to apply an equivalent trust to other adults in positions of authority.

In these circumstances, children trust adults not to abuse the power they have over them. Their knowledge that the various aspects of their emotional selves can be accepted and understood means that they will have the courage to feel their own feelings, think their own thoughts, and express these thoughts honestly and spontaneously.

Children in care: an interrupted process

Children from dysfunctional families, no less than the children of good-enough families, form their emerging identities from the experience of being owned in infancy by their parents or carers, through attempting to take reciprocal ownership of them, and through their reliance on them to organize and make sense of their experiences. These first carers hold the key to understanding their children's emerging identities and helping them to make sense of who they are, through toddlerhood, childhood, and beyond.

When children are removed from their first carers at an early age, the process through which they may be developing a sense of self, and a capacity to belong in a sense other than that of possession and control, is traumatically disrupted.

When they are removed at a later stage, they may or may not have passed successfully through this early process; in situations of dysfunctionality and stress they will be unlikely to have an experience of parents who are in a position to model insight, collaboration, and the capacity to resolve disagreements.

Whatever their age, the trauma of separation will be deep. How children cope with the trauma of this separation will depend very much on the stage of emotional development they have already achieved.

The deficits of a dysfunctional upbringing

Some children who are taken into care will have had a good-enough experience of reciprocal ownership to make use of the ordinary good parenting of long-term foster carers and adoptive parents; they may be sufficiently integrated to be able to describe what they have gone through, and to know something about their own feelings. They may have been given sufficient emotional attention by their birth parents to have the courage to feel their own feelings, think their own thoughts, and express them honestly and spontaneously. They may have a capacity for insight into their own feelings, and for sympathetic understanding for the feelings of other people. But this is not usually the case.

A lack of emotional attention may have deprived them of the tools for naming and organizing their disparate feelings. They may have had parents whose own neediness prevented them from submitting themselves to being owned by their babies. Instead, they may have tried to control their babies' behaviour without the capacity to offer empathy. In such circumstances, babies and toddlers will experience being owned as a tyranny rather than as a benefit, and they will not have the capacity to describe or make sense of their experiences. Without the ability to speak for themselves, they will be psychologically as dependent as babies are on the emotional availability of the unfamiliar adults who undertake their care. However, these will be adults without the detailed knowledge of the children's earliest experiences, who are not in a position to make sense of their fragmented feelings and help them to organize these fragments into an integrated narrative, to describe on their behalf the emotional consequences of what they have experienced, or to resonate instinctively to the fantasies that may be preoccupying them.

In addition, early experiences of abuse will not predispose children to believe in the existence of benign authority. Their carers' assumption that they have a right to exert their authority as adults will be met by hidden or overt resistance. They will lack the foundations for comfortable belonging that are taken for granted in children past toddlerhood who come from good-enough families.

Sometimes this is obvious from the start. Foster carers and teachers may describe a child as "attention-seeking" or "controlling" and may complain that they can give no reason for their volatile behaviours or that they show no remorse. Such children are demonstrating that they have not achieved the emotional learning that might be expected for someone of their chronological age. They are behaving in ways that are normal for babies and toddlers, who legitimately require their mothers' full-time attention, who need to control her as an auxiliary self, who do not understand the meaning of their own feelings or the causes of their behaviours, and who do not experience themselves in one mood as the same person that they were in another. This can be hard for new carers to understand in a child who is chronologically far beyond toddler stage.

For children in this predicament, the boundaries and discipline that adults usually impose on an older child will be inappropriate: punishments may serve to enforce compliance, but they will be experienced as incomprehensible cruelty and injustice. For other children, the damage may be more deeply hidden.

Dissociation

For most looked after children, the trauma of being taken into care is the latest in a series of ongoing traumas. Even as babies, they may have become accustomed to protecting themselves from frightening external events by cutting off from the possibility of feeling and thinking and by withdrawing into a private world. As toddlers, they may have learned to behave in any of a number of ways that will fit in with the needs of parents who are struggling with their own difficulties or preoccupied with the volatility of their own relationships. They may have had to learn to respond intuitively to the moods of the adults around them and, in this way, to take on some of the responsibilities of parenting their own parents, long before their own needs for empathic parenting have been met. For social workers who remove these children from dangerous or neglectful situations, it can be hard to distinguish a numb, unreachable state, combined with an enforced submission to the needs of adults, from the compliance of a normal, trusting child who is happy to accept adult authority. This state is called "dissociation", and it is familiar to all of us as the temporary consequence of shock or tragedy. But for children whose lives are a succession of frightening, unpredictable, and painful events, dissociation can become normal—a necessary and automatic way of dealing with a frightening and incomprehensible world.

What is more, dissociation can be infectious. This can cause significant problems among the adults entrusted with the care of such children. In the face of a child's unconscious determination not to think about, experience, or remember painful feelings or events, adults may empathically join them in becoming numb and unthinking. A child's apparent lack of distress may mislead even experienced professionals into a view that a child has survived without significant damage, or to go along with a belief that there is no real explanation for a child's actions.

The lack of shared fantasy

Where there is more of a sense of self, children may still be struggling with the outrage of toddlerhood even though they are chronologically much older than toddlers. In dysfunctional families, they may not have had the opportunities for shared play that most parents offer their children. They will not have developed an imaginative language they can share with adults that might help them to moderate their extreme emotions. In such circumstances, children of any age may never have learned to make a clear distinction between fantasy and reality, though they may succeed in hiding this confusion from an unsympathetic world. They may remain dominated by grandiose, vengeful, or terrifying (conscious) fantasies or (unconscious) phantasies that adults will not recognize as belonging to the same stage of development as that of a 4-year-old.

Case examples

Jessica: a possession without a self

One 8-year-old girl, Jessica, had been in care since she was 3 years old. She seemed to change her identity completely as she was moved from one placement to another—becoming in turn a sports addict, a dedicated academic, and a cosy little housewife, keen to bake cakes and nurse dolls—according to the personality and preferences of her foster carers. She had been assessed as resilient and with no problems around attachment, and, indeed, she appeared to attach all too readily. But somehow, each set of foster-carers had a plausible, practical reason for moving her on: the illness of a relative, a new job in a different part of the country, reaching retirement age. It was hard to escape the conclusion that beneath Jessica's apparent compliance was a set of unnameable, hidden feelings that made everyone who tried to get close to her feel deeply uncomfortable, but which she had no conscious way of communicating.

Children who dissociate will not themselves be emotionally available, and they will find it hard to make use of the emotional availability offered to them by the adults around them. Jessica was like a baby who knows how to mirror a mother's face and take possession of her mother's superficial characteristics— but that was all she knew. She had been neglected throughout infancy and toddlerhood by a mother who had become progressively more addicted to drugs and alcohol, and although she had loved Jessica, it was in the way that a little girl loves a soft toy: more for her own comfort than through a wish or capacity to meet Jessica's emotional needs.

Jessica had no coherent sense of self, and no way of naming or thinking about her own feelings. She had learned to cut off from her feelings, and she had therefore no capacity to communicate them in a way that evoked understanding in her foster carers. But a child's unfelt feelings are powerfully transmitted to anyone empathic who tries to get close to them. Jessica's need to numb herself was in itself infectious: the professional network around her became desensitized, and they found themselves ignoring the depth of trauma that she had suffered. However, she did successfully communicate a sense of constant unease: something nightmarish that no one felt able to describe, explain, or think about. This was probably an accurate description of her own predicament. She had no access to her own fantasy life.

Jessica had numbed herself from babyhood onwards. Another child, Terry, is perhaps a good example of a child who may have had a less damaging infancy but seems to have been denied any possibility of shared fantasy as a way of mediating the extreme rage of toddlerhood.

Terry: the rage of dispossession

Terry had been in a long-term foster placement for several years. He was described as friendly, quiet, unimaginative, a bit stolid, never any trouble. He was just 18 years old when, one night, he went into his foster mother's bedroom while she was asleep and hit her over the head with the handle of a screwdriver, concussing her and causing substantial bruising.

Terry was not a child that the professionals had ever worried about. When his social worker and I looked at his history together, we learned that Terry had first come into long-term care at the age of 7, because of ongoing physical abuse from his step-father. In the many years since then, no one had thought or talked with Terry or his foster carer about his past. The professionals around him had all been infected by Terry's own ongoing refusal to think about it. Terry was now about to leave his placement and live independently, and his old room was being prepared for a new foster child. He had helpfully offered to put up new shelves in the room: that is why he had the screwdriver to hand. Terry was unable to give any explanation for what he had done—he said he must have done it in his sleep, as he couldn't remember anything about it.

Terry had more of a sense of self than Jessica had. He had been the only child of a single mother with whom he may well have felt some reciprocal and successful sense of ownership. But then, when he was 2 years old, a new partner came along and, shortly afterwards, a new baby. Neither his mother nor his step-father knew how to cope sympathetically with his ordinary toddler rages and jealousy at these new intruders: instead, he was punished with increasing severity by his step-father. His retreat into dissociation and apparent compliance was the consequence of what must have seemed to him a monstrous injustice. However, he managed to numb himself sufficiently to the past to cope with life in a busy foster home, where he took on the role of helpful "big brother" until he found himself in a situation that replicated the original trauma: his foster mother had agreed to take on another child because he was about to move out into independent accommodation. Whatever internal fantasies might have alerted him or others to his buried sense of outrage had been kept deeply hidden and inaccessible. So for Terry, for his foster mother, and for the professional network around them, this attack came "out of the blue": so thoroughly had Terry cut off his memories and feelings about the past that no one had been able to figure out what had triggered this attack, let alone predict it.

Terry had had a rude awakening from the belief that he owned his mother and his mother owned him—that they were one another's undisputed possessions. He had been given no opportunity to think about his feelings, or to use shared play and fantasy to moderate the extremes of his emotional responses to traumatic events. For him, the fantasy of killing his mother had become a "phantasy"—an idea that he could not consciously own or understand—that intruded into waking life as a piece of incomprehensible behaviour.

Some children may oscillate between periods of dissociation and times when, like 4-year-olds, they immerse themselves in games of "let's pretend" to the exclusion of the real world. However if—as was the case with Terry—their fantasies cannot be shared, understood, and moderated by sympathetic adults, sensitive to their concerns, they may seep uncontrollably into these children's everyday lives in the form of action. Without any parental figures to make sense of the symbolic meaning of their secret fantasy life, they may find it impossible to explain why they have behaved in unacceptable ways.

David: secret fantasies

David wrote this story at school at the age of 10, for a new teacher who had given the class a first line to start them off: "It was a beautiful sunny day, and I was on my way to . . .".

This is how David completed the story: "I was on my way to . . . nowhere in particular and someone tapped me on the shoulder. It was the CIA. He said they were spying on me. 'We've come to get you, David!' David knifed him. Then he went home and killed the old lady. His girlfriend was really hot, hot, hot. He knew where she lived. So he stole the police helicopter and landed it there. 'Quick, David, get into the car, and we'll snog! The cops are after us!' 'Don't worry I can drive faster than they can. They'll never find us now!' The End."

David's teacher was interested in thinking about the emotional difficulties of the children in the class. She showed me this story, pleased that David had actually produced some written work for a change, though rather disturbed by the content.

This is what she knew of his history. David had been permanently removed at around the age of 4 years from a teenage mother
who was a prostitute and drug user and had probably allowed him
to watch her having sex with her clients. David's episodes of violent
behaviour were more frequent than Terry's: after a few weeks or
months of compliant behaviour, he would lash out indiscriminately,
in a pattern of escalating aggression. At times, he had caused serious injuries to other children or to the adults who tried to restrain
him. As a result, he had been moved from one foster placement to
another and had been excluded from a previous school.

David's story demonstrates how his sense of belonging was still
focused entirely on the mother he had lost at the age of 4. Nothing
that had happened to him since then seemed as meaningful as
this early relationship, or had touched him at so deep a level. He
still felt that he belonged with her, and with nobody else, and that
she belonged to him: she was his "hot, hot, hot girlfriend". In his
fantasy life, the foster carers who kept him from her became "old
lady" gaolers whom he would kill without compunction. Other
children and adults became spies, like the CIA and the police in his
story. David's apparent compliance to authority figures was built
not on respect or love, but on fear. He felt that they had the means
to enforce his obedience, but they did not have the right to his trust
or his loyalty. However, faced with a new and sympathetic teacher,
David still had enough courage to reach out with an account of his
fantasy life, in the hope of being understood.

David was—more clearly than Terry—a boy struggling with
internal rage, which he tried to keep out of sight and out of mind.
At times when he was not "losing it", he was a charming and
likable boy. Neither he nor the adults around him seemed to feel
the need to find any explanation for his outbreaks of violence. His
behaviour at each new placement was described as "being silly" or
"being naughty"—until his violence escalated, and he was placed
with new carers.

As was the case with Jessica and Terry, David's attempts to
dissociate—the only way he could stifle his impotent rage—had
infected the professional network. Like David, his teachers, social
workers, and foster carers had come to regard each explosion as
an inexplicable piece of "silliness" or "naughtiness," and they were

not able to make sense of it in the light of David's history, any more than David seemed able to do. Because there had been no continuity of care, no one person had a sense of what motivated David's violence. There had been no sympathetic adult to moderate David's extreme sense of injustice about being taken away from his mother, or at being punished for his steadfast loyalty to her. Instead, the ongoing response to each outburst was a non-comprehending imposition of further sanctions.

For children like David, who have not been helped to make sense of their own stories, and of the emotional consequences of what has happened to them, the boundary between fantasy and reality is flexible: fantasies that are not understood on their behalf by an empathic grown-up are likely to get acted out in real life—with disastrous consequences.

Adolescence

Adolescence severely tests the solidity of a child's emotional grounding as he struggles to establish a new identity as a young adult in the adult world. The failure of a solely behaviour-focused strategy becomes apparent as children proceed through their teenage years, and their carers are no longer as able to apply sanctions and constraints as effectively. For Jessica, Terry, and David the prospects are deeply worrying.

A child like David is ruminating about his past through fantasies acted out in the present. While David clearly could not be allowed to assault another child, the reasons for this assault needed to be understood, and the emotions behind it needed to be moderated, if a punishment was to make any sense to him. Responding to this assault simply as inexplicable naughtiness will have re-enforced David's underlying fury, resentment, and distrust of authority.

However, without sufficient specialist knowledge, the psychological work involved in providing in-depth understanding while keeping children safe, and keeping others safe from them, cannot easily be provided. It is unsurprising that the professional network often prefers to settle for an approach directed simply at behaviour, encouraging compliance and punishing naughtiness, whatever the long-term consequences of this may be for a child's emotional development. However, it has dangerous repercussions when children reach independence as young adults.

A child like Jessica, for instance, will be vulnerable to anyone who offers her superficial attention: in return for feeling wanted, she may let herself be used sexually or emotionally by others who are as unscrupulous in their neediness as her mother was, and as unable to meet her needs. David will be easily seduced into criminal activities, which will feel to him to be an appropriate revenge on a corrupt society that has deprived him of his mother and punished him for resenting their interference. Terry may continue to appear compliant, but his unacknowledged murderous rage may break out unexpectedly at any time, and he will have no insight into what has provoked it. For all three, the need to fend off painful emotions that they cannot understand or share will make them more likely to turn to drugs or alcohol for temporary relief.

Children like these may be able to control their behaviours temporarily to fit in with the expectations of those around them, but fundamentally they will not have moved from a conception of relationships as based on the rights of property and control, to the capacity for a more mature sense of belonging. When they come to have children of their own, they will be unable to provide them with insightful parenting and appropriate concern for their individual needs and complexities. Instead, they are likely to repeat the mistakes of their birth parents.

Enforcing compliance

The scarcity of resources and the intense pressures on all professionals within the caring system are such that the provision of any long-term in-depth psychological support is becoming increasingly rare. Social workers have to struggle with ever-growing caseloads, extensive record-keeping, and gruelling inspections, which makes it hard for them to hold on to being in touch with their own feelings, let alone those of others. They can sometimes feel that they themselves live in a climate of enforced compliance, where they are required to dissociate in order to get on with the job.

Teams change, social workers come and go, and it is unusual nowadays to find a child who has kept the same social worker for more than two years at a time. This makes it increasingly difficult to maintain a self-reflective culture, a working environment where people feel safe and comfortable enough to share their feelings, model insight, and resolve disagreements over complex cases. It can even preclude professionals from finding the time and energy to read through what is often many long pages of reports, correspondence, and other documentary evidence, in order to gather up detailed information about a child's early life. Recent endeavours to shorten the time allowed for decisions around children's placements have exacerbated these problems.

In these circumstances, overstretched professionals will more easily turn to a strategy of enforcing compliance from "naughty" children through sanctions and boundaries and assume that compliant children, who are causing only minimal trouble, are doing well; in so doing, they will collude with the children's determination to ignore their underlying problems and retreat from the thinking necessary for emotional learning.

Learning to belong

The task of helping looked after children to feel that they are separate, autonomous individuals who at the same time truly belong to loving carers is very complex. It involves carers providing the same degree of emotional availability that they would provide for their own baby; however, in doing so, they are likely to find themselves experiencing a mass of confusing and often very painful feelings that their own baby would not have evoked in them, because their own baby would not have been similarly traumatized. It involves making sense of a variety of behaviours that may have nothing to do with the relationships they themselves are trying to build with the children they care for; instead, they will be the consequence of the children's past relationships with birth parents or early carers—people that their present caregivers may never have met, and may know very little about. It involves building up a detailed picture of a child's early history—and often the early history of that child's own parents and grandparents—in order to understand why his first family was unable to look after him appropriately. It involves using this accumulated information to reconstruct imaginatively the traumatic experiences that children may not be able to remember or to talk about themselves. This work is emotionally draining, time-consuming, and requires great patience, insight, self-reflection, and expertise on the part of all the carers and professionals that surround the child. Workers and carers rarely have access to the training, supervision, or therapeutic support that could help them to provide such depth of emotional availability and insight.

In the absence of thinking time, self-reflective practice, and support for an approach based on emotional availability and understanding, foster carers and residential care workers are routinely offered strategies that encourage or enforce behavioural compliance. These may be useful tools in some circumstances, but they are counter-productive for children who have not reached an emotional stage to experience them as just or caring. Nor will it meet the needs of carers or professionals looking for help with feelings and resonances that they cannot understand, evoked in them by the children for whom they are trying to build a home. Instead, they too are increasingly judged on concrete measures of behaviour and regulated paperwork requirements.

For them, as for the children, this is not an environment or a system that fosters insightful or mature belonging.

Adoption

The prevalence of this climate causes particular problems for adoptive parents, who automatically lose the network of supportive professionals as soon as they adopt. Without the ongoing presence of the network, which holds so much of the child's history, and with so great a desire to make the child their own, they can easily find themselves colluding with an over-optimistic belief that all the traumas of the child's past life can be wiped out by giving the child a normal, loving experience in the present. They may also buy in to an expectation that they should be as capable of managing this on their own as they would be with children born into their families as babies, or with children whose lives, up to that point, had been untouched by trauma.

This means, however, that they may fail to do the work of reciprocal understanding through which they and their child can grow a sense of belonging to one another. It may also mean that they will never seek the help they need, or will do so only when their relationship with their adopted child is nearing breakdown and mutual bitterness has become entrenched. Adoptive parents can easily find themselves locked into a battle for control that takes precedence over providing intimacy and a curriculum for emotional learning. It can be hard for parents who look back with affection at the strict boundaries they remember from their own upbringing to understand the still greater importance of what they cannot remember: the intimate attentiveness they received as babies that underpinned their acceptance of parental authority.

Adoption can have tragic consequences, too, with dissociated children, whose compliance can be so easily misinterpreted. One girl, for instance, adopted by parents who were school teachers, worked hard for her exams and got good results: then she locked herself into the bathroom and took an overdose. This was an expression of unconscious fury and resentment. She had complied with what some hidden part of her felt to be her adoptive parents' narcissistic requirement: that she should succeed academically in order to enhance their prestige—as their possession rather than for her own sake. She was taking her revenge, in the only way open to her, by trying to rob them of the fruits of their achievement.

While children from good-enough families will appreciate being "owned" by parents within a benevolent hierarchy, children from backgrounds of neglect or abuse will mistrust and misinterpret adult authority and adult intentions. They will remain deeply identified with the early carers who provided them with whatever sense of their own identity they possess. This is likely to bring them into intense conflict—either consciously or unconsciously—with adoptive parents, who naturally wish to "own" their children as any parent would wish to own a baby that is born to them. In these circumstances, overt battles may offer more hope of eventual mutual understanding than apparent good behaviour.

Finding a way of making sense of the meaning of such battles without getting locked into an entrenched dynamic of control is hard work. But it is worth the effort. For adoptive parents who are able to work alongside their child to achieve a mutual understanding of the experiences of dissociation and trauma, the authenticity and depth of their consequent relationships and the happiness of watching their child growing towards true emotional maturity is a reward far beyond superficial compliance.

The following case study is an example of one such family's progress, which I hope provides a demonstration of how much can be achieved by sensitive parenting.

Lily: braving the feelings and sharing the fantasies

Lily was fostered at the age of 14 months and was placed with her adoptive parents, Tom and Sally, when she was 2½ years old. Her files refer to an extremely violent relationship between her parents. The police had been called to the house on several occasions, and when her birth mother was hospitalized with broken ribs, Lily was taken into care. She was subsequently released for adoption when her birth mother chose to return to her partner rather than reclaim her little girl.

Lily's first foster carers, as well as having a large family of their own, specialized in looking after babies and toddlers who were awaiting adoption. They were kindly people, but they had a very matter-of-fact attitude to their foster children: it would have been impossibly painful for them if they had become very attached to each child who was staying only temporarily in their care. Lily was described by her foster parents as a good, easy baby and a quiet, well-behaved toddler who never gave any trouble, but her adoptive parents found it hard to get close to her. They described how, once, when she had hurt herself on the stairs, she had picked herself up and run up to her bedroom—she hadn't run to them. She didn't like to cuddle.

After being adopted, Lily was fortunate in having adoptive parents who did not give up in their attempts to create a more intimate relationship with her. Their ongoing attentiveness had an impact on her that they had not expected: she began to throw violent tantrums. Her rages seemed impossible to withstand and continued for hours on end. She would break the furniture, pull down the window blinds, hurl crockery against the walls. Tom and Sally were incredulous at their own inability to manage her when she went into a rage. They couldn't reach her or talk her down or do anything but wait—restraining her between them, if neces-sary—until the tantrum had passed.

She was 6 years old when they asked for professional help. They felt that they were losing sympathy with her and that they needed support if they were to continue to maintain a state of mind in which they wanted to understand her rather than engage in a never-ending battle for control.

The problem, they said, was that Lily seemed to have no inter-est in learning to think about her feelings. She seemed relentlessly superficial. Her favourite bedtime story—which she asked for again and again—was one they found trite and facile: a tale about a fairy whose magic wand has been stolen and who is imprisoned by Jack Frost.

This seemed to me to relate symbolically to Lily's own pre-dicament. Whether as a baby in a volatile household, or in foster care with kindly but matter-of-fact foster parents, she had not felt allowed to take control and own her carers with the magic wand with which babies need to feel they can command their parents' total attentiveness and empathy. As a result, she had become frozen—a fairy in Jack Frost's prison of ice. This interpretation helped Lily's parents to think more sympathetically about Lily's cold response to their attempts at affection and understanding. However, it did not decrease the violence of Lily's tantrums.

Tom and Sally described how they could usually see the warn-ing signs when a tantrum was on its way: they felt she was working herself up into a storm. But when they tried to speak to her about it, ask her to calm down and control herself, it seemed to make things worse. And once the storm was over, she refused to talk about it—she'd put her hands over her ears and shout them down.

We discussed over many weeks the meaning of what they were describing: how it must have felt to baby Lily to watch her parents fighting, hurling missiles at one another, absolutely powerless to protect herself from scary objects flying around the room. We began to wonder if Lily was acting out a situation where she was power-less—exposed to the storm that was overwhelming her and the household—something she couldn't possibly control. If that was the case, it would not be helpful to make comments that seemed to blame her for the tantrums that swept her away, or to suggest that she should—or could—take control of them.

Again, this understanding seemed at first to be more helpful in changing her parents' state of mind in relation to Lily than it was in decreasing Lily's tantrums. However, a couple of weeks after we had arrived at this thought, Tom and Sally reported that Lily had become fascinated by a DVD of the *Wizard of Oz*: she watched it over and over, again and again.

Lily had intuitively responded to a different state of mind in her parents. She was beginning to wonder about the way that she, just like Dorothy, the little girl who is the heroine of the film, got swept away by a tornado into a strange and different world—"somewhere over the rainbow".

From then on we found ourselves engrossed in the world of Oz, on Lily's behalf, trying to understand what the story meant for her.

In Oz, Dorothy discovers that when she landed she had inadvertently killed the Wicked Witch of the East; as a result, she and the three friends she makes there are being pursued by the witch's vengeful sister, the Wicked Witch of the West, who is intent on killing them.

Sally—who bore the brunt of Lily's furious attacks—came to the recognition that, when Lily was blown away into her tantrum world, she saw Sally as this Wicked Witch: a vengeful figure intent on destroying her. She described how, at these times, Lily would kick her and hit out at her mercilessly. It was hard to hold on to loving feelings for Lily in the face of Lily's determination to cast her as a wicked, vengeful witch.

We speculated on the meaning of this fantasy. Had Lily felt that her passionate emotions had inadvertently destroyed her mother and her first foster carer, as Dorothy destroys the Wicked Witch? Perhaps she couldn't think about feelings because to do so threatened her with unbearable feelings of guilt.

We thought about the three creatures that Dorothy meets in Oz and who become her friends: the scarecrow without a brain; the tin man without a heart, who is rusted into paralysis until Dorothy pours oil on his joints; and the cowardly lion, too scared to roar and to assert his true identity as King of the Jungle.

All three of these friends of Dorothy's are, I think, suffering the consequences of trauma and dissociation—much like Jessica, Terry, and David, who were similarly unable to think, to feel, or to find the courage to assert their own needs and develop their own identities. We thought that these friends represented aspects of Lily, parts of herself that so much needed help to come to life and express themselves authentically.

Over the months, Sally became increasingly concerned to realize how much her relationship with Lily had deteriorated because of Lily's insistence on seeing her as a Wicked Witch. She had not given any attention to other aspects of the story—how in the film all Dorothy wants is to leave the scary, brightly coloured world of Oz and find her way back to her stern but kindly adoptive mother, Aunt Em, and her adoptive father, Uncle Henry; how much Dorothy longs for the safety of their home in Kansas, which is photographed in gentle shades of sepia, black, white, and grey—in contrast to the highly coloured world of Oz, where emotions are so extreme and so dangerous.

Thinking about this was a turning point for Sally in her relationship with Lily. She found herself more able to be aware of the moments when Lily was timidly signalling her capacity for neediness. She noticed, for instance, how interested Lily was in the early part of the film—the storm scene—when Dorothy makes frantic attempts to open the door to the safe refuge, under the house, where the rest of the family are sheltering from the hurricane. Sally started to wonder whether Lily felt that Sally was not helping her to open the door, and she, Sally, became preoccupied about what she could do about it.

This preoccupation seemed helpful enough in itself: Lily was quick to intuit her mother's feelings. Within a few weeks she had started to make a den under her parents' double bed. We could all see the connection: Lily had found the safe refuge that could shelter her from the hurricane.

Frank Baum, the author of the original book, was a sensitive, sickly child, home tutored until he was 12 years old. He was then sent to a strict, all-boy military boarding school, where he was deeply unhappy. After two years there he seems to have experienced some kind of breakdown—either emotional or physical—and was taken back home. So he knew something about the impact of trauma, in a context where there are no parental figures able to help a child make sense of fantasy, but only strict boundaries to enforce good behaviour. His World of Oz seems to me to describe a primitive, scary infantile world, into which he was thrown back by his exile from home and his exposure to a highly disciplined military regime.

Lily's parents had the sensitivity and imaginative capacity to become absorbed, alongside Lily, in the World of Oz that Frank Baum describes. They watched with increasing interest and understanding as Lily started to identify with each of the characters in turn, and to play games about them. They invented bedtime stories together, based on the characters. Sally was able to bear Lily's hatred more sympathetically at the times she morphed into the Wicked Witch in Lily's mind. She even began to find moments when she could tease Lily about it.

This was the point at which Lily's tantrums decreased. She amazed her parents by going to them spontaneously for cuddles and by starting to talk about her feelings in a completely new way. She told them, for example, that she now realized that, deep down, she thought that she had always felt like Dorothy.

This seemed an acknowledgement of how, like Dorothy, she knew that she had not been able to find her way home to them until she had helped her friends—the dissociated parts of herself—to find the feelings, the thoughts, and the courage that could allow them to come to life and to be authentic. It was only when Lily-Dorothy had enabled these traumatized and dissociated aspects of her identity into assertive existence that she realized that she had been wearing the magic ruby slippers all along, which enabled her to go home and to belong to her adoptive parents.

The improvement in her relationships at home coincided with a new thoughtfulness in Lily about her own past. She started to ask questions about her birth mother, and her foster carers, to think with Tom and Sally about why her parents had not been able to look after her, and to express feelings of concern about what might have happened to her birth family in the years since she had been removed from them.

This new liveliness and thoughtfulness was reflected elsewhere. Her teachers reported that she was fitting much better into class activities, doing well in her studies, and was much more able to make and sustain friendships with the other children.

Lily and her parents had found a common language for a reciprocal conversation, through which they could understand the primitive nightmare world of Lily's early experiences, even though Tom and Sally knew only a few details about the facts of her history. They had made their own thoughts and feelings available to Lily, and Lily had come to the recognition that her adoptive parents were trustworthy possessions, able to act as ancillary minds and make sense of her feelings and fantasies in the past and in the present. As a consequence, Lily felt less vulnerable to being blown away by inexplicable storms of emotion. She felt that she belonged and that she could trust her parents—and other adults—to take up ordinary adult authority.

Conclusion

The mature concept of "belonging" depends on a belief that we are held in a system of mutual and collaborative understanding and respect by those around us: that we are not "belongings" to be owned and exploited for the gratification of others, but autonomous individuals within a group of other individuals. All of us, adults as much as children, can accept and even welcome control when we believe in the benign nature of the authority that imposes it, and that the boundaries and regulations that are imposed are intended to serve our own long-term needs and the best interests of the group to which we belong.

The foundations of this belief in benign authority are laid down in babyhood by parents who offer their time, their minds, and their energies to servicing their babies' needs and who do not abuse their babies' dependency by cruelty or neglect—whether it be intentional or unintentional.

This emotional availability offered by ordinarily attentive parents is intuitive and based on shared experience. By the time most small children reach an age where they can put their feelings and fantasies into words, their parents will have acquired an empathic understanding of what has shaped their children's inner worlds, and they will be more or less able to find an appropriate response. They will have already moderated some of their children's extreme emotions and given them a sense of the link between events and their emotional consequences; through this process, they will also have helped to decrease the anxiety that accompanies feelings that cannot yet be named, thought about, or understood.

Dysfunctional families are rarely able to provide such secure foundations. When children from such families are placed with foster or adoptive parents, they need a very different quality of attentiveness from that which would suffice for children of the same age from more stable backgrounds—and a more sophisticated attentiveness than would suffice for an ordinary baby. For these children, emotional development may have been stalled by deprivation, derailed by terrifying experiences, disrupted by a change of carers, and paralysed by the dissociation that accompanies trauma.

When such children begin to access their frozen emotions, these are still the extreme and unmoderated emotions of very young infants and toddlers. They will be expressed through behaviours and fantasies that are likely to seem shocking and incomprehensible to carers who have not shared the experiences of which they are the emotional consequence. These children will not be able to provide explanations for their behaviours and fantasies: they will not have received the emotional education through which they might be able to name or understand the meaning and significance of their feelings and actions, or be able to manage the anxiety that accompanies unprocessed responses. Behaviours that might be an expression of wilful naughtiness in another child may be the impulsive expression of legitimate reactions to past events of which they have no conscious memories, and about which their present carers may have been given no information. In such cases, sanctions need to be married to an in-depth and compassionate understanding. Punishing such a child for his behaviours and fantasies will be as inappropriate as it would be for a baby—it will be experienced as a cruel or meaningless injustice. Either way, it will confirm a mistrust in adult authority and, at best, will push the child back into a frozen state of apparent compliance.

If these children are ever to reach a mature concept of belonging, foster and adoptive parents are likely to need expert help that goes beyond behavioural regulation: they will need to make sense of the aetiology of their children's behaviours. Rigid boundaries may temporarily enforce acceptable conduct. But in any family, it is the mutual exploration and benevolent understanding of fantasy life—either through conscious explication or intuitive empathy—that is the basis for feeling comfortably at home with one another. For fostered and adopted children, it is an essential requirement if the adults who care for them are to lay the foundations that will prepare them to feel at home with themselves, with their new families, and ultimately within the adult world.

CHAPTER SIX

Belonging inside:
a child in search of herself

Becky Wylde

This chapter arises from my work as a child and adolescent psychotherapist working within a specialist CAMHS for looked after children. Many of the children who find their way into this specialist care system arrive with a very thin and insubstantial sense of themselves and with little or no feeling of belonging in relation to a physical home or emotionally in relation to others. Many have had extraordinarily confusing and unreliable care, often abusive, and the places where they have lived or been accommodated have been fractured, through multiple transitions, placement moves, and losses. Multiple foster placements will have presented them with a tantalizing experience of transitory stability in other people's homes with other people's families, only then to be moved on again into yet another new context. It is not surprising, therefore, that in psychotherapy such a child will bring us the tattered shreds of memories of different people and of the different homes and places in which he or she has found him/herself. But the narratives that we hear are not consistent, and their stories about themselves lack depth. These children look to the outside world in their search to try to find ways of fitting in and of belonging, but their inconsistent external world does not supply them what they need to know: who am I, and where do I belong? Of the thousands of deprived children within the looked after system, only a very small number make their way into psychoanalytic psychotherapy. One such child was Laura.

When I first met Laura she achieved a sense of belonging by either clinging to or intruding upon others. In this chapter, I hope to describe how the therapeutic journey led her to gain knowledge of herself so that she could achieve a sense of belonging that started essentially within herself rather than outside herself.

Belonging and identification

For me to understand the process of change within Laura, it was important to recognize how she acquired her sense of belonging. The discussion later shows how in theoretical terms she made a shift from a desperate adhesive identification, with attempts at intrusive control, to the formation of an inner world that could begin to support a rudimentary sense of her own identity.

Containment

From Bion's (1962a) theory of infantile development we understand that infants are not born with a mechanism to think about or understand their experiences in the world. They are reliant on the function of an external (primary) object. This external object—usually the mother—needs to function as a "container" for the baby, taking in and making sense of the baby's painful sensations and feelings. In this way, and through multiple experiences of this function, the baby gradually takes into himself this process of discrimination and mental digestion. This process opens up a space inside the infant which will hold this example—or prototype—of the transforming mother, and thus the infant will begin learning to understand his feelings and to relate to an internal sense of himself. Bion stresses that in this process of early containment, it is vital the mother uses her own "mental equipment" to give meaning to what feels meaningless to the infant. In some cases of early emotional deprivation, when the mother's own impoverishment and emotional disturbance means that she is unable to offer containment to her infant, the child himself is unable to grow a containing function within himself. Gianna Henry (1983) says that:

> We are often confronted with patients, especially amongst the ones who have missed out on the early experience of containment as described by Bion, who do not seem to have developed such mental equipment. [p. 83]

When these processes of internalization do not occur, the child may look outside himself to make sense of his unresolved feelings and to form an identification.

Identification

Margot Waddell (1998) clearly describes the possible modes of identification available to the developing child as of the adhesive, projective, or introjective kind. She goes on to say:

> In any one child it is usually possible to discern the underlying predominance of one mode over the other, despite shifts and changes. It is the predominance of one of these modes over others that determines whether learning takes place by way of imitation, of mimicking, parroting, adhesive kind; or by the child's anxiously seeking to be someone that he or she isn't . . .; or by the child resiliently seeking understanding by engaging with his or her own experience of a secure, inner sense of self. [p. 106]

When the adhesive form of identification is predominant, the child's sense of safety and survival depends upon adhering to those around him. There is a thinness of self, a flatness inside, with no place for holding thoughts or memories.

This is described by Meltzer (1974), who sees adhesive identification as a failure to form an internal space, resulting in two-dimensionality:

> . . . the two-dimensional surface relationship to objects in which there were no spaces and in which therefore identification processes could not take place and development did not seem

to occur because they could neither use projective identification, which required a space to get into, nor introjective identification, which required a space that you could take something into. [1974, p. 348]

Laura was driven by her need to belong. She either attempted to look outside herself to adhere to various characters from fiction or public life or used methods of intrusion in an attempt to have control over others. However, these attempts failed to bring her any substantial relief as they led either to terror of her own emptiness or to distressing sexualized fantasies. Her attitude to progress was always ambivalent as she had to start to relinquish the mode of identification that had helped her survive in the past. This meant the painful recognition of the deprivation that she had started from. She then had to struggle with her fears and memories of past abuse to discover how she might find a safe place to belong in a relationship with parents. However, slowly she began to build and then internalize more reliable and benign characters and, despite external circumstances that kept her in a state of transition, she did begin to feel she belonged to a therapeutic home and family. The thread of stability for Laura was provided by the consistent psychotherapy sessions. She used this process of interest in who she was in order to grow a greater internal sense of self.

Laura: a child with no identity

I worked with Laura for four years. In that time she had five foster placements. Latterly she had two temporary placements, both of which lasted for well over a year. In both of these foster homes, there was the initial possibility—of which Laura was aware—that they could become long term. This depended on them going well or, as Laura put it, "if they want to keep me". However, in both placements she had the experience of knowing six months or so into the placement that she was to move on. The pain of this situation is difficult to imagine. She knew she had been rejected and would not be a permanent member of the family, having for untold months to continue to live as if she were. This appeared as a kind of unbearable twilight, in which she was provoked by the pain and fury of rejection while being encouraged to be part of the family. She saw this hypocrisy, saying, "they say they treat you as if you are part of the family but it's not true, they don't". The task that faced us was how it might be possible for her to grow an identity while in transit and despite these provocative external circumstances.

History

Aged 8 years, Laura was taken into care. She had lived most of her life with a mother with learning disabilities and a personality disorder. However, her life was transitory, sometimes staying with aunts or her grandmother. A picture emerged of a mother unable to distinguish herself from her infant, not able to recognize and digest Laura's anxieties. No doubt the infant Laura experienced this as her mother's identity intruding and leaving no possibility of separation between them. There were shorter periods during which her alcoholic father lived with them. Laura was sexually abused by him and exposed to sexual violence between her parents. As a consequence of many locality moves Laura frequently changed schools, and she fell through the net of the protective services. One school reported concern that she didn't seem to be able to eat solid foods at age 6, as if she had not been weaned. They reported her overall presentation as being learning-disabled with a confused sense of reality.

Aged 9, she was referred for psychotherapy. She was living in a short-term foster placement. On first meeting Laura, I was at a loss to understand her feelings, and she seemed to lack a containing internal object. Her confused state of mind, mimicry, snatches of songs, and fragmented stories reminded me of a distressed and restless infant in desperate need of containment. She brought scraps of memories of life before coming into care, which formed very watery pictures. Given attention, these seemed to seep away from us. However, although she was often confused, disoriented, and at sea in her placement, she did consistently show interest in me and the psychotherapy process.

At this time, Laura's survival seemed predominately dependent on an adhesive mode of identification. Her interest in me seemed like another possible raft to which to stick herself .

Beginnings

At the outset of the work, Laura was in her initial foster placement. She spent every third weekend with her birth family, who were close-knit and religious. Contact with this family was important to Laura. However, while it made a contribution to her sense of identity, it was also confusing for her. Exploring this confusion, Margaret Rustin (2008) mentions that it creates a conflict of loyalty for the looked after child and increases disturbance, "because it very often entails exposure to emotionally intense conflicts and stirs up distressing memories which intrude into present realities" (p. 78).

Laura's first foster carer, Stacey, was a highly organized single mother who specialized in having very young children in foster care who were being prepared for adoption. When Laura arrived, there were two toddlers in placement. Although arriving confused, Laura quickly appreciated the regularity and structure: bedtimes, mealtimes, order, and predictability—so different from the chaos that she had known with her mother. She was cleaned up and began to look neat and tidy and very much like her foster carer and the toddlers. This appeared to be an adhesive adaptation to create a family likeness.

Assessment sessions

Laura talked in her first assessment session about having glasses now she is with Stacey and hoping she will see things clearer, comparing this to living with her own mum's "blurry sight". Throughout these sessions, she thought a lot about babies inside and outside and about the great confusions of feelings of entangle-ment with her mother. She described the shock of finding out that her own mother was pregnant when she brought Laura a photo of the scan to their contact meeting. She wasn't able to see the baby in the picture, but her mother insisted that Laura could see it. Furthermore, she wasn't able to see its eyes, nose, or mouth. She was frightened by her feelings of ambivalence towards this invisible inside baby. During these sessions, I had a growing discomfort due to Laura's depiction of this mother-figure, who seemed to insist that Laura saw the world through her eyes. They seemed merged as one, without separate identities. Laura's thoughts of a place inside, an internal space, were crowded by an unformed baby, giving rise to a battle over ownership of their mother and a space inside her. She brought a dream of *herself giving birth in a state of terror, while the toddler foster sister laughs at her, and the baby is born wet and covered in mess.* I saw this as a dream depiction of a terrible disaster, no maternal containment, no safe place for babies to be detoxified and cleaned up, no receiving relationship to be born into and belong.

She told me how she wished she was like the babies at Stacey's, who were lucky in believing Stacey to be their mother. She could not believe this because of her terrible difficulty facing how to be sure where and to whom she belonged. The separation from her intrusive mother had painfully exposed her lack of an independent identity.

The intruding girl

As the twice-weekly therapy got under way, she began to turn her attention to how to take in the therapist-mother. She employed a mixture of intrusiveness and adhesiveness. She often got too close and wanted to touch my face and lips. She made sudden raids on my jumper buttons with the Play-Doh, to try to form imprints of them, which she then wanted to hoard. She used my language and repeated back my words, sometimes weeks apart, as if they were a store of stolen treasure. As I said above, the aim of this type of intrusiveness is to control the other and to treat that person as an extension of the self, thereby avoiding separation. For Laura, intrusion in order to dominate might also be understood as a re-enactment of her sexual abuse, as a rudimentary attempt to discover the internal space of another person through a forced entry. I think that these two psychic aims—that of dominance and a more developmental attempt at discovery—were in tension with each other.

In those early months of therapy there was a superficial atmo-sphere of fascination and desire for her therapist, which lacked any depth of curiosity. She hoarded what she took from me but did not take it in meaningfully. However, she did seem to like my thinking about her, and sometimes she seemed able to reflect a little on what I had said and what it might mean. There was a half-term break after four months of our work together which initiated Laura's work on the painful task of separation. Before the break she had made an attempt to construct an exclusive telephone line between us to obliterate the difficulty of the forthcoming separation, but after the reality of this break she set to work differently. She had drawn a picture of the clinic in a previous session, which seemed to suggest that, by fixing it on paper, she could somehow have pos-session and control of it. After the break she returned to this image wanting my help to draw the *inside* rooms of the clinic. When this attempt continued to frustrate her, she started to construct a row of houses in a street. One of these was mine, another hers, and she worked on how they linked together. She added a back to them, with doors that opened, and then tried to construct an interior to the houses. She peopled my house. This creation began to fail as a comfortable solution when she suddenly realised that she had given me a "Mr. Therapist". Her thoughts then ran to a house full of children with her standing bereft and deprived outside looking in.

She had started to imagine internal space, but all the space was projected into me, leaving her with a terrible sense of her own deprivation and internal emptiness. Laura's hard work to discover internal space was painful and frustrating. A less painful alterna-tive for her was the search for new identities to cling on to. These were figures from stories or public life.

A cast of possible identities

Having projected aspects of her internal life into me, her therapist, Laura was left looking in, feeling great envy and emptiness. This put her in touch with feelings of wanting to steal and of being stolen. Suddenly this led to Laura talking about the stolen child Madeleine McCann. She felt the terror of the child being stolen away by an adult. She asked, "how would you know if it was a social worker or a burglar?" Her dilemma was whether and how they might be the same. At this point she felt a desire to be the burglar, who steals a child from the therapist's house and takes it away, to then—cuckoo-like—insert herself in its place.

The Madeleine McCann motif stayed with her for many months. It surfaced in a different form later after the disastrous breakdown of her permanent placement. At that time, she was in a very fragile state of mind and had lost her bearings so significantly that she was terrified that she was indeed Madeline McCann herself, since she could find no internal evidence of who she was otherwise. Putting herself forward as the lost child, whose discovery and return was nationally so longed for and mirrored her own longing to be found, seemed like a hopeful possibility to her. During this time, when I talked about flying in the face of facts, Laura seemed to have no facts about herself, no grounding knowledge, as if she believed she could be Madeleine—or, indeed, anyone.

Never Neverland and mermaids

In the first year of her foster placement, Laura had not only witnessed two of the toddlers she lived with moving into adoptive homes, she had become aware of the birth and adoption of her own baby sister. It was tantalizing and unbearable waiting for her turn to be found a permanent home, a long-term foster placement. She had even made a determined bid for one of the adopting mothers: she had sat squarely on the mother's lap and explained seriously that she was in fact the toddler's big sister so this available mother should obviously adopt both of them together. Eighteen months into our work, Laura was facing a three-week summer break. She started to tell me about the ideas of flying to Never Neverland like Peter Pan, taking another foster child with her and avoiding all adults and family.

This fantasy was both exciting and frightening. Making herself a lost child by taking herself away to Never Neverland felt exciting. She was also fearful that at night Peter Pan might come for her, and she really would have to fly away. Then, in her progressively messy drawing of this fantasy, it became the therapist flying out the window and leaving her forever—off to "never–return–land".

Laura now started drawing Siamese-twin mermaids, their tails entwined and heads stuck together. For Caroline Case (2008), the mermaid is a symbol of the child's fantasy of remaining an inside baby, as it represents her entanglement with her mother and the resistance to separation. Laura had struggled to manage a faltering hold on a maternal therapeutic figure, and with the threat of the break she seemed to ditch all need for adults and in her mind evacuated to Never Neverland, where children live without the pain of their dependence on parents. However, as her anxieties grew, so did the thought that she might be the one who is left behind in this obliterating world. She was drawn again to her more primitive form of identification through an intrusive merger, sticking the tops and bottoms of the mermaids together.

Signs of progress: composing a maternal object

Over the two years in her first placement, there were signs that Laura was beginning to internalize a safer sense of boundaries, as well as of safe spaces between people. In her thoughts about others, she saw safe rules between people, and she was less drawn to intrusive behaviour. This became clearer to me when one day she came to her therapy session unusually anxious and stated she supposed that I was 38 years old. When I wondered why, she said it was the age of her mother. I said she seemed to be deciding all mother people are the same in age and capacity. I expressed that this might not be the case. Slowly and with great confusion, she described a dilemma.

Her grandmother had told her to keep a secret: when she next stayed at grandmother's she would have a sleepover at her auntie's house, which had not been designated a safe place to stay by her social worker. She knew her social worker would not allow it. By asking me to keep the secret implicitly, I was to be like her mother, careless of her safety and sometimes dishonest. I talked about the need for rules to keep Laura safe, the great importance of adults who can come together and really plan and think together in her interest and stick to the rules. With a great sigh of resignation, and some relief, she understood that I would pass this information on to her social worker. Then she asked me what the social worker might do about it. When I said I didn't know, she speculated that if I could get inside her social worker's body, then I would know and would control the social worker. I then talked about what a great muddle this would be, leaving both myself and her social worker with no mind or body of our own. She began to giggle and started to draw an amalgamated mother person—a mixture of limbs, body parts, and the facial appearance of her social worker, her birth mother, and myself. She gave this picture a composite name using letters and part names from all three of us. The picture emerged with some surprising beauty about it. Although it had begun as an attempt to entangle us all together, its completion suggested something different. Together we speculated on how this type of mummy-person, with the combined qualities of the social worker to keep her safe and the therapist to keep the thinking going, could curtail her mother's dishonesty and enable the kindness in her mother's nature to be received. At this point, I began to divine the beginning of a new type of identification. Laura had designed a maternal object with various good aspects. I hoped over time she might internalize this good object, learn to relate to and rely upon it, so as to feel eventually that it belonged inside her and formed part of her identity.

Time to move: becoming aware of her intrusiveness

Laura had been in her first placement for two years. Having lived through the many transitions of others, she was finally told that a match had been made and that she was to move to live in a permanent placement with a single carer named Denise and her 15-year-old daughter.

Denise had only recently trained as a foster carer, and Laura was to be her first foster child. Introductions began, and I was asked to meet with Denise to help build a picture for her of Laura's psychological difficulties and emotional needs. Denise was a warm and nurturing woman, and it was clear she felt genuine concern for the awkward and confused Laura and wanted to offer her affection and comfort.

Laura felt great anxiety about the transition and what might be expected of her in her new home. In her therapy, she started to make accusations about the harshness of Stacey's care, which culminated in accusing Stacey of taking away her bed and making her sleep on the floor. Her accusations were not substantiated. They were precipitated by her fears about moving and an attempt to manage this by splitting the world into one cruel, rejecting mother and another whom she wanted to be all sweetness and light. During this period of intense anxiety, Laura became very disturbed in the outside world, which continued after she moved to Denise's home. In her sessions, she acted out terrifying scenarios of witches who needed to be drowned and of mistakes made when children were drowned instead of these witches. The story of Rapunzel held a special significance, particularly the witch's action of stealing the little Rapunzel away from her family. She became quite paranoid and persecuted. She stared at me intensely, and said she could imagine my underwear. I talked about her need to know what someone was truly like underneath, who someone really was, her fear of being tricked and kidnapped, and her terror of not knowing. Overall, we tried to understand how her raised anxieties drove her attempt to control those around her through intrusive fantasies.

Laura became preoccupied with her sense of an atmosphere of indulgence in her new foster home. She told me about "pamper parties" and "girls' nights- in". She pleaded with me: "I'm not a girly-girl, I don't think I am a girly-girl, am I?" She was very frightened about what was expected of her. In her sessions she again became very confused and highly sexualized. It seemed that the offer of closeness in the new family felt like seduction to Laura. She became very preoccupied by babies and sexual intrusion, and a terrible muddle re-emerged with fantasies of intrusion into a mother's body precipitating a collapse of her fragile sense of separateness from the maternal object.

Breaking down—moving forward?

The placement rapidly broke down after only eight weeks. Laura was removed to an emergency placement. Denise had found the strain of a very disturbed Laura overwhelming. It had reactivated a serious underlying neurobiological disorder. Laura was devastated, shocked, very frightened, and concerned that she had caused such damage to her carer. She had been unable to sustain a sense of identity in this transition. Therefore, because she did not feel she could belong to herself, she could not begin to see how she could belong in this new placement. After a week in the emergency placement, Laura was placed in another temporary placement— a robust couple, Rachel and Matthew.

Attempts to triangulate: fear and hope

In this new placement, Laura was faced with the challenge of living with a couple. Her only experience of living like this, in her early childhood, had been the short periods that her father had lived with her mother and herself. As mentioned above, her natural infantile development from total psychological dependence on a mother towards inclusion of a third, the father, had been grossly derailed. Laura had not been able to establish a reliable and secure relationship with her mother in her early months. This was then followed by actual sexual intrusiveness by her father with her mother's collusion, neglect, and incompetence. Paradoxically, with this background the couple in Laura's new placement represented a terrifying prospect for her.

We know that resolving the oedipal situation is a key developmental stage for the child and sets the stage for the ability to separate and establish an identity. Britton (1989) writes:

> A third position comes into existence from which object relations can be observed. Given this we can also envisage being observed. This provides us with a capacity of seeing ourselves in interaction with others and for entertaining another point of view whilst retaining our own, for reflecting upon ourselves while being ourselves. [p. 87]

Britton went on to describe the terrible difficulties the child has in facing the oedipal situation if he has not been able to internalize a containing and stable maternal object. In Laura's case, the experience of the couple seemed to threaten her very existence. In a similar vein, O'Shaughnessy (1989) writes:

> The combined parents—a cruel structure in these cases—demand sexual watching, threaten invasion or suction into their perpetual intercourse, stimulate envy, and enormously increase anxiety and depression. Because the patient lacks an internalized figure that can contain and modify this nearly overwhelming state of mind, he feels alone with an intolerable psychic load and threatening chaos. To disburden his psyche and re-enter his object, the patient in phantasy inserts himself between the combined figure, pulls the couple apart, and projects himself into one or other of the separated pair. [p. 149]

In the two years prior to being placed with Rachel and Matthew, any success Laura had achieved in creating internal space for a good object collapsed in this double crisis of a further experience of rejection and the prospect of living with a couple. It became, as O'Shaughnessy described, "an intolerable psychic load" such that in her placement, and in her sessions, she became increasingly disturbed.

She had been living in her new placement for a month when, coming to her session, she tried to grab and plunder a storage cupboard in the corridor. Once in the room, I talked about her trying to grab what isn't hers. She threw herself violently into an upside-down position on the beanbag, her legs flailing in the air, her skirt falling back and knickers showing. She was all upside down, with her crotch being where her thinking head should be, as if she were showing me that her head was full of sexual thoughts. Hearing this suggestion, she got up and danced, emitting squeezed baby-like cries, loud guttural grunts, and snatches of disembodied voices and stories. She was terribly confused and seemed to be enacting or embodying the combined parental couple. She sucked water into her mouth and tried to talk to me through it as if drowning or choking. My words and thoughts didn't appear to reach her, until she managed to accuse me of incompetence and collusion by saying, "you drive a car round and round the toilet and wet yourself". My response was to talk to her about the failure of this mummy person-therapist who seemed stupid, unable to clean up and get her out of the mess, but got messed up herself. She laughed at this, saying "you drive round and round the potty too and you fart in Dad's trousers, and you have Dad's trousers in the potty". I replied that there was a horrible mess in the trousers and talked about grown-ups all muddled up in their mess with the baby's mess and no one keeping this mess in the right place.

She suddenly became very serious for a moment, asking, "is that what was wrong with my Mum?" I talked about the very important job of knowing the difference between babies and grown-ups, in being able to clean the mess and not muddle it further, and her Mum's difficulty with this. She then came very close to me and suddenly pulled up my trouser leg, touching my leg and shouting that I had black socks on. I tried responding to this sudden intrusion, but Laura started to giggle and wriggle and dance away from me, saying, "Fart in Dad's trousers and the fart goes in your mouth and then you slide down the Dad's trousers because you are tiny, tiny-miniature".

What we see here is Laura in the grip of what O'Shaughnessy described—as if she felt that she belonged in the very heart of this intrusive and violent couple. She was in terror of being pulled in, sucked in, and annihilated, and her compulsion was to be right inside the combined object. We see that if she pulls free she must then identify with one or other of these parents who had intruded upon her. In this case, she identified, in her intrusiveness towards me, with the abusing father. I think she was also describing the terrible and unthinkable alternative, which was identification with the abused little one (so "tiny, tiny-miniature"), such that she felt just a droplet slipping and sliding forever downwards into oblivion. Laura's internal conviction at this time was that she either belonged to/was caught up with the intrusive parent or would be dropped forever. Gripped by intrusive identification, she was unable to manage any thoughts of separation, and without any separation it is not possible to achieve a triangular relationship with parents. Britton's "third" position in the oedipal triangle can only be achieved if the child is held by, and holds herself within, a relationship with both parents. In this state of mind, Laura had no sense that she could find a comfortable "third position"—a place of belonging in a relationship with a couple who could be parents to her as well as being a couple.

Some progress

However, over time the intense arousal from being with a couple began to settle a little: a space for thinking began to open up in which we were able to discuss her difficulties with being with the couple. In one session she said, "do you know something, I feel left out when I am with Rachel and Matthew", and she started to rapidly tell me how unfair it was when she got sent to her room because of the noises she made. She elaborated that Rachel explained that her noises interrupted them, but, Laura said, "I feel left out! Why do they always want to be together?" She then told me she would like to send Matthew away. She laughed and said that he was working away from home soon and "Hurray—it will be just me and Rachel together!" I talked to her about how difficult living with a couple felt to her and that all she seemed to feel was pushed out and not included, and she couldn't enjoy it. Furthermore, that if she did get rid of Matthew, I doubted she would feel good but maybe horrid and scary too. She said, "well, I can't because Rachel loves him and they are a married couple", and I agreed. She then started to question me urgently again about if there *was* a Mr. Therapist, my husband. We talked then about how in her mind the world was just brimming over with Mr and Mrs's and she just couldn't see the right place or space for where a child should be—but the concept of such a place and relationship had begun to be thought about.

As her anxieties and terror of living with the couple slowly subsided, we found ourselves struggling again with the problem of the lack of internal space. Laura had begun to achieve a rudimentary knowledge of being a child with parents both in therapy and externally, but her sense of identity and of a relationship to the couple were still very fragile and fleeting.

A family to belong to: a hope betrayed

Matthew and Rachel had adult children, and they often cared for their 4-year-old grandson, Kenny. Rachel reported that, on the whole, Laura (now 12 years old) played well with Kenny. She felt Laura regressed happily in her play.

In therapy, Laura talked often about Kenny. He seemed both a useful example of how to be a secure little child that she could use as a model, and a painful reminder of what she hadn't had. She felt her deprivation acutely at these times. In parallel, in her therapeutic work, she was endeavouring to understand the nature of being in the therapy family as well as the external everyday adaptations of being in Rachel and Matthew's family.

Eric Brenman (1985) describes how the process of psychoanalysis develops a "psychological home" for the patient to belong to. I have come to understand that extending this concept from "psychological home" to include a "therapeutic family" is exceptionally helpful for looked after children in transition. Laura often called to me "Hello Mum-not" or "Hello therapy-Mum" as I collected her from the waiting room. She had really taken to and enjoyed the idea of being in a therapeutic family. This had been a very helpful concept during her various external transitions, providing a consistent sense of family to belong to.

For one session, after my unexpected cancellation of the week before, she brought in some photographs . There were pictures of herself with Rachel and Matthew, and of herself and Kenny playing on the beach. They both had similar buckets and spades and were digging holes in the sand. Indeed, Laura did look very like a little 6-year-old girl. She watched me carefully as she asked me, "Don't you think Kenny is sweet?" I said she seemed to be wondering if I had a preference. "No", she replied, and I said he seemed lively as he seemed to be digging energetically. "Yes", she said, he had made her laugh. Then she then told me that there had been two spades, and she had had to have the pink one and it wasn't fair because she didn't like pink. She also told me that Kenny's spade had somehow got damaged and she had been blamed, unfairly she felt. She suddenly was full of resentment and anxiety. I talked about mixed feelings and how something nice had become spoiled with envy. Laura didn't seem to be able to hear, and she started to talk about being very scared by seeing starving children in Africa on the television. It seemed she had felt the cancelled previous session as a loss, as starving her, putting her in touch in a frightening way with baby Laura who had really needed more and better food. I talked about how hard it was to see Kenny getting the right sort of food and love for a little one. "Yes", she said "and . . . Rachel sometimes doesn't treat me like her daughter but like a foster daughter". I linked this to the deprivation of a cancelled session. She said: "Yes you had family problems and you had to go away, but why? Your family needed you . . . couldn't you say no?" I said that she felt I had left her when she needed me, so had not treated her like a daughter either. She said, "No . . . have you told your family about me, do they know?"

Clearly Laura was growing a sense of belonging to the therapy family. However, she also struggled with being both a therapy child and a foster child and with the truth that neither of these identities is the same as a birth child. She therefore questioned the value of this dual status. In the therapy room, she would find constant evidence of my involvement with other children. She determinedly tried to recruit a child she met in the waiting room as her "Therapy Sister", and she was later devastated when this patient stopped coming. While she glimpsed at the value to her own truthful status, Laura easily slipped into categorizing the evidence that she was treated harshly. Thus, her grievance and resentment interfered with the small moments of achieving a place to think about herself and her true identity or, as Britton described, the third position of reflecting on ourselves while being ourselves.

Sadly it became clear that Laura was not able to stay with Matthew and Rachel on a permanent basis. They felt her resentment of their couple relationship, and the sexual remarks she made to them at home, were a potential indicator that she might make a false accusation against Matthew. Matthew worked as a teacher and therefore felt a potential allegation was too great a risk. It took eight months for a new placement to be identified from the moment Laura was told of the decision that she would have to leave.

Moving on, but with more inside

Knowing her social worker was actively looking for a suitable long-term placement, nevertheless—and understandably—Laura continued to struggle with mixed feelings of anxiety and resentment during these eight months. Her struggle was increased by the unfortunate reality that I had become unwell and was off work for four months. During this time she was held by my colleague, who had been offering parent-work to Laura's carers. My colleague now helpfully and skilfully included Laura in a series of sessions along with Rachel to help them think together and make sense of my absence and its effect on Laura, the impending move, and her fear of what the future held. I am sure that this work helped Laura extend her reflection and not to resort to splitting, turning Rachel and Matthew bad in her mind, as she had done in previously similar circumstances with her foster carer Stacey. Although the move was disturbing for her, it did not result in an emotional crisis and collapse, as had happened before. There was a sense that, this time, Laura had more of an identity inside herself to take with her.

Laura was moved to a new placement with a couple, but with a big and lively family around them. There was a teenage birth daughter living with them, and also a teenage foster child who was in placement with her own new-born baby. The atmosphere and culture in this busy family was very different from Rachel and Matthew's quiet home.

When I returned to work I found Laura, now approaching 13 years old, anxiously trying to fit in by trying to change her appearance and interests. She had changed her style of dressing and wanted to appear more like the teenagers. She described hairstyles and colour, make-up, and shopping outings that she had enjoyed with her new carer, Paula. She appeared to be attempting chameleon-like to belong and become as one with her new foster family. However, we were also able to struggle with the truth that the roots of her hair would remain her birth colour: that the roots of herself, the essence of who she was and where she came from, could not be covered up or changed.

Laura continued to make desperate attempts to identify with and belong in her new surroundings. However, her old, painful familiar feelings of resentment and rejection were very close to the surface. Three months into placement, she acted in an impulsive and abusive way towards Paula's 4-year-old niece. This precipitated Paula's family's decision not to agree to offer Laura a long-term placement. However, she was to continue to stay there. Laura found herself once again living in the intolerable and difficult situation of being in transition while making a semi-permanent home.

External changes threatening internal home: will the inside hold?

Six months later, Laura was still waiting for news of a new placement when our CAMHS had to face its own transition. The need for budgetary savings centralized local provision into one main clinic. This meant a move of the therapy base and therapy home for Laura. By this time, Laura had been in therapy for nearly four years. This move was a very significant experience.

At first, this further loss seemed to push her into a disintegrated state, and she became very confused. After a while, I came to realize that she had made an assumption that she would be allocated a new therapist at the new clinic. This would be replication of a foster placement move, with all the changes of the home, the family, and the primary object. I felt shocked and devastated when I recognized this assumption as an indication of the brutality she had really experienced in the care system, of actual losses and the absolute severing of attachment. Despite nearly four years of the therapeutic relationship, during which due care and attention had been paid to preparation for holiday breaks and thinking about the pain of unexpected breaks and separation, Laura was still able to believe that there would be a total abandonment and a careless exchange of a person.

As time moved on and the shock seemed to settle a little, she became more able again to hold together in her sessions and even to have some interest and enquiring thoughts about the new clinic. She also recognized that I, too, was to become a displaced person during this move, although I would be attempting to remain a secure object for her throughout the transition.

I began to notice that although Laura still had very confused states, she was starting to have more thoughts about herself, about who she was and how she might grow. One day she told me she felt she wanted to live "opposite to normal" and described herself as a grown-up Laura having pink hair, a multi-coloured cat on a lead, and wearing pyjamas to go shopping. I said it all sounded very confused and distorted, but as we discussed these ideas together I came to understand that she was trying to describe to me how different and "opposite" she felt to the "ordinary" people around her.

Laura now seemed to be able to perceive how she had attempted to superficially match, to adhesively attach, herself to her different foster families in the past. This way of doing things did not seem so available to her any more. The alternative for her was a beginning to see and understand her real disabilities and deprivations, and the losses that she had experienced that could not be glossed over. In the last session at our old clinic, she brought in her iPod and wanted to show me pictures of her birth family and also to take photos of the clinic and our room for her album. This felt like a joining-up of history we were able to continue to think together about, a bridge between the past and the future, the loss of the familiar, and the apprehension of the unknown new place. Laura was growing a sense of a relationship with her own history. I think the iPod, with its capacity to store all these pictures, represented to her a useful model of an internal space for memories and personal history.

Predictably Laura felt that the new clinic was a disappointment: she thought it was shabby and cold, and she felt uncomfortable and restless there to begin with. Her feelings of grievance about her foster home and complaints about the new clinic rose to an all-time high. I talked with her about how she felt the space I now offered her was impoverished and depriving and how I had become a cruel, depriving parental provider in her mind's eye. She agreed angrily with me that this was true. She was also quite reckless in her climbing onto furniture, and I had to be very firm and strict in containing her dangerous behaviour. However, one day a month or so after our move she told me that she had been swimming with her school at the leisure centre very close to the old clinic. She described her sadness and longing for the old place, and she seemed to be able to stay alongside me for a little while with this painful feeling without immediately resorting to blame or grievance. She simply said she felt sad and wished we could go back there. I said that it was sad and sad that she had had so many losses in her short life. And this led her to a sudden memory of living with her birth mother and how she felt she was the one in charge and not her mother. She said she remembered how she had made her mother put her on a dangerous parapet outside their second-storey flat. Laura then started to wonder, "Why did I want to do that? I don't understand—why?" We then began to think together about Little Laura's need to communicate the danger she was in to the outside world and about her struggle with knowing the poverty of her mother's capacity to keep her safe.

I thought there seemed to be a discernibly different quality in Laura's ability to think and wonder and to have some ideas about herself as a younger child and, as Britton (1989) says, to reflect upon herself while being herself. I was struck later by the poignancy of this image. In her memory of herself, Laura did not have a safe place inside her home in the real world. A dangerous and unthinking mother who recklessly but passively provided instances of terror for her young child inhabited the "inside" that Laura described. How would it have been possible for that child to have internalized a safe maternal object from which to begin to grow a sense of internal space to "home" herself?

Conclusion

I have tried to describe Laura's psychotherapy journey, show-ing the shift she has made from searching *outside* herself for an identity towards being able to know who she is from the *inside*: a move in mode of identification from an adhesive type to a more introjective kind. In order to make this shift, she has had to start to recognize her own drive to control others and to face her terror of the abusive couple. Her progress, as I have described, is not secure, and setbacks regularly destabilize her; however, she is now able to think about herself with an emerging sense of who she is and of her own history. She can locate herself inside herself and can look tentatively into her own past and can now have hopes for her own future. While Laura was driven to rely upon an adhesive or intrusive identification, she was unable to form a sense of belonging through developing a relationship either with an external object or with herself. As she began to experience herself and others as separate from each other, she found she began also to develop a self to belong to.

The work Laura has done to build an internal identity has, sadly, not been secured by external stability—there is no happy ending, no permanent settled home. At the time of writing, Laura was still in transition and remained extremely vulnerable with a fragile identity, and it was likely she would face the undoubted storms of her adolescence without a stable, safeguarding home.

Laura's story is the story of one child, yet she represents many children in our care system. There are thousands of children like Laura, who live with the same internal deprivation and poverty of identity. The psychoanalytic treatment that I have described can be slow and demanding for both the child and the therapist, but the benefits of the internal changes can enable a child to develop deep knowledge of his or her identity.

The severe budgetary cuts facing our mental health services directly affect society's most vulnerable and deprived children and are resulting in the loss of long-term, specialist psychoanalytic treatment for looked after children. It is difficult to imagine how less in-depth, shorter treatments could achieve a similar outcome. It is with great regret that I report that the specialist psychotherapy treatment service for looked after children—the service in which I was able to see Laura—has now been closed.

CHAPTER SEVEN

The smell of belonging

Lesley Maroni

his chapter looks at the role that smell—the scent of the other—might play in helping or hindering children to develop a feeling of belonging to a new family. It asks how children removed from their birth family can form this feeling of belonging when the smell of the caregiver is foreign and unfamiliar and competes with any olfactory memories, implicit and without words, that might have developed previously between birth mother and infant.

I discuss the difficulties of forging a new link to the other from the point of view both of the child and of the carer. The caregiver also has to be willing to belong to a child with a different set of genes and thus a different set of smells. I illustrate this with an example of an adoptive mother who could not tolerate her daughter's scent, and I examine the daughter's reasons for wanting to keep this state of affairs from changing.

The clinical examples given in this chapter are taken from my work in an inpatient unit for families sent by the courts for parenting assessments and from a community CAMHS. In all of the cases I describe, it was helpful to think of smell as an unconscious communication about belonging, especially when the placement was precarious or when a child was in transition.

Smell is one of the most primitive senses: it is the primary form of sensory stimulation between mother and newborn (Schore, 1994). We are all familiar with the power that a long-forgotten smell caught in the air has to transport us instantly to a time beyond time. The sense of smell is directly connected to the limbic system, the part of the brain that is responsible for processing emotions. Advertisers have long known about the close link between smell, memory, and mood; they lure their customers in with subtle, almost imperceptible scents that are associated with luxury and well-being. Estate agents advise making fresh coffee and baking bread before a viewer comes to see a property. It is standard practice for supermarkets to use such olfactory tricks as pumping out the smell of cinnamon to persuade people that their bread and cakes are home-baked.

People perceive all sorts of interesting things about one another through olfaction. We choose our mates partly because of the way they smell. The body odour of one person may smell disgusting to some, but others will be smitten by it. One's nose can help identify a genetically suitable partner whose DNA will be different enough to ensure that any offspring will be robust. Interestingly, when men are asked to smell anonymous sweat collected on T-shirts, gay men tend to prefer the sweat of other gay men and heterosexual men the sweat of women (Everts, 2012). Newborns can smell the lactating breast just as the mother may recognize her newborn by scent, something that the father cannot usually do. People can smell anxiety and fear. Pheromones are unlike other chemicals we secrete because they trigger behaviours in others rather than affecting our own.

These behaviours are particularly relevant when it comes to understanding some fostered children's initial reaction to their new homes and carers. While they may say very little, there may also be a secretion of pheromones unconsciously communicated to signal alarm or to stop people from getting too close to them. Once a placement is secure, then pheromones may be a factor in the establishment of a bond between carer and child, which would help to foster a stronger sense of belonging and, ultimately for the child, a less fragmented sense of identity.

Olfactory conflict between primary and foster family

Children are removed from their birth families only as a last resort, but in my experience this does not stop nearly all of them longing for a return to their original family. Even when there has been trauma and/or abuse, a child is capable of splitting off the abusive part of the parent from the part that is perceived as good to keep the relationship viable. Smells associated with the "good" parent are likely to give the child a nostalgia for what was or might have been. As Freud (1939) says, "Whenever [people] are dissatisfied with their present surroundings—and this happens often enough—they turn back to the past and hope that they will be able to prove the truth of the inextinguishable dream of a golden age".

The smells of the primary relationship may remain with the child at an unconscious level, to be triggered and brought back to consciousness at unexpected moments. A smell may also be clung on to in a desperate attempt to give the illusion that the absent one is in fact present. In *The Son*, a novel by Michel Rostain, there is a moving description of a father taking his son's duvet to the cleaner's not long after his death from meningitis at the age of 21 years. The father cannot bear to relinquish the bedclothes, and he buries his nose into the folds in an attempt to recapture the smell of his son and bring him back to life. He is immune to the stink of the duvet, which has never been washed. What in life may have been an offensive odour becomes in death an almost unbearable memory.

One highly observant little girl in long-term foster care, who had been in therapy with me for some time, sniffed the air and observed that I both smelt and looked different from usual, "as if you're going to a wedding". Her envy of me for having an occasion filled with family members to go to, even if only in fantasy, put her in touch with her feelings of maternal loss. She exclaimed that she wished she was a fairy so that she could magic her mother into being a good mother who would look after them all and they could be a family again. She put her head on the table and wept.

The little girl had had a troubled start with her first foster carers, who suddenly decided they did not want to keep her because she failed to "show any warmth or affection to us". They diagnosed her as a "psychopath" and a "pathological liar" as she did not respond to their attention in the same way that their own children had. These foster carers were particularly inexperienced and inappropriate, but their attitude raised an important question: can carers be helped to develop their maternal capacity to belong to a child who has an unfamiliar/un-familial scent?

The role of olfactory neurons in facilitating attachment

In a recent study at the University of Pennsylvania led by Minghong Ma (Lee, He, & Ma, 2011), mice pups' olfactory sensory neurons were monitored from birth to Day 30 of development. It was found that they quickly transitioned from having a relatively indiscriminate response to different odours to becoming highly attuned to one specific smell. Given the choice between their mother and an unrelated lactating female, newborn mice pups chose for the most part to suckle from their mother. However, this depended on the presence of an olfactory marker protein (OMP). In the absence of this OMP, newborn pups failed to make the distinction between the mother and an unrelated female. According to Lee, He, and Ma, mice are not hard-wired at birth but, through the maturation of olfaction, "learn to find their mother, home, and siblings, and to stay alive". This behaviour is not only seen in mice pups. Newborn human babies, too, are able to recognize their mother's scent from Day 6 and, according to Macfarlane (1977), "discriminate the scent of their mother's breast pad from that of another woman" (quoted in Schore, 2003a, p. 155). Schore suggests that olfactory communication occurs between the mother's and infant's right brains and that "the processing of olfactory/gustatory information is dominant in the perinatal period" (p. 156).

While oxytocin, a neuropeptide found in the hypothalamus and limbic brain regions, is not a smell as such, it is released in response to sensory stimuli such as smell and taste. Gaze, touch, sound, and sucking also contribute to the release of oxytocin. For example, a dog gazing at or being patted by its owner has increased levels of oxytocin in its urine (Fonagy, 2009). Oxytocin has also been shown to play a role in promoting and maintaining maternal behaviour. Where the mother has a secure attachment with her infant, a subjective bond develops in her when her baby smiles, leading to a rise in oxytocin levels. "Secure" mothers show an enhanced oxytocin response when interacting with their infants, whether the baby is happy or sad (Strathearn, Fonagy, Amico, & Read Montague, 2009).

It is not the same for mothers with insecure attachment patterns, especially when they are dealing with a baby in distress. A lack of response or a too-intrusive response from the "insecure" mother will not lead to a rise in oxytocin levels and will interfere with their ability to establish a secure attachment to each other. "Insecure" mothers have often been exposed to childhood maltreatment themselves, and this is associated with decreased oxytocin in women aged 18–45 years, particularly for emotional abuse (Heim et al., 2008). Of course, the cycle of abuse is likely to be repeated with their own children unless there is some form of parent–infant intervention to break the cycle.

A clinical example from an inpatient unit

I saw this particular pattern repeatedly when working in an inpatient unit for families sent by the courts for parenting-capacity assessments. These women often gave the impression that they had no real sense of belonging, either to a place or to a person. They invariably came in to the hospital with their third, fourth, or even fifth child, having produced one child after another in an effort to quell the emptiness inside them. They all believed that the next baby would give them the love that they had not received themselves. The tragedy was that, of course, their babies did not have the capacity to respond to their mothers' projections of need or neediness, which left the infant with what Bion (1962a) called "nameless [or un-nameable] dread". This nameless dread was the very thing that these mostly young mothers were trying to escape from themselves.

The cycle *can* be broken: a young woman aged 24 came in to the hospital with her fifth child, a baby boy of 4 months. Her other four children had been removed because of neglect and non-accidental injury. The mother either walked around failing to protect her baby adequately as she swung him through doorways, narrowly avoiding hitting his head on the doorframe, or she made derogatory comments to and about him, often regarding what a "stinky" or "pooey" boy he was. She saw the baby as wilfully hating her. The baby kept his eyes firmly closed; in fact, he hunched up his whole body in an attempt to give himself some protection in what must have seemed to him a very unprotected world. There were small changes, however, over the course of the next few weeks, leading to a breakthrough when the mother was able to put her baby down on the play mat and look at him for the first time as if she liked him. She smiled at him. He relaxed his whole body and evacuated into his nappy. He returned his mother's smile. She called him "stinky boy" but with a new gentleness in her tone, which caused him to smile again. This only happened because for the first time in her life this mother felt that there was someone (her therapist) who was genuinely interested in getting to know her and the contents of her mind. She could even begin to tolerate her baby's smelliness.

One can assume that in the case of this mother there was a natural increase in secretion of oxytocin, initially caused by the burgeoning of trust towards the therapist, which improved eye contact from mother towards the therapist and then to her baby. This probably led to "dopamine-associated reinforcement pathways" (Strathearn, et al., 2009) in both mother and baby. From a more psychoanalytic point of view, one could speak about the mother taking back her projections of the baby being somehow toxic in his wilful hating of her as she began to relate to him as a defenceless infant who needed her in order to survive. Against all the odds, this mother and her baby were eventually rehabilitated, and they continue to do well.

Strathearn found that when oxytocin is administered intra-nasally, "it produces a broad range of social effects, including enhanced social memory, improved eye gaze when viewing faces, increased recognition and memory of facial expressions and identity, and increased manifestations of trust" (Strathearn et al., 2009, p. 2657). The application of oxytocin intra-nasally is an area of research that looks promising in its potential to aid mothers who fail to form an attachment with their babies, as well as to aid adoptive parents and foster carers to form new attachments to children who have had to be removed from their birth family because of

THE SMELL OF BELONGING 163

neglect or abuse. In all cases, one can imagine that the children would benefit. A secure attachment leads to a more secure sense of belonging and thus a stronger sense of identity.

Second-skin formation

How babies and children are cared for is, of course, of fundamental importance for their psychological as well as physical growth throughout their childhood. In early infancy, a prerequisite for healthy development is the "mantling" function of the mother's voice, gaze, and familiar smell. A mother (or main caregiver) will use her capacity for empathic reflection to absorb, or digest, her baby's distress and try to make sense of it without swamping the baby with her own fears and projections. It is astonishing how helped infants can feel simply by sensing that there is a mind available to think about them. Bion (1962a) has the rather lovely term "reverie" to describe a mother's state of mind when observing her baby and puzzling about meaning. Winnicott (1965) calls it "primary maternal preoccupation", an equally vivid term that demonstrates how the complicated and passionate feelings aroused in a mother when watching her infant are, and should be, given priority. All of this is optimal for healthy development: a baby who feels held (or contained, as Bion terms it) both emotionally and physically by a mother who can make her mind available to him will have increased levels of oxytocin, and this, as we have seen, will lead to the strengthening of the bond between the two.

But what are the consequences when this goes wrong, as it so often has for children removed from their birth families and placed in the care system? Winnicott (1971) described the pseudo-maturity of patients who have developed what he termed a "false self". Esther Bick (1968, 1986, 1987) described a similar defensive strategy that she named "second-skin formation", which is probably a more primitive and earlier response to a lack of maternal containment. Both were referring to the pathological manoeuvres used when a child does not have a mother/carer to contain and make sense for the baby of his confused, chaotic, and anxiety-ridden world. The 4-month-old baby who came with his mother for a parenting

assessment protected himself from danger by hunching and tens-
ing his whole body well before he was mature enough to begin to
separate from her.

If there is little belief that the mother can hold the infant
together, then fundamental anxieties of dissolving and disintegrat-
ing will never be far away.

> The need for a containing object would seem, in the infantile
> unintegrated state, to produce a frantic search for an object—a
> light, a voice, *a smell*, or other sensual object—which can hold
> the attention and thereby be experienced, momentarily at least,
> as holding the parts of the personality together. The optimal
> object is the nipple-in-the-mouth, together with the holding
> and talking and *familiar smelling* mother. [Bick, 1987, p. 115;
> emphasis added]

Smell therefore could be considered an essential sensory function,
both to help mother and infant find each other to ensure survival
of the infant and, when the mother is unavailable, for the infant
to latch on to in an attempt to create the illusion of being held
together.

A clinical example of holding on
to a smell sensation

A 5-year-old girl in intensive psychotherapy who had been
severely neglected in infancy would, whenever unbearable sensations of being abandoned were triggered in her, remove her pyjama
top and urinate on it, before picking it up and burying her nose in
the hot, wet material. It usually happened at night when her foster
carers turned off her bedroom light and shut the door, leaving her
to imagine that they had also gone from the house and she was
alone in the dark. This transported her back to a pre-verbal stage
of sensation where, in reality, she had been left in a urine-stained
cot in a dark room for long periods of time. In the absence of what
Bick calls the "optimal object"—that is, the mother—she was desperately trying to recreate a familiar warm smell of her own to ward
off fears of disintegration. As I was working with her foster carers
to help them understand this troubled little girl, it was relatively
easy to suggest that they left a night-light on and the door open at

bedtime. However, it was harder to persuade them to think of her, and therefore treat her, at times like these more as an infant in need of reassurance than as a 5-year-old.

Foster carers generally need help in understanding the triggers that might send their child spiralling back to a primitive state of fear and confusion, making the child incapable of using his brain for rational thought. Many foster carers exclaim, "But he's 5 years old (or 6 or 7). He shouldn't be acting like a toddler at his age", as if the child were wilfully misbehaving and had some control over his functioning if only he chose to use it.

The caesura in the memory of children who have had a traumatic start in life can impede the development of a feeling of belonging that permits the formation of new relationships.

Sugar and spice and all things nice

The pressure on teenage girls, and to a certain extent boys as well, to disguise their natural smells with synthetic scents remains as strong as ever. Advertisements bombard us with products designed not just to make our bodies smell fresh and clean but also our clothes and houses. We inhabit a world of synthetic "freshness".

There is no escaping the fact that faeces smell, as does urine. One of the first things that a baby needs to experience is a mother who will accept and tolerate these bad smells while being able to do something about them. Many fostered children have not had even this basic need met. They will continue to feel unlovable if they then fail to find a carer who can tolerate their smell, especially that produced by flatus or faeces. It is no wonder, then, that children who come in to therapy often have the idea that they are hiding a disgusting smell inside them that they must keep in at all costs but which nevertheless escapes at times, causing extreme embarrassment. Burping and farting in the therapy room is a way of communicating this.

Sexual activity also produces its own range of smells, which children who have been sexually abused may find excruciating. Alternatively, they may imagine that such smells still linger on them because it was somehow their fault and they will be punished for it.

As we have seen with pheromones, there can be secondary gains from producing an off-putting smell, whether consciously or unconsciously. This will certainly put an obstacle in the way of a carer getting too close to a child. But a child who lets herself start smelling of neglect again—and this often happens when children are moved suddenly to a new family—needs to be taken seriously as it may be an attempt to communicate a renewed sense of deprivation and loss.

One of the reasons why abused children tend to do well in child psychotherapy treatment is that it gives them the opportunity to begin to process terrifying, un-nameable emotions that can sometimes be acted out in the therapy room in a concrete emission of bad smells. If their smells can be tolerated by the therapist, the child will have the sense that she can begin to form a secure relationship based not on idealization—"all things nice"—but on a warts-and-all sense of reality.

Toxic smells

An adolescent girl, Louise, had been placed in foster care when she was 3 years old because of extremely poor parenting from her birth mother. There was no father around. Louise had three foster placements before being adopted at the age of 5 years by a middle-aged couple with no children of their own. From the start, Louise liked her adoptive father but had problems with her adoptive mother. It was Louise's account of her adoptive mother finding her smell unbearable that made me consider the role that smell might play in facilitating or hindering the *carer's* capacity to attach to a child, rather than the other way round.

There was a poignant reference in a file written about Louise when she was first removed from her birth mother to her liking to snuggle in to her mother to be hugged and cuddled. One can easily surmise that smell played a large part in the unconscious memory of her primary relationship. Here is an extract from a session.

Louise started by saying that she realized that she really did love her adoptive father but there were still major issues between her and her adoptive mother. Whatever she did she could not manage to feel close to her mother, nor, it seemed to Louise, did her mother feel close to her. She gave me an example of when she had come back from the gym and the first thing her mother said to her was that she stank. She told her to go and shower before being allowed to sit at the dining table to have her supper. Louise said to me indignantly that she did not "stink"; she could not have done because she had only been doing floor exercises to tone her stomach and had not even broken into a sweat. She added even more indignantly that she had gone to have a shower and had then put on some perfume that her mother had bought her, only to be told again that she stank and that her mother could not bear the smell of the perfume, even though "she chose it specially for me". She apparently objected to any aerosol deodorant Louise used as well. It made Louise feel that there was something intrinsically "stinky" and revolting about her that her mother could not tolerate, and this revoltingness would seep out even when masked by more pleasant scents.

There is clearly strong oedipal rivalry between mother and daughter. This is always more complicated between adopted children and their parents as there is no genetic taboo to inhibit union. The pheromones secreted in Louise's sweat were perhaps being identified, completely unconsciously, as genetically suitable as a "partner" for her father, which would, of course, have the potential to threaten the marriage and break up the family. It is hardly surprising, then, that her mother experienced her smell as repulsive. There are anecdotal accounts of foster placements breaking down, ostensibly because the child is said to be displaying inappropriate sexual behaviour but more probably because unbearable sexual feelings have been aroused in the father. But the interesting thing about Louise is that the secretion of pheromones that may have been attractive to her father also prevented her adoptive mother from getting too close to her. This was exactly the effect that Louise wanted, although she had no conscious control over her smell.

She told me that she liked her body smell—or "the stink", as she called it. She felt it confirmed the difference between her and her adoptive family, which allowed her to maintain an identification with her birth mother and to hold on to her idealized memory. However, in order to keep this relationship psychologically alive, Louise had to think of herself as bad or stinking or toxic—all the qualities associated with her birth mother that had led to Louise being removed from her.

It is uncanny how thoughts such as Louise's can become concretely communicated in the form of an odour. I have had direct experience of a smell being conjured out of the ether. This was while working with Sabine, an adolescent girl who had a severe eating disorder.

Sabine

Sabine described to me how for months she had hidden half-eaten food in odd places in her bedroom where it would gradually rot away, and how amazed she was that her mother never once commented on the horrible smell. As she was talking I noticed that the therapy room had filled with an unpleasant odour similar to that of the rotting food in Sabine's bedroom. At first I thought my powers of empathy were so great that I had created it out of imagination. But I then saw Sabine taking surreptitious sniffs and wrinkling her brow. Sabine was one of the most fastidiously clean people I knew, but this also went with being able to live and sleep in a room that stank of rotten food. I drew her attention to the smell and interpreted it as being a concrete example of her wish to expel everything bad inside her so that she could remain internally pure and unsullied. The rot would then be external where it could be commented on or, in her mother's case, ignored.

Once the smell was out in the open, both literally and metaphorically speaking, it was there as a shared memory between my patient and me. As Canham (2003) says, "a detailed and honest description of a moment or a memory can open it up, and . . . subjecting this moment or memory to scrutiny can be both transforming and liberating" (p. 190).

When thinking later about where the smell actually came from, it is probable that Sabine silently and without allowing herself to be aware of it turned her internal "badness" into flatus. It is always a communication when children expel wind as it can signify extreme anxiety as they test to see if their bad smells make them unacceptable and therefore unlovable.

The mechanism Louise used was similar to Sabine's, although Louise was invested more in keeping the bad smell, as one might call it, inside her as a way of holding on to her primary family, as well as transmitting it externally to disgust her adoptive mother. The difference was in the two mother's reactions: Louise's mother openly expressed her disgust, whereas Sabine's mother did not comment.

Lexi

I would like to return to the little girl I mentioned at the beginning whose first foster family had called her a psychopath. Lexi had an air of insouciance, an "I don't care . . . nothing can affect me" quality, which misled many people into thinking that she had no feelings. Lexi had been hoping to stay "forever" with her foster carers, and she had made a kind of shrine with a candle in it which she said she would light as soon as she heard officially that the parents had been approved to keep her long-term. Instead, she was abruptly removed at the wish of the carers and placed with a new family. I saw her a few days after she had changed family. When I went to the waiting room to collect her, she gave me a big false smile and proceeded to introduce me in a grown-up way to her new carers. Her bright chirpy voice sounded completely insincere as she kept the conversation going all the way down the corridor and into the therapy room. Yet I was struck by how pale she looked. The word "shell-shocked" came to mind. She also had a curious air of neglect about her, although her school uniform was clean and ironed and her hair was brushed back in the usual way.

In the room I talked about how understandable it was that she needed to protect herself from the sadness and disappointment of what had happened, and how it might remind her of earlier times when she had been so confused about where she belonged and who she belonged to. (In fact, this sudden removal mirrored her first removal from her birth mother because of alleged sexual abuse by mother's partner.) I also took up the fact that Lexi kept trying to talk over me in that bright, false adult voice so that neither of us had to think about these difficult things. Lexi quietened, then she crumpled onto the floor and sobbed. I used my voice, the tone more than the actual words, to wrap her up metaphorically, rather as a mother does with a distressed baby. She asked me to give her a tissue from a box of hygienic wet-wipes that was kept in the room, and after wiping her eyes she held the tissue over her nose and breathed in the scent. She nodded when I suggested that she was remembering the familiar smells of before. We then shared memories of past sessions when Lexi had used the wet-wipes in her play. There was somebody—her therapist—who could help her to feel "re-membered", with the meaning of being put back together again psychically, to counteract her earlier sense of fragmentation of identity. By the end of the session, Lexi had picked herself up, so to speak, and although she still looked pale there was a more robust and authentic quality about her.

* * *

These clinical examples share a common theme: in all three, the girls' emotional well-being is seriously compromised as they grapple with a confusion about where they belong and who they belong to, although all are at different stages in the process. Lexi was the most confused because of an actual rejection by her foster carers; Louise was muddled about whether she belonged, or should belong, to her idealized primary family or to her adoptive family with all their faults; Sabine could not work out whether she had a space in her mother's mind to be thought about and remembered. She was left adrift among the putrid smells. When there is doubt in children about the carers' desire and capacity to want them, therapy can provide a secure place in which to feel they belong.

Smell and taste in the forming of memories

Memory is central to our sense of identity. The mature brain has two distinct memory systems each with different functions, one situated in the right prefrontal cortex, the other in the left prefrontal cortex.

The memory system situated in the *right prefrontal cortex* is fully operational from birth. At this stage, communication takes place through the auditory, visual, gustatory, and olfactory senses, with, as we saw above, the olfactory sense being the most primitive. The right-hemisphere memory system involves non-conscious memory, also known as implicit or non-declarative memory. Experiences processed by the implicit memory system cannot be remembered or verbalized, but they can be somatized. To put it another way: the initial emotion activates a body response that is unavailable to consciousness and therefore uncontrollable. What may be controllable is the regulation of the feeling once engaged. The caregiver's primary role in the initial stages is to regulate the infant's affects until the infant's brain is mature enough to be able to self-regulate by naming the feeling with words of his own.

Picture a baby who cries: his face will go red, tears will form, he will tense up his body and so forth, all of which will be completely outside his control. However, his mother can regulate his emotion by holding, rocking, and soothing him, which will help him to become calm. Bion (1962a) names the same process—that is, the mother's regulation of her infant's emotions—"alpha functioning", only he uses the metaphor of the digestive process, wherein the mother digests the infant's experiences and turns them into "food for thought". As Bion goes on to say, if alpha functioning fails, which it is likely to have done with children who have been removed from their birth families, then sense impressions and emotions remain in their original state and can only be evacuated. These evacuated emotions he calls "beta elements".

The ability to name feelings with words is controlled by the memory system situated in the *left prefrontal cortex*, which does not begin developing until near the end of the second year of life. It is responsible for the rapid growth of language during this period. The left hemisphere involves conscious memory, otherwise known as explicit or declarative memory, because it enables a child to start to describe and give specific meaning to events in life. Imagine the baby in the previous paragraph, whose brain was not developed enough to be able to soothe himself, now aged 2½ years. He knocks his head on a table and cries. However, at this age he can run to his carer and tell her what has happened. "Naughty table!" he might say, thus using words to make sense of the hurt.

Memory and brain function

It is important to note that children who have suffered trauma and/or abuse at a pre-verbal stage of development will neither be able to remember nor repress their experiences, as the structures concerned with explicit memory are not yet mature. These will remain at the level of early, unrepressed unconscious experiences. Neuroscientists now think that dissociation occurs to reflect "the inability of the right brain to recognise and co-process or integrate external stimuli . . . and internal stimuli" (Hart, 2008, p. 266). We saw earlier with the 5-year-old how quickly she could be transported back to a time of disintegration simply by her carers turning off her light and leaving her to sleep.

It is not surprising that so many fostered children have no explicit memories of their first years, as there may so easily have been a disruption or an actual trauma during this time which will have to be split off in order for them to retain their sanity. But because smell is so closely linked to primitive emotions, a familiar odour smelt in the present will fill the child with a feeling that cannot be given a name or explained. This can be terrifying for a child who has been abused.

One cannot talk about taste and smell without reference to the most famous description in literature of it being able to transport one back instantly to a forgotten or unremembered time. I refer of course to the passage in Marcel Proust's *A la recherche du temps perdu* when the narrator has his first experience of involuntary memory as a young adult. Like many of my patients, Marcel had very little memory of his childhood apart from the anxiety caused by his mother: would she grant or deny him a goodnight kiss? This is his conscious memory, but buried deep in his unconscious is all the rest, and it is triggered and brought very painfully into consciousness by a taste sensation—the dipping of a *"petite madeleine"* (a little cake) into a cup of tea. This takes him back not only to early childhood but, indeed, even further, to an uncovering of the unconscious and the repression that has to be stripped away to allow it to surface. However, the hero of the book is a middle-class child who lives with his parents, not a fostered child who has been abused. Whereas Marcel repressed his memories, abused children do not repress pre-verbal memories; they have a body response to emotions that feel uncontrollable. As Bion (1962a) stated, all a child can do with an undigested emotion is to evacuate it. The evacuation might take the form of faeces, which, of course, will smell horrible and may well alienate the carers. Quite understandably, it is hard for carers to keep faith in a child who soils and smears. The question is whether carers can continue to want a child to belong to them when the relationship is suffused with bad odours.

A heightened sense of smell at times of transition

It was decided at a professionals' meeting that two brothers aged 10 and 8 years who had been sexually abused by a member of their family needed to be placed with different foster carers. This was after two years with the original carers, who received their own therapy and other support to help them understand and care for these horribly abused boys. In spite of all the efforts, the carers continued openly to show their preference for the younger child and their dislike of his older brother. Both children had been in once-weekly psychotherapy for the two years that they had been with their foster family.

The following extract of clinical material illustrates how sensory impressions, especially that of smell, become heightened at times of extreme stress, when children may revert to a more primitive mode of functioning to help them survive psychically.

Josh, the older boy, was seen for once-weekly art therapy by a colleague, who discussed the material with me in supervision.[1] She had remarked a few days after the move on Josh smelling somehow "greasy" and "unwashed", which may have been an unconscious communication of how neglected he felt. In the following session, however, it was Josh himself who complained of the smell:

Josh sat down beside the sand tray, took off the lid, and pushed his hands into the damp sand. He exclaimed with heightened emotion, "Oh, this sand stinks! It's disgusting!" He pulled his face into a contorted shape and repeated several times, "It stinks! It's disgusting!"

Josh asked me about the smelly, stinky sand and why I had not replaced it with clean fresh sand. "The stink", as he put it, was so bad that he could not bear the feel of the wet sand but had to cover his hand with a number of tissues in order to continue to work with it. As he built the sand into a sculptural form, he protected his hand by constantly adjusting the tissues. It was as if he was working blind, as he had turned his head away with his nose up in the air. He told me that I really should change the sand and that he wanted to be there when the change happened.

While I was trying to think about this, Josh turned the sand sculpture into a head. It was a distinctive face with slits for eyes, no ears, a strange nose, and a faint mouth. He told me that it was the face of a "dark character" in a book he had read. The smell was not referred to for the rest of the session.

While Josh's expression of disgust came out during his session, and seemed to belong more to feelings of anger towards his therapist for not protecting him, his brother started repeatedly to complain about the smell emanating from their escort and his taxi when they were brought from school to their sessions at the clinic. It seemed probable that an olfactory memory had been triggered that was somehow connected to past abuse. The smell might well not have been noticed at a different time but when combined with the stress of having changed families, it became intolerable. Both boys felt psychically threatened at this point, which must have heightened all their senses and made them hyper-vigilant to any perceived danger, especially of abuse.

It is not improbable that however unpleasant it had been at their previous foster home, for Josh and his brother it was a familiar setting, which would have given them some sense that this was a family they belonged to. For these children, starting again with yet another foster family can revive all the old defences. It is essential for the therapist to be able to tolerate and digest the children's emotions during this process. There is nobody else who carries the memory of how they were and the hope of how they might be in the future.

The interpretation of smell
for children in the care system

Mary Dozier undertook a study of fostered children versus children staying with their birth families (Bernard, Butzin-Dozier, Rittenhouse, & Dozier, 2010). She found that although foster care involves disruptions in children's relationships with parents, the children "are better able to regulate their neuroendocrine systems when living with foster parents than when they continue to live with neglecting birth parents". This does not prevent nearly all children longing to be returned to their birth family, even though they might know that it is not possible. However, they can be helped to come to terms with the disruption if their foster family is stable and sensitive to their needs, both spoken and unspoken.

I have given examples of fostered children in psychotherapy who show that when under stress they will resort to more primitive functioning, including expelling intolerable feelings in the form of flatus and generally making bad smells. While this can be processed in long-term psychotherapy—and abused children often need lengthy treatment to address their developmental deficits—foster parents may struggle to cope with a child who displays repulsive behaviours such as farting, soiling, spitting, and so on, or who withdraws from them. This appears to be especially true when caretakers are not given enough information about what behaviours to expect. They need help to reinterpret their foster children's signals and to be aware that a child who has been neglected or abused is not acting in a deliberately defiant way but is utilizing survival techniques to ward off perceived or real threats.

Dozier, Peloso, Lewis, Laurenceau, and Levin (2008) use an attachment-based intervention for foster carers, which is delivered in the foster carers' home. The children are helped to develop self-regulatory capacities, but also—and perhaps more importantly—there is a focus on the foster carers' own issues that might be affecting their ability to parent. The goal is to change foster parent behaviour, which in turn brings about changes in child behaviour. Children will only be able to develop a sense of belonging in conjunction with the foster parents developing their own capacity to attach to their child. Ideally, a short-term intervention such as Dozier's would become compulsory for all foster carers.

Conclusion

In this chapter I have considered the implications of smell and its role in assisting or impeding a sense of belonging in fostered and adopted children. Smell is vitally important in the forming of new relationships, but it is often neglected or ignored. Professionals need to be alert to the messages smell can communicate and sensitive to its impact on vulnerable children, especially when they are under stress. We need to start considering smell as one of the factors in attachment and ask what can be done if the carer simply smells wrong to the child, or vice versa. A mismatch of smells may well hinder the child's feeling that she can belong to a new family and may also draw attention to the biological difference between the child and her carer.

While it is already clear that carers need practical training in order to be able to foster a sense of belonging in a child and to develop their own capacity to belong to the child, it would also be interesting to explore whether the administering of oxytocin nasally might help facilitate this process. Could a rise in oxytocin levels produce a more positive response to a child whose smell was off-putting, as happens with a securely attached mother regardless of whether her child is happy or sad? This is a potentially fruitful area of research.

If those caring for children were more aware of how primitive the sense of smell is and how instantly it can affect memory and mood, they might be able to discuss this issue more openly. Children do sometimes have a smell that is unattractive. This can come from an unconscious desire to keep people at bay or be a signal of alarm, for example. Or it may be the result of a child's desperate need to communicate a sense of deprivation. Whatever the reason, smell is always worth taking seriously as a communication of a child's emotional state, especially so when the child's sense of belonging to a particular family is fragile.

Note

1. I would like to thank Jen Bromham for her permission to use material from a session with a fostered child in therapy with her.

CHAPTER EIGHT

Fostering relationships for looked after children

Sara Barratt

I work in a specialist multi-disciplinary team that is part of an NHS CAMHS providing therapeutic services for children who are "looked after", have been adopted, or are in kinship care. We also provide consultation to professionals. Referrals come from GPs, social workers, and other organizations involved in working with this population; while the majority of children referred to us live in London, we also take referrals from many different parts of the UK. Adoptive and foster families referred to our service do not usually have a biological link to one another, and they are thus in the process of thinking about how they belong together; our work is often to help them work out their relationship together. Developing a sense of belonging and the ability to form attachments is essential for the emotional health of children and adults. This chapter describes our work with foster families considering complex emotions that arise through developing a sense of belonging both for the families that re-configure to include, as is often the case, a non-biologically related member and for that child who is thus included. As a team, we find it important to draw on a range of different therapeutic modalities in order to provide a service that fits for the children referred and their caregivers. Although not discussed in detail here, we include systemic family psychotherapy

and child psychotherapy, eye movement desensitization and repro-
cessing (EMDR), mindfulness, and mentalization. We also run
groups for children, parents, and carers.

Children come into care because of a failure of parenting. The
dominant culture in local authorities is that successful social work
keeps children out of care; thus decisions may have been delayed
because of these constraints, and children may have suffered more
long-term harm by a failure to act. Some children are fostered by
members of their extended families and the majority by foster carers. Many foster carers feel they have very little influence on the
decision making about the children placed with them, and placing
social workers may have worked hard to prevent children from
coming into the care system. On 31 March 2014, there were 68,840
looked after children living with foster carers (DfE, 2014), of whom
some were family members or friends. This chapter discusses the
experiences gained from working in our specialist fostering, adoption, and kinship care team.

We aim to work with children and their carers together and separately and are mindful that for many children who have entered
the care system, referral to yet another set of professionals can
increase their sense of anxiety. While for adoptive families step-by-
step work is important to develop a sense of belonging together as
a family, kinship families may have ties that can provide a sense of
continuity. For foster carers and children, the work can be complex
in that the child's future care may still be undecided. Children
may be referred to us at a point of leaving birth families, at times
of transition, and because they are struggling to make sense of
their lives. This chapter considers the dilemmas for foster carers
and children in investing and believing in the future of a relationship that is determined by others; it also considers the process of
developing a sense of belonging for looked after children and their
carers. This relationship is contextualized by the placing agency
and the messages that children and carers have about the plans for
their future relationship alongside the constraints afforded by past
and present relationships.

Relationships are the bedrock for who people are and what
they become. However, relationships and the process by which
people relate to each other are complex. They can be the source
of security, belonging, and intimacy; they can also be the source

of disappointment, anxiety, and frustration. For most people, it will be a combination of the two. How children and adults experience any current relationship will be a combination of two things—their needs and expectations in the present, and the models they bring with them from past experience. There is an important struggle to construct a reality in the present where the determining and distorting expectations of the past are kept to the minimum. Both the child and the foster carer have to adapt to each other's expectations about the current reality and, in the longer term, the impact of the past and what might be possible in the future. They will need to have flexible and realistic expectations of themselves and the other. Where children are concerned, their relative developmental immaturity as well as their past poor experiences will always need to be taken into account. There is an important imbalance in what can be expected and may be required of adults and children.

Terminology

The 1973 *Shorter Oxford Dictionary* has a number of definitions of "belong", including "to go along with, as an adjunct, to pertain to and to be the rightful possession of". These definitions infer a proprietorial factor in "belonging" which does not fit easily for children who are looked after. Children are in foster care because their "belongingness" to their biological families is such that they will remain in care rather than moving to a different family through adoption. Thus, although their biological parents or their families are not in a position to parent them, children may remain in a more ambiguous position in relation to "belonging". This begs the question: would they feel disloyal to birth families if they started to settle, allowing a sense of belonging with their carers? The social care system usually has parental responsibility, which is delegated to foster carers; this cannot *not* influence the relationship and sense of belonging between children and carers.

Defining the mental health component is complex, as the age span for "looked after" children is from birth to 18 years and, in a modified form for some, into early adulthood., This is compounded by the fact that the age when children enter the system, the length of time they remain, their pathway through the system, including moves from carer to carer, and their exit out of the system are all variables that impact on development and outcome. In my 45-year career of working with vulnerable children, terminology has changed; the term "foster parent" in common parlance in the 1970s changed to "foster carer" at the same time that the term "corporate parenting" arrived. These subtleties of language have a profound effect on the definition of the relationship. The word "parent" creates different expectations from "carer". The current structures in which temporary foster placement can convert to long term creates new possibilities for children and foster carers to feel that they "belong" together.

The context for our work

Children in care will have met and worked with a number of different social care and health professionals who are interested in different aspects of their lives. They are referred to our special-ist CAMHS because their social workers, schools, or carers are concerned about their behaviours and relationships with others. For many children, referral to us is upsetting and difficult; often they have not been told the reason for coming to our service, and for many it brings back the fear that they will, once again, be rejected. We have to be very careful about how we start to work with children, how we play with them, and how we try to help them make sense of their early lives and its impact on their present circumstances. Some children are with new foster carers, some are awaiting a move to a "permanent family", and for oth-ers there is uncertainty about what would be best for them in the long term, raising questions such as: Should they be in foster care because contact with birth families is significant? Should they be placed with siblings? Many children have a stronger sense of belonging to brothers and sisters than to their parents, who may have been physically and/or emotionally absent. Can a sibling group's needs be met if they are placed together and if there has been significant neglect and maltreatment? Many children are referred to us whose future is uncertain and who are confused about with whom they belong.

Minnis, Bryce, Phin, and Wilson (2010) say that maltreated children can rapidly develop secure attachments when placed in the care of a sensitive and secure foster carer, regardless of the severity of their behaviour problems. Furthermore, the authors state that the security of attachment in foster care is also related to the degree of commitment of the caregiver to the child: if a foster carer considers the placement to be temporary, the child is less likely to develop a secure attachment than if the caregiver sees herself as having a life-long caregiving role. They go on to say that placement instability, such as we see in many local authorities in the UK, has a detrimental effect on mental health, reinforcing the importance of early decision making about permanence.

While children's experiences with their biological families are deemed to be the basis of symptomatic behaviour, their care history is also of fundamental importance. The care system and the financial implications for local authorities considering permanency for children means that decisions can be delayed; this is illustrated in the case of Hamid.

Hamid

Aged 9 years, Hamid was referred to us because of anger and challenging behaviour. He immediately told me that he had been in eleven different families (seven of whom were foster families). He could name each one and where they lived. For Hamid, there was no reason to invest in building a relationship with his new foster mother, who shared his religious culture but was from a different ethnic group, which led to some reservations for the social workers. Hamid had no reason to believe that he would remain there. The transitions, alongside the abuse and disruptions of his early life, meant that a referral to us was, for him, a reinforcement of his idea that he was bad and unworthy and would probably be sent to another home. Fortunately, Hamid was living with a foster mother who, from the beginning, "claimed" him and spoke about how they would, together with his younger brother, be building a family together. Through the commitment of the foster mother and her perseverance in helping Hamid to manage very painful memories and complicated messages from his birth family, and through her openness in joining the therapeutic work with him, Hamid is still in his placement four years later. Children are often referred to us for individual psychotherapy in the hope that, through being with someone who can help them think about their emotions, they can start to make sense of their lives; while this is often very useful, it is also a way for adults to distance themselves from the children's experiences, often leaving the child with a more powerful sense of emotional belonging to a CAMHS professional than to the person they live with. We emphasize the need for foster carers to be involved in the work we undertake with children, in order to develop a sense of belonging and to create a shared story. We work hard to build a relationship with carers and children, together with their social workers; the support of the latter is essential to our work.

Training and support

A New Zealand study into the training and support needs of foster carers (Murray, Tarren-Sweeney, & France, 2011) reflects the feedback from foster carers we meet in our service. These foster carers would like more specialist support from social workers and training to help them manage the behaviour and understand the mental health needs of the children in their care. Many training packages focus on the ability to manage behaviour. While developing techniques to respond to children's challenging behaviour is helpful, it is also essential to develop the ability to connect with and understand children's emotions in order to help them to use language, rather than behaviour, to let people know how they feel. This makes the difference in developing a growing relationship between adults and children. Some foster carers are unsure what they are being trained for, and many we meet feel confused about what is expected of them. The inevitable uncertainty about how long children will be living with them makes them more uncertain

about how much of themselves to invest in developing a relationship with the children in their care.

In a training course that I ran for a local authority, foster
carers described their confusion about whether it is their role to
develop relationships with the children or whether they are "care
takers" for the local authorities while decisions are made about a
child's long-term needs. One said: "I am not sure if I know how
to talk to children about their feelings. I leave that to people who
are trained. I think my job is to provide a home and feed and
care for them. And to keep things nice." This foster carer, like
others, was worried about managing children's emotions when
they "kick off", and she worked hard to keep things level and
calm for the sake of all the children living in the family. This begs
a number of questions: What do professionals expect of foster
carers? The role of social care may get in the way of the opportunity for children and carers to develop a feeling of belonging
with one another. Can belongingness be transitory? If the possible outcome of a placement is for children to return to their
birth families, can it be beneficial for a child and carer to invest
in a relationship that can provide a child with a positive sense of
self to carry with him in subsequent living arrangements? These
questions come to mind when I think about the complicated and
contradictory messages we give to foster carers about our expectations of their relationships with foster children.

Expectations

The earliest experiences of being cared for influence children's
future relationship to being looked after, and their sense of identity is bound up with their experience of belonging to their biological family. Children I have worked with often feel confused
about the reason they came into care; they may feel worried
about birth parents who are vulnerable because they suffer from
mental ill-health or addiction, and many have been parental to
their parents. Foster carers are employed by agencies and local
authorities to look after children whose parents have, for all sorts

of reasons, failed them. The children, by dint of being placed by agencies employing the foster carers, "belong" to the agency: it is a contradiction for us to expect the foster carers to "love" the children placed with them—they will have different feelings for different children. I work with a number of foster carers who have looked after many different children over the years whom they were able to care for and prepare to move on, but then they have a child placed for whom they have very different feelings. They can develop a sense of belonging with a particular child that they have not felt with others. Wilson (2006), in her research into the relationship between carer and child, talks about the importance of the child's response to the foster carer, which influences the future of the placement. In describing one child, James, she says: "Slowly he was giving more and more and he was starting to trust. And he started calling me mum. And I just couldn't let him go. James would always give you something back which made you feel good about the relationship you'd got. He'd come each day and stroke [her husband] John's leg, and say, 'Are you all right, John?'" (p. 502). It is this kind of feedback that helps carers feel they have a child who is relating to them and gives them the optimism to reciprocate, forming the basis of a sense of belonging.

Relationship

I have been working with Caitlin, who has been fostering children for many years and has a 19-year-old foster son, Kevin, living independently but who is still very much part of the family. She has now decided to adopt two sisters, Annie and Isobel, whom she was fostering. I asked her what was particular about her relationship with them. She writes:

"When I started fostering 13 years ago I had no intention of adopting or having 'permanent' children. I liked the thought of having children in my life and parenting children but with a 'get out clause'! I could return to my holiday-rich, child-free existence whenever I wanted! Friends & family would often say that they knew I'd adopt children one day but I was pretty sure I wouldn't!

"Kevin started to feel like he belonged with us in a very gradual way. He came to us on a weekends-only respite basis as his mum was terminally ill. When she died everyone in the family wanted him to come and live with us, which we resisted for a long time. We felt that we didn't want 'permanent, full-time' children & that respite fostering suited us perfectly. We loved Kevin very much, but we felt he 'belonged with' his birth family; however, over time we feel that he very much belongs with us and is part of our family together. With Annie and Isobel, I absolutely felt like I was the best person to take care of them and that they therefore 'belonged with' me. I don't mean this in a way that I was doing it for them, more that I could see and feel the very strong bonds we all had with each other and I couldn't imagine ever being separated for any justifiable reason. I've fostered children before whom I have loved dearly, but I don't think I've ever felt that for them to stay with me was 'the best' or only justifiable outcome for them. But with Annie and Isobel, I felt from an early stage that if they didn't return to their mum then their 'place' should be together, with me, my partner, & Kevin. I'm not sure where that feeling came from but I just know that I love them hugely and that this feels reciprocal and I absolutely can't imagine life without them (in a way that with my other foster children I have missed them terribly at first, but then it passes and life returns to 'normal'). I can't imagine a 'normal' life without Kevin, Annie, and Isobel.

"I agree that all relationships are different and that has been evident in my differing relationships with all my foster children. But I also think my relationship with each of 'my' three children is different. I also think there's sometimes an expectation that foster carers 'should' love the children they care for. I don't agree—largely because I think that's impossible to control. I don't think you get to choose who you love or don't love and the same goes for children. I absolutely think foster carers should make children feel loved but they can do this even if they don't actually love them. And in fact, I don't think I'd use

the term 'belong to' but 'belong with'. I don't think children
do belong 'to' their parents, even though most of them belong
'with' them."

I think Caitlin makes a very important point about belonging, in
making the distinction between "belong to" and "belong with". But
she does more than just this. Within her distinction, she points to
the ownership of another through belonging to and the mutuality
of belonging with.

The contradiction of belonging

Becoming a carer for somebody else's child is one of the most challenging roles and relationships for anybody. Whether this is for a
short period of time, an uncertain period of time, or in some cases
permanently, it provides an opportunity to make a real difference
to a child's life that is unequalled. It also has risks attached to it:
the child may be difficult to care for, may pose problems for the
carer that the carer cannot manage, or may stir up issues with other
members of the family that create tension and a conflict of loyalties.

Loss

Whatever the balance of positive and challenging factors, there
are significant adjustments that both carer and other members
of their family are likely to have to make. There are also likely to
be significant adjustments for the child. It is a process of necessary change and adjustment for everybody involved, and this can
include powerful experiences of loss. While some of these issues
may be predictable, based on a foster carer's past experience and
understanding, others may come as a surprise. Some issues may
reawaken deeply buried memories and others may seem more
routine, but whatever their source their resolution will depend on
the adaptability, creativity, strength, and resources of the carer and
the other people in the family and wider network.

Disloyalty

Do we expect foster carers to take children into their home for an indeterminate period of time, relate to them as if they "belong", form close emotional bonds, and make themselves emotionally vulnerable when children leave? Children who are in contact with their biological parents may feel disloyal to these families if they become too drawn towards their foster carers. Sibling groups have different relationships with their biological families: one child may be clear that she does not want to return to the biological parent while another, who may have been in line for more punitive treatment, may be communicating more clearly a desire to remain in the foster home. Managing these different needs and the different relationships with children is a constant struggle for carers and social workers.

The biological family

The current coalition government emphasizes the importance of adoption and criticizes social workers for delay in decision making. Taking a decision that parents are not and will not be able to meet their children's needs within the children's timeframe is a very complex one: the relationship between children and parents is an important factor, and foster care is, in many cases, a way to keep children safe while continuing their relationship with their biological parents. In talking about looked after children, such decisions are made because children's primary sense of belonging is to their biological family, either because their age means that they would want continued links to this family and adoption would be inappropriate, or because, as a sibling group, it may be more important for siblings to stay together as their identity and sense of belonging is to one another.

In recent years, the expectation of fostering is that it is a short-term relationship, despite the knowledge that many children remain with foster carers throughout their childhood. However, when the decision that children will remain with foster carers is not explicit, there is a detrimental effect on the developing relationship and sense of belonging between children and their foster carers.

Sometimes policy determines that indecision about permanence is better than declaring that a child's needs will best be met by their carers, as making this explicit may lead to local authority managers noticing and changing placement because of policy rather than the best needs of the child. For example, Samantha, who was referred to us at the age of 8 years, came from a close-knit, white-British London gangland family.

Samantha

While in foster care Samantha had contact with her aunts and uncles, who gave her many presents and who said she would soon be home. However, the level of abuse she had suffered from her biological parents and their associates made it clear that she would not return to them, and the local authority plan was for adoption. During the course of our work with Samantha, we met four different family-placement social workers who were seeking adoptive parents; each change of social worker led to delay in family-finding; Samantha was aware of this, and she was probably aware that no family would take her because of her violent outbursts. By the time she reached the age of 10 years, she had been in her short-term placement for three years. Her very experienced foster carers felt it would be best for them to offer to care for her long term, but the local authority did not accept their application. When the placement broke down because of challenging behaviour from Samantha, by then aged 11, who was also violent in school (hitting and kicking other children, teacher, and carers and trashing the school office), the only option was a specialist inpatient unit. The tragedy for Samantha was that delay because of changes of social worker and rigid policies by the local authority meant that the carers, who felt a strong bond with this child, could not claim her and that the remainder of her childhood would be spent in psychiatric or residential care.

The failure of decision making meant that Samantha's need to belong with a family was not met; she could only react by using anger to push everyone away. It is often safer for children to use anger to push away those whom they may trust than to risk allowing people close and then get let down and rejected.

Bewilderment

Children often come into care in an emergency and then have a change of placement. I have heard children describe their bewilderment when talking about their experience of coming into care. Martin illustrated this for me very vividly.

Martin

Martin was 8 years old when he was removed for the last time from his mum. He came from a white British–South Asian background, although his mum couldn't tell social workers anything about his father. Social workers had been involved in his life for as long as he could remember. He longed for them to notice the bruises on his skin and to take action; however, they listened instead to his mum, who had mental health difficulties, telling them how hard it was for her because he was such a difficult child—and then going away again. I met him when he was 10. He spoke to me about the day he came into care:

> "I was at home and my mum was screaming at me and I was in the bath. The social workers came and took me to an office. I was there for a long time. They didn't say why I was there; they didn't talk to me. Then at night time I went to a stranger's house where there were other children and a dog. I spent some days—no, weeks—there and then I went to another family and then to the family I am with now. I remember the day I went to the first foster carer. There was a room full of people who were watching television, and a lady met the person I was with. I think that must have been a social worker. I have not seen her since. I was shown my bedroom and given something to eat. I remember I was hungry—my mum didn't feed me much. The house smelled different. . . ."

When Martin spoke about the day he was taken into care, he said no one had explained anything him. He didn't know what was happening—why, on this particular occasion, he was taken away from his mum, when nothing had happened on other occasions when she had really hurt him—but he thinks the neighbours told the social workers. Martin conveyed his feeling of loneliness and bewilderment. He likes the foster carers he has lived with for the past year. He is in a new school and hasn't many friends. He sees his mum every month in a contact centre; sometimes she turns up, sometimes she doesn't.

Martin was referred to our service because he was getting very angry at his foster home and at school. He got other children into trouble by reporting misdeeds to the teachers, and he was starting to remember some of the things that had happened to him when he was living with his mum. He was in a foster family with two biological adult children and two foster children, one older and one younger. Martin was nearly 9 when he came to his current school, and he did not want other children to know that he was in care. He was worried about the questions they would ask and believed that other people think foster children must have been bad to be in care. Martin really did not want to come to our CAMHS, but his social worker and school were anxious for us to try to help him manage his angry outbursts.

Martin's foster mother, Sylvia, was an experienced carer who was acutely in tune with the moods of the different children living in her home. She worked part-time, and her husband was out of the home for long hours, often working away from home. In our service we usually expect carers to attend the initial sessions with us so that we can underline the importance of the family's understanding of a child's problems and ensure that difficulties are discussed openly. For Martin, little was known about early experiences, other than that there was serious neglect and physical abuse and that the family of mother and son were open to a series of male "partners" who lived with them for short periods and then left. There was a sense of confusion about his early childhood and a gap that no one can fill. While the community mental health team worked with his mother, they had not considered Martin's needs.

His foster carer attended our early sessions with Martin, but, with other needy children in the family, she did not see herself becoming part of the therapy. It was clear that Martin had suffered greatly in his biological family, and we felt we needed to work with him and his foster carers so that we could start to create a coherent account of his early years, in relation to emotions and experiences, and try to piece together the basis for the emotional outbursts and rage that Martin was showing every day. By playing and talking together with him, he began to feel safer; he started to feel better about coming into our building, and, with his foster carer coming with him, the feeling that he was about to be abandoned diminished. For looked after children, the experience of coming to a clinic can be terrifying. They cannot be sure that the adult caring for them will remember them sufficiently to take them home; they cannot trust that they won't be left. With Martin's experience of coming into care, he was always very frightened that adults would abandon him without explanation. Having carers staying with him to be part of the work led him to feel that they were committed to him, and he allowed himself to feel that they were committed to him.

Putting language to these fears was difficult and painstaking, and without the commitment of the carer Martin could not have continued. Belonging starts with developing a belief that the adults around you are trustworthy. We find that, once children begin to trust their caregivers and begin to relax a little, they can become more angry and aggressive because of the fear that, if they start to trust, they will be let down again. Thus, I often put a positive spin on descriptions of violent outbursts, trying to reassure physically and emotionally bruised carers that the violence and rage is a "positive" sign. The work with Martin also included regular meetings with the social worker and school, so that we created some coherence in the support system around him and his foster mother.

Siblings

Children we work with are frequently more concerned about their relationship with their siblings than with their parents. One young person who had looked after and fed her younger brother spoke about the way things changed for her; as someone who had, while with their parents, been anxious to make sure she could meet his needs as far as possible, once safely placed she would be outraged if she thought he had more chips than her. After the intense anxiety that these children have experienced, allowing themselves to relax enough to become children again and to be cared for is a big change that has to be managed sensitively by foster carers and carers. Such children may also feel that it is their responsibility to parent younger siblings, which can undermine the authority of foster carers; they may also hold on to the feelings of loyalty to birth parents. We find ourselves managing the tensions between children and foster carers in showing an understanding that the "carer children" have taken on the role of parenting and could not trust "outsiders" to care for them and their siblings. It takes time and patience to enable children to allow their foster carers close enough to parent them; if they are able to allow themselves to cry or be cuddled, they are on the way to allowing themselves to belong to their foster family.

Professionals are often concerned about how to make the decision about whether to place children together or separately. Children coming into the care system tend to have a larger sibling group than the general population, and it is complicated to decide whether they should be placed together or separately, and in which combination. Alongside this, as Rushton, Dance, Quinton, and Mayes (2001) describe, resource issues are also a factor, and the availability of foster placements may well determine whether children can be placed together. Lord and Borthwick (2009) talk about the importance of clear, measured, and transparent decision making in relation to the placement of siblings together or separately. As a CAMHS, we work with the consequences of these decisions; with the benefit of hindsight, we sometimes question the reason that young children can be placed with older, emotionally damaged, and needy elder siblings. They have sometimes left the family home prior to the birth of a sibling and feel that they cannot be the lovable small child that they see, and so they feel desperately jealous, angry, and, because of their behaviour, bad, which can lead to a spiralling of their behaviour. Foster carers may respond in a way that reinforces the child's feelings about herself, and we find that our work is trying to act as interpreters between adults and children, being highly mindful of the experience that behavioural problems and conflictual relationships with carers are highly correlated with destabilizing placements. For the children remaining with their siblings, there is continuity, security, and an affirmation of identity, so we need to have a more open mind when considering the issue of "together or apart" when considering sibling groups and the needs of individual children within their sibling group.

This can only come from a professional team who are able to talk and debate openly when thinking about making such decisions.

Rushton et al. (2001) found that children who had been rejected by birth parents had a better outcome when placed with their siblings. Children coming into care have often looked after one another; many children talk about feeding younger brothers or sisters and feeling responsible for them. The decision of who to place together is often a pragmatic one; however, the experience of caring for a sibling group can be very challenging. Foster carers have spoken about children fighting one another constantly until they intervene, at which point it feels as if the children then become a strong team united against their carers. Children who have suffered abuse and neglect have usually cared for one another to the best of their ability. Their sense of belonging comes from a shared history and cultural identity.

Damon

Damon was the eldest of three children, and, at the age of 6 years, was trying to provide food for his younger sisters in the absence of their mother, who had been out since the previous evening. The flat had caught fire, and the children were taken into care and placed separately. Damon blamed himself for the children coming into care, saying, "If I hadn't set the flat alight it would all have been OK". The children were of white British–African origin. Damon was placed separately with white British foster carers. When the decision was made to place the younger children together in an ethnically matched adoptive family, Damon's carer was very anxious that his contact with them would continue. His social worker also emphasized the importance of this. However, as we frequently find, once the children were adopted, their parents felt that they were distressed after contact with their brother and wanted to put it off until the children were more settled in their adoptive family. Following this, they did not respond to requests for contact and said that it was detrimental to their children. Damon was distraught and raged at his foster carers, blaming them for the loss of contact; he could not sleep or concentrate at school because his thoughts were taken up with worry about whether his siblings were being cared for properly and his need to see them.

Many children, usually older siblings, we work with are in similar situations and feel heartbroken at the loss of siblings who are their main early attachment figures. Children whose foster or adoptive parents can maintain open relationships and support contact with biological families, while responding to the children's changing needs for contact, are able to feel a more secure sense of self and may become able to describe their different emotions in relation to their biological family in which they can feel that they belong with both their past and present caregivers.

Themes from clinical practice

The majority of referrals to our service for children in care are in relation to sexual behaviour, stealing and lying, and dysregulated and oppositional behaviour at home and school; sometimes the referrals are for the management of tensions between different professionals and foster carers which impact on the care of children. Sexual acting out between children can create considerable tension for adults, and trying to find ways to help carers manage the behaviour and find the language to talk to the children in a way that helps them to moderate their behaviour is complicated. For some foster carers and professionals, sexual acting out from one child to another is an indication that a child will become a paedophile; for others, it is seen as a symptom of anxiety and powerlessness or as a possible indication of sexual abuse. We find that it may not be until children are settled (sometimes years) into a placement that they start to act abusively to others in the household, and foster carers can feel angry with the social worker who had not told them. We are aware that, given that most children come into care as a result of neglect, abuse is no longer "disclosed", but, from my perspective, sexual abuse has been an experience alongside lying for days in dirty nappies and being hungry, cold, and alone and thus cannot be distinguished from the other assaults on the body that they have experienced. It could be that sexual abuse was the only time for physical contact, and thus it may become the only way children have known physical proximity. Sometimes foster carers are in tune with children and manage to combine talking and behavioural management in a way that changes the behaviour;

however, for others there is a panic, and the child turns into a monster. Our interventions try to find a language, usually through play, for experiences that took place without language, to describe emotions that are expressed through anger and rage. Because talking about sexual feelings and behaviour is challenging for us as a society, we find ourselves helping foster carers talk about behaviour and actions in a concrete way, looking for language that fits for the child and can begin to ameliorate the behaviour. Farmer and Pollock's (1998) study supports our experience that, where there are high levels of sexual behaviour between siblings, there is a higher risk of placement breakdowns. Sexual behaviour is difficult to manage; foster carers are also sometimes worried that allegations may be made against them. Helping them to hold steady, to work with the behaviour, and, importantly, to see the positive qualities in the child that can be amplified and, where appropriate, work alongside the school to this end, can be a rewarding experience and can lead to greater confidence in their feeling that the child can "belong" with them.

Another theme in which we try to help foster carers "hold steady" and talk openly to children is around lying and stealing. As with sexual behaviour, there is a polarity in terms of what determines a lie. Some carers view taking a yoghurt from a fridge as stealing, others have found that children have used credit cards to take large sums of money; understandably, for many, the loss of money from purses or wallet creates a tension in the family and a lack of trust, which erodes family life for all. Once confronted, children's first response is usually to say it wasn't them. There is often a preoccupation about children telling the truth and lying, while for children this is not a concept that they can understand. Their previous experience may have been one in which what was said bore very little relationship to their lived experience. They may have been told by parents what to say to others/professionals/teachers who may have been concerned about their life at home; they may have had parents who did not communicate at all.

George

In working with 9-year-old George about stealing from his foster carers, he spoke about the death of his father when he was

5 years old and then living with his mother, who was an alcoholic. He remembered finding his lost coke can full of vodka; he said his mum would disappear for two days at a time leaving him at home alone, and he had no one to talk to about it until the police found him wandering the streets at 2 in the morning. In family sessions with him and his foster carers, he talked about his being worried about his mother's violent partners, her drinking, and her anger towards him. As he became more reassured that he would stay with his foster family and that he belonged with them, he began to relax more and to let us know more about his early experience. When, at age 12 he was found to be touching the granddaughter of his foster carers, they were able to hold steady, set some boundaries in place, and come with him to sessions in which he was able to talk about his envy of these children who knew they were loved and who belonged in the family in a way that he never could. Our work was to try to assure him that he would remain in the family, that he was loved, but that he could no longer be alone with these younger children. George was able to make a connection between his actions and his emotions, which was highly dependent on the ability of the social worker and his foster carers to maintain an open mind and to separate the child from his behaviour. Through the positions taken by those around him, George was able to start to like himself, and the behaviours that were found to be challenging stopped as he was also able to move into a peer group and to feel a sense of belonging in the family and with his friends.

Many children have not been spoken to or given explanations for events in their lives, either by biological families who do not have the language or by foster carers or social workers who do not have the confidence to talk to/listen to children. Child and adolescent mental health services have an important role to play in fostering understanding.

Conclusion

One positive aspect of current government policy is that it seeks to delegate more authority to foster carers so that decisions can be made about staying over with friends or school trips for foster children without recourse to permission from the local authority. There is a wish to increase the status and security of long-term fostering (Doyle, 2013) so that the foster carers' wish to apply to foster a child long term can be legitimized. Long-term fostering is once again on the map and may help carers and children to feel more "normal", in that they can make spontaneous decisions and thus be more parental in terms of authority, thus allowing a greater possibility of belonging together.

Children's and foster carers' relationships to birth families impact on the degree to which they feel they belong to one another. Although many foster carers seek to reassure children in permanent placements that they will continue to be in their lives into adulthood, children cannot quite believe this. A number of children whose foster carers feel that they hold back and seem reserved with them say that, in the end, the only place they can rely on belonging is with their birth families, in which they have a shared culture and experience. I have been concerned that children who give up on education are feeling that ambition for themselves would take them too far away from birth families and that it is safer to be loyal to their tradition. This is frustrating for foster carers and social workers, but some young people in care describe a very profound feeling of alone-ness in which, following their life in care, they feel neither part of a foster family nor part of their birth family. For children who have been in care, the ability to manage a sense of belonging as "both/and" rather than having to choose between one or the other is important for their sense of self. We need to help children form attachments and a feeling of belonging with friends, carers, and members of birth families. For us all, the ability to develop trust in others, to form attachments and thus a sense of belonging to friendships groups, individuals, work colleagues, and communities, is an important foundation for our mental health in adulthood.

Note

Many thanks to Clare Hewitt for her contribution to this chapter.

CHAPTER NINE

Existential yearning: a family systemic perspective on belonging

John Hills

This chapter discusses the experience of belonging as a basic existential yearning. It presents a systemic perspective on such yearning and considers its application through systemic psychotherapy with children in care. Systemic thinking describes the structures, processes, and interconnectivity of relationships as well as the elusive values sought, often unknowingly, from the drama of family life. Accomplishing the universal human quest for being loved, for being understood and made secure, and for love are the fruits of attached relationships. These are the unstated corrective goals of every placement for these children. While the "ghosts in the nursery" (Fraiberg, Adelson, & Shapiro, 1975) inevitably distort the pathway to every emergent and secure identity, this is an especially poignant phrase to describe the experiences of these children. A systemic perspective in particular helps to illuminate the life experience of the children since, for a variety of reasons, their sense of continuity, predictability, and certainty in relationships is highly fragmented. They experience little direct control over their living arrangements, and frequently those who take decision about their lives are not part of the family network.

The early part of the chapter briefly explores the idea of belonging. This is followed by an examination of the basic assumptions of systemic psychotherapy and their derivation and departure from individual psychotherapy. This acts as a backdrop and leads into a discussion of my work with Calvin, which was a collaboration with a child psychotherapist. Calvin's life was comprised of disrupted cultural roots, competing attachment dilemmas (as to "whose he is"), and daunting future prospects in a society increasingly based on a harsh individualism. We will see that Calvin's future will be determined by personal resilience, useful networks, and a disproportionate amount of good fortune. This is because the social scaffolding of care, safety, and psychotherapy that surrounded his 15 years is to be dismantled. His future now is alone, facing statistically established odds against him that challenge both the vulnerabilities and the strengths of his "self" that have emerged from his background life as a child in care.

Longing, belonging, and the "oikos" of family attachments and identity

We are existentially bound and driven and cannot escape from living in the "world" or by positioning ourselves relationally. This "world" includes the social world of human "others", without whom we would have neither existence nor personal identity. We exist in one another's perceptual experiences. Only through death do we disengage from the "world" while remaining an active presence in the minds of others, at least for a time. We are essentially "ontological creatures" ascribing meaning and value even in the face of troubled living. Hamlet's soliloquy "To be or not to be" is a deep reflection of just this.

The word "be-longing" is an extension of the word "longing". A longing is a desire for an experience or an object that can seem out of reach or which has been irrevocably lost. It is possible to long for what we have never had, obsessing that others have not been so deprived. Here, imagination and fantasy can fill the deficit of life's experience.

Longing

Some longings seem trivial; others fundamental to a sustainable, basic existence. For the poor of the world, the longings are for reliable sources of food, water, shelter, security, and healthcare—the "taken-for-granted" goods of affluent social networks. Longings for the flourishing of personal accomplishment through learning, training, and work; for education; for recognition; for exciting sexual encounters; for loving relationships; for dominance and control; for a better job, a car, win on the lottery; for a different partner, move from a locality; for justice, kindness, or care and tenderness. These all take their place in the personal meaning hierarchy of our lived experience.

Longing implies a deficiency, a deficit in our immediate access to goods, or the "good" elements of experience. Such experiences when met and satisfied produce the effect of the "existential validation" of self-love. Such validation is contingent on being significant in the mindful, attuned experience of at least one human "other". Winnicott wrote frequently on this theme that "good-enough" self experience depends on the quality of the interactive space between baby, mother, family, society, and the world to develop trust and self-confidence in living. Likewise, Bowlby's theory of attachment describes four kinds of relational patterns each of which has different effects in satisfying longings and desires (Bretherton & Munholland, 1999). The optimal experience of "secure attachment" from within a "secure base" enables "existential validation" in which a child's longings, desires, and anxieties go some way to being reconciled and held through expressive, "total dialogue". "Total dialogue" is a term used in systemic psychotherapy to describe the whole communicational exchange—overt and latent—through language, touch, and expressive receptivity that takes place in all relationships, of which family relationships have primacy.

Longing and loss

At the other extreme, within chaotic, disorientating relational experiences, the child's longings and anxieties have to compete with those of the adults, who therefore present themselves as neither containing nor reconciled presences. In such situations, chronic experiences of "existential, ontological invalidation" occurs, demonstrated by all manner of fragmented, disruptive, and troubled presence. In extremes of crisis, there may even be a longing for oblivion. This is most eloquently expressed by Shakespeare's Cleopatra, whose "secure base" of her love affair and marriage to Mark Antony collapses. Faced with political disaster and military defeat, she anticipates suicide—her "immortal longings". She feels the personal weight of loss and humiliation and sees her only release as a "flight to death".

The early family life of twentieth-century American folk singer Woody Guthrie was beset by tragedy. A sister died when the home burnt down in mysterious circumstance, and his troubled mother was eventually committed to the Oklahoma Hospital for the Insane, where she spent the rest of her life. These formative events contributed hugely to shaping the direction of his creativity and to his many folk songs filled with ontological themes of anxiety, escape, rootlessness, and homelessness. In the song "I Ain't Got no Home, he sings, "Now I worry all the time like I never did before, / 'Cause I ain't got no home in the world anymore".

Home and belonging

The etymological root of "ecology" is *oikos* the ancient Greek word for home and household. Guthrie's song conveys a sense that belonging, having a home, is essential to a meaningful existence. For Cleopatra's "immortal longings", the quest is for such a sense of belonging beyond the material world. Bowlby's (1988) notion of a "secure base" conveys the meaning of an existential *oikos,* a place of belonging to call home, a container of all desires and anxieties while affording safety and ease of being. This may be a mystical, mythical place, one that is "nowhere" in its geography. However, the longing for it is deeply embedded in the human psyche (the "soul"), and this inner place may be likened symbolically to the mythic voyage of Odysseus.

Many cultures' stories frequently embed family life in this archetypical longing for belonging, whether in religious iconography (the Holy Family, the Hindu deities, etc.) or in secular icons like the British Royal Family (as "meta-family") or many Hollywood "dream factory" creations like the *Wizard of Oz*. In the latter, the scenarios move between dream-fantasy good and bad magical figures (in colour) and the realities of Dorothy's surrogate household (in monochrome). Glinda, the good witch, tells the symbolic "lost child" Dorothy to repeat the mantra "There's no place like home" in order to return to belongingness. An "Englishman's home is his castle" is another folk idealization. However, there is a clear disjunction between fantasy and the existential reality of finding an authentic place of belonging, which requires struggle.

Home and difference

Oikos for the Greeks did not just mean a place but a household, a set of communal relationships that seem reliable, mindful, and attentive to others. From such a household, like all family groups, comes the degree of personal existential validation. In eco-systemic thought, how "difference" is perceived and reacted to is a crucial shaper of personal experience.[1]

There are many templates of "difference"—cultural, national, class, sexual, gender, religious, wealth, racial, ability, literate, to name but few. Just as we have differences, we also have affiliations: our sense of "tribal" identity. These multiple masks and identities are central to our search for who we are and where we belong, reached thorough painstaking "self-reflexivity". However, it is from "the family" (however we characterize this household)— the invisible loyalties and attachments that help comprise "who" and "whose" we are—that our personal centredness emerges and is held secure.

Oedipus and belonging

Another symbolic figure on this journey of belonging is coincidentally the same one Freud used to articulate the darker "family romance" of murder and incest: Oedipus. In Sophocles' drama *Oedipus Rex*, Oedipus' parents, Laius and Jocasta, King and Queen of Thebes, learn of the divine prophecy that their son will murder his father and marry his mother. They arrange for him to be put to death at birth. However, the servant assigned to do so cannot bring himself to the task. So through a variety of events he ends up in the household of King Polybus and Queen Merope of the adjoining state of Corinth. They are childless, so they raise him as their own without telling him about his origins. Unfortunately, in adolescence he hears about the prophecy and, fearing for the harm he might inflict on his "parents", he flees to Thebes and promptly enacts it.

His search for his true identity is disabled by close family figures around him. Fear and anxious beliefs drive their action (in systemic parlance, Oedipus is part of an "anxiety" or "fear-activated" system). Tragedy and suffering afflicts two families and Oedipus himself. As he gains personal insight, so, symbolically, he destroys his actual eyesight. The drama weaves many differences of character and social position and is rich in meaning. It celebrates the Greek heroic ideal of the pursuit of self-knowledge whatever the costs. He is certainly uncompromising in his search for self-empowerment and ontological validation. He may fulfil the prophecy but discover himself:

> Storms, hurricanes let them all come. I've travelled this far and now I'm determined to discover my identity. If my birthplace was the gutter I shall hunt it out! . . . My true mother is fortunate coincidence, my brothers and sisters the changing seasons, and I change with them as naturally as the trees. If that's my background who could ask for better? I am what I am. I have no wish to be otherwise. But who I am, that I must know. And I will know it! [in Taylor, 1998, p. 45]

Though guilty of two crimes, he is a true innocent, misinformed through secrecy of human guilt and fear, the plaything of those who base their lives around supernatural prophecies as accurate predictors of the future. It is a drama of the paradox of outcome from unintended consequence—he brings about what he is trying most to avoid. Much of this drama is mirrored in the traumatized lives and the quest for validated, integrated selfhood that many children in the care system experience. The Oedipus story, therefore, is an example for these children as they undertake the painful journey of self-discovery in psychotherapy.

The development of systemic and ecological thinking in psychotherapy

In the opening issue of the journal *Family Process*, the psychoanalyst Nathan Ackerman wrote:

> The family approach offers a new level of entry, a new quality of participant observation in the struggles of human adaptation. It holds the promise of shedding new light on the processes of illness and health and offers new ways of assessing and influencing these conditions. It may open up, perhaps for the first time, some effective paths for the prevention of illness and the promotion of health. [Ackerman, 1962]

Ackerman applied this "new level of entry" to his work in child and adolescent mental health following Bowlby's work at the London Child Guidance Clinic in 1947.

Bowlby and the family

In 1949, Bowlby gave what was the first account of what became known as "family group therapy".

> We see, furthermore, that to attain the end of a secure, contented and co-operative community in which parents can give love and security to their children, enabling them to grow up to be the stable and contented people, able to sustain and further a just and friendly society, no one point in the circle is more vital than another. The vicious circle may be broken at any point; the virtuous circle may be promoted at any point. [Bowlby, 1949, p. 26]

Both Ackerman and Bowlby drew on their psychoanalytic training with individuals, adapting it to working with family groups. Like attachment theory this has had a lasting impact on both the health and the social care services. In time, it gave birth to the Scandinavian "open-dialogue" movement based around the more radical use of reflecting teams (Andersen, 1987) and the community of responsive voices from open professional and family collaboration (Seikkula & Arnkil, 2006). This is what we might now term the "total therapeutic dialogue".

The 1940s saw a revolution of thought in modern science and technology. Information theory, cybernetic theory, communications theory, and systems theory converged with the better established discipline of ecology, which examined and described the interactive feedback and balances that living systems require for survival. The *oikos* in ecology is the "household" of the living planet. These movements were committed to models of pluralistic thought and of active and valued interdisciplinary working.

Bateson and ecological thinking

A central figure in this area was the British-born anthropologist and polymath Gregory Bateson [1904–1980]. An original thinker, his willingness to collaborate outside his own discipline resulted in fresh "levels of entry" into the fields of mental health, theories of mind, interactional patterns of behaviour, and social organization. Through his influence, systemic thought has developed as an approach and philosophy that looks as much at relational connection as parts.[2]

There are three main ideas from the ecology of systemic thought that need to be understood in the process of enquiry about change:

1. There are different, interacting levels of any system between the individual parts and the whole.
2. A situation, in its full complexity, requires placing different perspectives alongside each other to give a clearer picture (what Bateson termed the "double description"; 1980, p. 21).
3. In looking closely at patterns of organization, it is the live flow of information and communication through circular feedback loops that is crucial in seeking to intervene for change.

An example of these exists in the simple mechanical system of a central heating system. To work, the whole system must be joined between its component parts, and these parts all need to be set alongside each other as equal elements; it needs to be able to take in feedback about room temperature (via the thermostat) so that the flow of warm water in the system neither overheats nor is insufficient. Like Goldilocks' selection of "Baby Bear's" porridge, everything must be "just right", or "good enough". Such a mechanical system is designed to self-regulate through simple corrective feedback-information processes.

Working with families

Applied to a complex human system like a family, this model is simplistic and limited. However, there are some comparisons that can be made. A family in which violence and abuse seem part of its normative transactions, or one in which depression, psychosis, suicidal thoughts, and intentions seem to be the predominant culture, may be thought of as living in extremes of "discomfort zones". The culture of neither would pass the Goldilocks' porridge test, but with the skilled therapeutic application of interdisciplinary intervention both might be enabled to satisfy Goldilocks' rigorous requirements.

R. D. Laing visited Bateson in the US and developed his own thinking in a little-known pamphlet in 1969 entitled *Intervention in Social Situations*. Laing wrote perceptively:

> This situation [a case just described] is one of many which have the characteristic: *no one in the situation knows what the situation is*. If one stays in such a situation just a little, say for 90 minutes, we get more and more lost and confused, disorientated. . . . We can never assume that the people in the situation know what the situation is. A corollary to this is: *the situation has to be discovered*. [Laing, 1969/2002, p. 3; emphasis in original]

Very often, this is a family's "closed" experience of itself. It takes an outside perspective to help "reveal itself to itself". In what US family therapist Carl Whitaker termed "the family crucible" (Whitaker & Napier, 1988), family life is often a "collision of subjectivities". There are many different perspectives and judgements about the origins and nature of a "problem" (indeed, whether one exists); who/what is responsible for it; and who/what is frustrating a solution. These are at work in the operation of Bateson's "double descriptions" (though "multiple descriptions" might be more accurate terminology in the case of most families)

Double description is best understood when trying to understand the different complexities of a poem or work of art. Reading three or four critics' accounts may confuse you considerably. However, from different "meaning accounts" and your own curiosity, you will reach your own considered position and appreciation of the work. This is true when seeking to understand families through the process of enquiry you also help them understand each other. Their different realities "set alongside" each other help create a wider, clearer picture.

Levels of context

Ecological and systemic thinking helps us map and understand the organization, process, and structure of relationships: how they interlink and enfold in each other, like Russian matryoshka dolls, in different levels of social context and meaning. Each part of the social structure has a narrative about itself and a narrative about the "other". However, while systemic thought is largely descriptive in its analysis, it is not "power blind" about the dynamic process of relationship conflict. Goldilocks was well aware the bears could bite.

Body and the whole-self relationship

The first and closest level of relationship is with our bodies. Systems thinking does not have us as disembodied minds from body. "Mind" is everywhere in the intelligence of gut, heart, muscle, bone, eye ear, mouth, skin. We are a system of systems. However, this is a system with intelligence, with an alert consciousness that ties together all the different elements of being into an extraordinary presence.

Relational system: the family

The next level in system ecology involves those relational systems of "others" who direct our care and mentoring. This household community, comprising many different and discrete structures and forms, is the family system (the "family crucible"; Whitaker &

Napier, 1988). It reflects the "foundry" nature of its task of refining the "base material" of primal human nature (with its impulsive, often destructive passions) into something of use, beauty, and form. Reflected too is the "hot" characteristics of the process of doing so, the careful management and containment necessary as a prerequisite for a working *atelier*.

Relational system: the neighbourhood institutions

The next level of relational systems involves those social institutions that intersect with the personal and the familial. These can be readily identified from their commonplace, direct influence—nursery, school, religious places of worship and community, neighbourhoods with their shops, health surgeries, libraries, play-parks, as well as the direct community of neighbours.

Remote institutional systems

The more remote institutional systems are those of the police and law enforcement and legal advice (though such institutions are, for some families, embedded in their communal experience of regular living); housing "systems", private or local authority; the social security system; banking; the armed services; the judiciary; and, finally, the democratic guardians and legislators.

The State "Leviathan" and Crown Head of State

There exists the level of society often characterized by the more impersonal and abstract notion of the State power (a Leviathan like-being characterized by Thomas Hobbes) holding the whole social structure together through legislative enactment and enforcement, and governance of the social institutions. Every citizen has a relationship with the State through evidential proof of identity (passport, driving licence, etc.).

The global, international context

Beyond this level is the global, international context one in which State is in relationship to State for "good" (trading and intellectual exchange) or "ill" (support for warfare, use of cheaper labour, etc.).

The universe and the rest

Beyond this level is that of the cosmos, with all its endless vastness of cold, barely illuminated space, the spur to human wonderment, curiosity about the meaning of it, and the purpose of existence, generally and personally. From this wonderment at the deserts of empty spaces and the puzzlement of time, immeasurable and inestimable, comes the awareness of existential fear and dread at the insignificance of the personal self and its inevitable mortality. This emptiness can give rise simultaneously to feelings of ecstasy at the extraordinary nature and beauty of creation and to the fact of human consciousness to witness, describe, measure, and understand some of the complexities of the gigantic scale of its processes. And so we return full circle to the "embodied" person alone in a universe that may seem both awesome and absurd—the basis of our ontological insecurity and anxiety.

From such cosmic wondering, and with a consciousness of different levels of being and context, a systemic frame of seeing produces a different approach to psychotherapy. It asks questions of how we locate ourselves, what are our relationships with our "worlds", how do we define our identity, and what meaning and understanding we give to our experience. It is also a complementary framework for other psychotherapies seeing these as parts of an overall, if invisible, whole.

Connecting themes with individual psychotherapy

Though systemically informed psychotherapy is of recent origin, it has its roots in the traditions of psychoanalytic psychotherapy, which is itself an evolving and changing discipline. In an interview in 1987, Bowlby presented a context marker about family and systemic therapy:

> Freud drew attention to a whole range of issues. Much of what he wrote about was in terms of family interaction. The "Oedipus

complex" is concerned with family interaction. The development of object relations has all been in terms of human interaction. I would call it almost entirely in terms of attachment, caregiving relations and the emotions concerned with all those things. There's the whole area of defence against feeling and thought about those things. No other discipline has concerned itself with that . . . one of the tragedies of psychoanalysis I think has been that people have defined psychoanalysis not in terms of the phenomena but in terms of the particular theories Freud advanced 50–80 years ago. *No growing discipline has ever dreamt of defining itself in terms of any single set of theories.* [Bowlby, 1987, p. 9; emphasis added]

Calvin's story: collaborative working in the search for existential validation

My work with Calvin is an example of a collaboration between child and systemic psychotherapy, involving the whole professional network around a child in care. Before beginning the discussion I want to revisit what I have said so far, in order to bring to mind the backdrop for this work.

Children in care: an existential perspective

Many children in care are retrieved from the crucible of chaotic/disorganized family relational attachments featuring abusive violence either to themselves or between their care-givers, confusing sexual boundaries, and neglecting and neglectful interactions of care. They are the most vulnerable section of children in our community. Many often carry latent feelings of being an "existential error" and burdensome participants in an "Oedipus legacy" (their birth will foretoken the parental "catastrophe" of feeling overwhelmed by their constant needs for care). They also become "children of the State", which invests the responsibility for their parenting in their Local Government Authority. This makes their status uniquely different.

The early parental and family response to a new birth is an invisible "signature" to a child's birth, and it may be influential in the child's subsequent experience of existential validation. If the child's birth was desired, welcomed, and emotionally and psychologically embraced by the community around the child, then the developmental pathway for the child is likely to be optimized. She has a community of attachments. However, with children in care there is a diametrically opposite experience. This is well documented in publications and research pointing to a child's inner landscape beset by cumulative "existential invalidation". The child's inner landscape is in a state of constant and active feedback with its outer relational landscape. There are nuanced shades of experience between these poles for all children, but this is the basic ecology of development.

The reparative work and care that goes into creating a set of transformative experiences for an ontologically distressed child is considerable and demanding. It is seldom integrated, and in its disjointedness and disconnection replicates the child's original relationship sets. These "sets" become set indeed! To avoid this repetition is exactly what the child in care most needs, in the form of a collective, actively thinking, communicating community with a shared presence that seeks to correct the historically formed developmental process: one that seeks to replicate a beneficial working network providing an experience of secure attachment in which the child is "held" totally (Hills, 2005). This is what we hoped to achieve for Calvin through our work with him.

Calvin's background

Fifteen-year-old Calvin was first-generation black British. The youngest of five children, he was fostered with an older brother and sister at the age of 2 years. His foster father, Josiah, was first-generation Afro-Caribbean–British, married to Jane, a white British woman; they had a16-year-old daughter, Maisie.

Calvin's background was one of disruptive attachment and of two parental figures living on the edge themselves. His mother, Marcia, had herself grown up in care; his father, Robert, a Jamaican musician, rarely lived at home with them. The relationship between

Calvin's parents was volatile, at times violent. Marcia had become a chronic, long-term drug misuser.

Marcia would often go missing for days, without warning, and Robert would then take care of the children. The quality of care was described as basic. Robert died suddenly from a rare condition, activating social services' concerns about the care and safety of the children. Marcia accepted a place at a residential drug-rehabilitation unit for nine months with the two youngest children; the older siblings were accommodated elsewhere. Having completed the programme, all the children were returned to live at home. However, full Care Orders were obtained within three months, as Marcia began misusing drugs again, leaving the care of the children to daughter Amanda, aged 16. Marcia resisted cooperating with social and healthcare services. Calvin was 2 years old when he and his younger brother and sister were removed and placed with his current carers. Weekly contact was agreed, though Marcia attended sporadically. Calvin's brother returned to live with his mother when he turned 18.

Early life in care

When the children were first brought to the family, Calvin had a bad cough and cold. Despite this, he slept well at night and there were no other signs of anxiety. Apparently he gave up his dummy, which does seem rather remarkable for a toddler placed in a strange situation. Although he was noted to play well when he first came, he could be destructive with toys, often picking at things until they broke. He also picked at his clothes and his body. Calvin was a poor eater, only eating food like yoghurt, and was unable to eat any vegetables or food that needed much chewing. The children did not appear used to sitting at a table, nor using a knife or fork. Generally he had great problems getting off to sleep. This remained a problem at the time of my work with him. In the early days he could be destructive—for example, peeling wallpaper off the walls, breaking toys through his "picking" behaviour.

However, by the time of his third birthday, Calvin's development was seen as generally good. He was eating well and enjoyed playing and socializing. He was quite a cuddly little boy. His foster carers noted that, aged 3 years, Calvin had difficulty with remembering—again, something noted in my work with him. He was said to easily break into tears. He did not like changes in routine—yet again, something noted in the work with him.

Individual child psychotherapy

Child psychotherapy began when Calvin was in primary school and lasted for several years, until adolescence. His psychotherapist then considered he might benefit from having a male therapist and a systemic, network approach. This was because of his life stage and the complexities of his background culture. Marcia insisted he be brought up to respect the Rastafarian beliefs of his father, Robert, although Calvin had little identification with this. The professional system around him, like that of his family, was large and complex. One main concern was also about "whose he was"—that is, his sense of belonging and affiliations. At the closure transfer summary, the child psychotherapist wrote perceptively:

> For most of this time they have been weekly sessions, for a period it was fortnightly, and recently it has been less regular. Calvin has always made good use of sessions at a level appropriate for his age. He did struggle as a younger child to think about his feelings and to be in touch with reality e.g. when court cases were ongoing and there was a threat he might leave his foster carers. The uncertainties of his early years led to him being driven by an anxiety that it was hard to name but drove his behaviour, making him an active child who found it hard to relax, fully concentrate and focus. Despite this, there were more peaceful periods with no court cases, and he got a clear message when contact was reduced that his placement was where he would be staying. This made a powerful difference to how he seemed to feel about himself.

> From about the age of 11 years there were more signs of Calvin having developed a mind that could begin to grapple with his life experiences, make more sense of his emotional responses and behaviour. Real thinking together could happen at times in

therapy, although this was sometimes lost and all he wanted to do was be active in sessions and stop the thinking and understanding process.

Several times we talked about therapy reducing or stopping over the years, but then another crisis would happen or Calvin would resist it very strongly, displaying more worrying behaviour at home or school . . . for the last year or so he has shown his anger more at home as well . . . I do not feel it is his anger per se that needs addressing or even managing because it is fairly normal for a youngster of his age to be rebelling and expressing strong feelings about things he sees as unfair in his life. As a looked after child, Calvin has a lot to come to terms with, in particular why he had a mother who was a drug addict, a father who died when he was a baby and why he had to come into care at the age of two years . . .

The relationship Calvin continues to have with his male carer, Josiah, is particularly important at this stage of his development and the fact that Josiah is black and of African-Caribbean origin is an additional positive factor in helping Calvin with his sense of identity . . .

Despite his attachment to myself I believe he has been attempting to achieve some separation from myself and his therapy but is fearful this will lead to me rejecting him . . .

Having built up a relationship over many years it does feel important that he knows I will continue to be here, be interested in his progress and be available at a later point should that be helpful.

The transition from individual to systemic psychotherapy

There was a careful handover between myself and his child psychotherapist. I met Calvin and his carers and found him charming, witty, shrewd, sharp, easily bored, and slightly disengaged in the therapy process. We talked about the long working relationship with his therapist, its losses, the differences of our gender, but that both of us were white and could not share any obvious racial affiliation with him. He seemed to accept this change and the differences, although reticent to voice any unease.

I began by working with him as an individual within a systemic context. We worked out an agreement for the sessions. He enjoyed playing Monopoly, as he had before. He played aggressively to win, which he did frequently, though he got bored realizing that I was not effective opposition. We took another direction using the Internet in sessions to track down the story of Bob Marley and discuss the YouTube clips of him. This seemed to connect with him, and he came alive. As noted above, his father had been a Jamaican musician and Rastafarian. We shared our different interests in black music, mine in the Blues. He began wearing a wristband with the Jamaican flag on it and showed growing interest and pride in Jamaica's achievements at the Olympics.

However, his carers were clearly getting very anxious not just by Calvin's behaviour (fire-setting in his bedroom, staying out late some nights, defiant attitudes to their boundary-setting), but also about the two other children in placement (one of whom was Calvin's sister). The third child, Luther, also black, was showing similar behaviour difficulties. Both would sometimes stay out late together without negotiation. Luther's therapist and I worked together with the carers to help them find effective conduct boundaries and ways of communicating with the two boys. It was clear that as a couple they felt stressed and disconnected from each other. This also formed part of the open dialogue, though the couple were less comfortable talking about this.

After eight months, at the end of the summer term, Calvin announced he no longer wanted individual therapy from me. He did accept my invitation to work jointly with his wider care system and family of origin. His local authority, in response to the placement crisis, provided a mentor for him and a local systemic clinical practitioner who undertook to carry out some work with him and his family of origin. It seemed an "all hands to the pump" strategy to keep the placement going, but without much coordinated dialogue.

However, I linked up with the systemic clinical practitioner, and we tried to develop a schema of joint working. To me, Calvin was at a crucial point of transition. He had a confused and self-hating sense of himself, which was apparent from drawings he made and concealed. He had deep anxieties about his future—this had a basis in reality. In an open session with his carers, we talked with him about the "self" of his drawings. I accepted his "sacking" and our renegotiation to work with his "whole system" and stay in touch. This would include "joined-up" work with the local systemic clinical practitioner, himself, and his oldest sister, Amanda, who seemed a likely ally in any open dialogue with the family since Marcia was struggling increasingly with mental health difficulties.

His carers were eager to help develop his curiosity and confidence in forming questions to put to the family. His child psychotherapist also expressed enthusiasm to join in this open dialogue with his family at home. Calvin was especially keen.

Meta-narrative

I wrote a meta-narrative for everyone in the system as a preliminary to arranging open meetings

> I have wanted to put on record my observations and thoughts from working with Calvin and his network. I have been seeing Calvin for just over a year for individual therapy. However, he made it apparent at a meeting a month ago that he no longer wished to continue in individual therapy. I said to him that I would want to remain connected therapeutically with the wider system around him to seek, with others, change that would benefit his long-term well-being. He seemed eager for this to happen.
>
> I have met with or liaised with, at different stages, his carers with whom he has been brought up for about 80% of his life. They are de facto his family in terms of attachment relationships, psychological identification, personal mentoring, his direct cultural experience, and his personal history. However, he has another family affiliation, with its separate connections and narratives that are less tangible, more sporadic and influential in less direct ways. His carers have been meticulous and boundaried in respecting the rights and beliefs of his family of origin. However, this has not been easy for either family on

each side of this difference, and particularly so for Calvin, in the "no-man's-land" between the two family systems. He struggles to grasp a clear sense of his emerging identity and to trust the capabilities of his intelligence. It is difficult not to see his split identifications and loyalties as contributing significantly to his struggle to find a secure sense of himself and to begin to imagine a future.

"Who am I and where does my future lie?" is a question which, though not articulated with such precision, is conveyed through how he has related to me when we were working together in individual work and was my sensing beneath the common confusions and normal preoccupations of adolescence. We developed in therapy the use of the computer to search out and explore his curiosity about the objects that attracted him, about Rastafarian culture and the music of Bob Marley in particular. Calvin spontaneously searched out more about Bob Marley without prompting from me, between sessions.

I got a sense that his direct knowledge of his father's background as a musician was fragmentary—as, indeed, was his knowledge of his family background generally. His facility in finding his way around a computer was in striking contrast to his lack of open curiosity about his roots and background. This, I thought, probably derived from awareness that questioning key family figures too closely might lead him and his prospective informants into areas of emotional difficulty, discomfort, and potential conflict. He is highly attuned to this potential at home with the care family and tends to deal with emotional issues through avoidance or deflection. His main, and secure, family experience is with these long-term carers, who share elements in their own background. However, this does not bridge the information gap from the background family life to which, anyway, he may return in the near future.

I have discussed some of these issue with Claire Brown, Clinical Practitioner from his home-base CAMHS, and we have explored the idea of setting up a couple of meetings at home with significant members of their family to see if we could help clarify some of Calvin's questions.

It is clear that, for some time, his carers have been stressed and distressed, like most, by a number of life events, one being how to manage holding the well-being of their relationship in the face of four young persons, some of whom are especially challenging. I have always been impressed with the positive role model that his male carer, Josiah, as a successful and accomplished black male, has provided for Calvin. He communicates directly and by example the positive messages he has been able to give Calvin in the face of the moments of racial "put downs". However, my sensing is that sometimes he misjudges Calvin's confidence and resilience, formed from a less accomplished family life start to that of his own. Both carers find great difficulty in managing Calvin's behavioural "acting out" at present, one of the effects of which has been to undermine their perception and confidence in the strengths and values they have brought to Calvin through their relationship.

I have suggested, after further discussion with others, that reflective work to help support the couple through this current difficult situation and transition is essential and should be fairly prompt.

Calvin is in many ways both an attached and an unattached teenager. It is not quite clear where the planning for his future is heading. He is caught between two different family structures, each with different claims on him: one from direct experience, the other from his historical roots. These family systems are very separate and not in direct communication. This situation is not helping to contain his huge life uncertainty and confusion about how and where to locate himself in the coming years. I feel some fairly urgent work needs to take place to have the kind of dialogue with him, Marcia, and his family of origin to clarify a number of issues on his behalf. I have suggested that joint work at his mother's home with myself and his local authority workers in consultation with his current carers should be undertaken.

The carers should have some therapeutic help to think about and prepare for their own transition at the same time as that of Calvin's. Fostering is a complex, relational task as "corporate parents", and access to skilled therapeutic consultative work is just as essential for carers as for all parents in the community.

I would be pleased to discuss this further with all involved to help develop an agreed therapeutic intervention plan and a timetable. I repeat the offer made to Calvin at the time of finishing individual therapy: that I remain available for any single session of consultation he might seek, whilst accepting he tends to deal with personal and situational anxiety and difficulty by withdrawal.

The foster carers were especially eager for this to take place, though wary of joining themselves and anxious about criticism from Marcia and other members of Calvin's family. However, unexpected developments occurred that kept this meeting in abeyance. Luther left the placement. The foster carers reported that Calvin became more settled in the family, less defiant and more engaged with local life and his social environment. Everyone seemed to relax, and a more harmonious "virtuous circle" (Bowlby, 1949) "feedback loop" seemed to have replace the "vicious one". It appeared that a wider, more open, narrative communication may have shifted the "system" from "crisis activated" to one that was more integrated. Calvin and his carers now seem more freed to accept the primacy of this setting as his secure base, for the immediate future at least. It remains open to Calvin to continue to explore at some future time in his life should the impulse to curiosity and discovery become more insistent. T. S. Eliot pointed out in an oft-quoted section from the *Four Quartets* that our existence is a journey of exploration of meaning that moves backwards and forwards over time until we return to its beginning and understand it differently for the first time. This is a similar experience of self-realization over time to that shared by Louis MacNeice in his poem "The Truisms".

At first, Calvin demonstrated little settled ease about where his *oikos* is located. From conflicted loyalties and out of some confusion, he has sought to honour his mother's wishes about his deceased father and preserving his heritage. In his surrogate "family of attachment", his carers have sought to be fair and "neutral", respecting his mother's expressed wishes; but they also have a strong sense of love and belonging for him. The local authority social work department—his legal parents—had no decisive view about what should happen for him. No one in the adult system around him has struggled to arrive at a satisfactory consensus as to how he is to be best "held in mind" (Hills, 2005). He, a contemporary, teenage equivalent of the fifteenth-century drama *Everyman*, is beset by different and conflicting voices from which he must decide which fits him best.

As a black teenager with, as yet, no academic qualifications, a return to London would seem to be risk-laden choice for Calvin. In 2012, the *Guardian* reported:

> More than half of young black men available for work in Britain are now unemployed, according to unpublished government statistics which show the recession is hitting young black people disproportionately hard. . . . The youth unemployment rate for black people has increased at almost twice the rate for white 16- to 24-year-olds since the start of the recession in 2008. [Ball, Milmo, & Ferguson, 2012]

Into this kind of statistical evidence Calvin must somehow find a route to a meaningful, productive life of personal well-being and be expected to transcend the constraints of his conflicting life experience so far. This seems a "big ask".

Conclusion

The conjoint work with Calvin also demonstrated systemic psychotherapy as primarily a collaborative complementary, open, and pluralistic psychotherapy. This is part of its methodological strength and its free movement in between analysis and synthesis. Such a methodology is embodied in its use of live supervision, reflecting teams (Andersen, 1987), and open dialogic working (Seikkula & Arnkil, 2006). It is firmly rooted in democratic process and respect for "situationalism"—that is, it seeks to address the whole unique organization of the situation (which R. D. Laing describes, as I mentioned earlier in this chapter). Complexity is valued and examined in the light of abundant practice evidence that change results from sustained and focused work. It assists in mapping the whole sets of relationships, loyalties, life-cycle transitions, and communications from which the subject of the thinking—the child in care—may be helped to experience better existential validation from his enfolding community. It enables focused, open, shared integrated working to repair the ontological damage to the roots of the child's secure being and his family relationships. These are often further distressed by poorly connected conjoint working.

Systemic psychotherapy draws its ideas from a synthesis of attachment-based thinking, the methodology of social anthropology, an existential phenomenological world view, and the communitarian awareness (Hills, 2013). It also incorporates the political view, though not in any partisan way, that systems are all politically directed at both macro- and micro-levels. Social inequalities generate slow-burning but lasting systemic damage to interpersonal well-being (Wilkinson & Pickett, 2009). These are the invisible partners to therapy and social care. Systemic analysis is a total framework, which omits no level of human society in its consideration.

It does indeed "take a village to raise a child". Being personally and professionally open to a child's ontological needs for a sense of *oikos* is the key to helping the transformative process. As Isca Salzberger-Wittenberg (2013) put it after a lifetime of understanding the process of belonging, enforced estrangement from one's roots, and helping others find the emergence of a true self from the drama of fragmented personal attachments:

> . . . all of us may, at times, have to struggle to hold onto hope, to keep our hearts and minds open and to remain grateful for having been given life—and with it the opportunity to experience the wonders of the world as well as its tragedies. [p. 13]

There may be nothing "over the rainbow" except the joy of appreciating it for the wonderment it is.

Notes

1. There is a full and helpful dialogue about this between family therapist Robin Skynner and comedian John Cleese (see Skynner & Cleese, 2011).

2. It is beyond the scope of this chapter to explore the extent of Bateson's contribution to the new ways of family and systemic psychotherapeutic

work, for he was not himself a psychotherapist. There are many introductions to family and systemic psychotherapy (e.g., Burnham, 1986; Carr, 2012; Draper & Dallos, 2010; Gorell Barnes, 1998; Hills, 2013; Rivett & Street, 2009). All describe the history and principles. Bateson's originality of thought is best expressed and found in his own writings (see Bateson, 1972, 1980; Ruesch & Bateson, 1951).

Endpiece

This book has brought together various ideas that help us understand the attachment of children and young people to their foster carers or adoptive parents. This attachment is fundamentally different from that between children and their biological parents, largely because it is an attachment to strangers. It is a second attachment for them and one that brings with it a prior separation from their biological parents. Unlike the post-natal attachment to biological parents, this new attachment usually comes after at least some cumulative experience of attachment to the birth family from whom they were separated. Thus, in addition, it is a relationship entered with the child's sense of loss and trauma to be accounted for. This is rarely the case for children remaining with their birth families.

The emotional and psycho-social complexities that result from the experience of attachment, separation, and the expectation of attachment to a new family would be difficult enough to fulfil, but they are made more so by the trauma that many children suffer before they are taken into care or placed for adoption. Various forms of neglect and abuse have their toll on these children, so that by the time they arrive in their new families they are usually too disorientated to begin the process of integration with what is then a new family reconstituting itself. For various personal reasons, these families have offered themselves as adopters and foster carers and have successfully completed pre-screening and the training for their roles. Nevertheless, frequently both mental health and social care practitioners see stark evidence of ambition for these children, which comes more from the family than from the child. As part of the corporate parent, the family is tasked to treat the child as if their own. Often, this remit is followed in such a way that the new parents' own aspirations slip into their wishes for the child's development and future. This slip occurs through their blinding themselves to the fact that the child is actually not theirs from birth and arrives with them already shaped by experiences. This disappointing reality usually comes home when they realize that the child is not attaching to them in the way that they would like in order that their wishes be fulfilled. Attachment then tends to be the term used to describe what they feel *should be happening*. Closer observation, however, suggests that belonging is at issue and not attachment *per se*. New families want children to *belong* to them, not simply to attach and make use of what they have on offer.

Belonging is not a concept that is recognized sufficiently to be part of the currency for training mental health and social care practitioners. This is very surprising, given that most of these professionals would no doubt agree that a sense of belonging is essential to the establishment and maintenance of emotional well-being and mental health. Because of its lack of academic recognition, the full extent of its meaning has not been explored by researchers. However, the children and new families live their parts in the problem of the expectation of belonging, and the difficulties in developing a sense of it. It has been a main undercurrent of this book that a sense of belonging is underexplored and is thus a poorly understood essential lens through which to discover the meaning of adoption and foster-placement success and thus failure.

A book such as this on the sense of belonging—which is a widely understood feeling but one that has hitherto been only partially constructed as a concept—opens up huge possibilities for its contributors and readers to explore ideas and link them together. Consulting a dictionary leads to various definitions of belonging: to be somebody's property; to be in a proper situation; to be attached by birth, allegiance, or membership; to be an attribute or function of a person or thing; to be owned by, be the property of, be part of, be a member of, be associated with, relate to, go with. These are very near those put forward by mental health practitioners as a feeling of fitting with some group or set of ideas one feels an affinity with, and a sense of identity that is both a cause and product of this fit, leading to an integrated self. But these definitions, as helpful as they may be for guidance in such a turbulent emotional territory, do not convey the liveliness of the individual's development of a sense of identity. They do not really help us see just how difficult we, as a society, find it to develop the concept so that it has the same academic and colloquial purchase as attachment and attachment theory.

The book's authors have been prepared to push the boundary around this concept and lead us to new and interesting possibilities. What is clear from this is that it is not possible to see the development of this sense outside a relationship, and that this relationship is very complicated. A sense of belonging directs us at observing and understanding the child's inner world, the way the child approaches and recognizes being approached by the external world, and how the external world itself comes to the relationship. This is the basis of the matrix introduced in this book. Its simplicity covers the depth and width of the complex territory we must enter if we are better to understand how to help adopted and fostered children develop their lives, now and for the future.

REFERENCES

Access All Areas (2012). *Action For All Government Departments to Support Young People's Journey from Care to Adulthood.* London. Available at: www.thecareleaversfoundation.org/sitedata/files/ Access_All_Areas_Complete.pdf

Ackerman, N. (1962). Family psychotherapy and psychoanalysis: Implications of difference. *Family Process, 1* (1): 30–43.

Adams, P. (2012). *Planning for Contact in Permanent Placements.* London: BAAF.

Anant, S. S. (1966). The need to belong. *Canada's Mental Health, 14:* 21–27.

Andersen, T. (1987). The reflecting team: Dialogue and meta-dialogue in clinical work. *Family Process, 26:* 415–428.

Ball, J., Milmo, D., & Ferguson, B. (2012). Half of UK's young black males are unemployed. *Guardian,* 9 March.

Barratt, S. (2006). Systemic work with children after adoption. In: J. Kenrick, C. Lindsey, & L. Tollemache (Eds.), *Creating New Families: Therapeutic Approaches to Fostering, Adoption, and Kinship Care.* London: Karnac.

Bateson, G. (1972). *Steps to an Ecology of Mind.* Chicago, IL: University of Chicago Press.

Bateson, G. (1980). *Mind and Nature: A Necessary Unity*. London: Fontana.

Baumeister, R., & Leary, M. (1995). The need to belong: Desire for interpersonal attachments as a fundamental human motivation. *Bulletin of the American Psychological Association, 117* (3): 497–529.

Berlin, I. (1969). *Four Essays on Liberty*. Oxford: Oxford University Press.

Bernard, K., Butzin-Dozier, Z., Rittenhouse, J., & Dozier, M. (2010). Cortisol production patterns in young children living with birth parents vs children placed in foster care following involvement of Child Protective Services. *Archives of Pediatrics & Adolescent Medicine, 164* (5): 438–443.

Bick, E. (1968). The experience of the skin in early object relations. *International Journal of Psychoanalysis, 49*: 484–486. Reprinted in: A. Briggs (Ed.), *Surviving Space: Papers on Infant Observation*. Tavistock Clinic Series. London: Karnac, 2002.

Bick, E. (1986). Further considerations on the function of the skin in early object relations. Reprinted in: A. Briggs (Ed.), *Surviving Space: Papers on Infant Observation*. Tavistock Clinic Series. London: Karnac, 2002.

Bick, E. (1987). *Collected Papers of Martha Harris and Esther Bick*. Strath Tay: Clunie Press.

Bion, W. R. (1959). Attacks on linking. *International Journal of Psychoanalysis, 30*: 308–315. Reprinted in: *Second Thoughts*. London: Heinemann, 1967; London: Karnac, 1984.

Bion, W. R. (1961). *Experiences in Groups*. London: Tavistock Publications.

Bion, W. R. (1962a). *Learning from Experience*. London: William Heinemann.

Bion, W. R. (1962b). A theory of thinking. *International Journal of Psychoanalysis, 30*: 306–310. Reprinted in: *Second Thoughts*. London: Heinemann, 1967; London: Karnac, 1984.

Bion, W. R. (1967). *Second Thoughts*. London: Karnac, 1984.

Bion, W. R. (1970). *Attention and Interpretation*. London: Karnac, 1984.

Bowlby, J. (1949). The study and reduction of group tensions in the family. *Human Relations, 2*: 123–128.

Bowlby, J. (1958). The nature of the child's tie to his mother. *International Journal of Psychoanalysis, 39* (5): 350–373.

Bowlby, J. (1960). Separation anxiety. *International Journal of Psychoanalysis, 41* (1–3): 89–113.

Bowlby, J. (1969). *Attachment and Loss, Vol. 1: Attachment*. London: Hogarth Press; reprinted Harmondsworth: Penguin, 1971 (2nd edition, 1982).

Bowlby, J. (1987). Bowlby at 80—Part 2: The Bowlby Interview. Conversation with John Byng-Hall. *The Association for Family Therapy Newsletter, 7* (No. 2, May). [Warrington: AFT Publishing]

Bowlby, J. (1988). *A Secure Base*. London: Routledge.

Brenman, E. (1985). Cruelty and narrowmindedness. In: E. Bott-Spillius (Ed.), *Melanie Klein Today* (pp. 256–270). Hove: Routledge, 1988.

Bretherton, I., & Munholland, K. A. (1999). Internal working models in attachment relationships: A construct revisited. In: J. Cassidy & P. R. Shaver (Eds.), *Handbook of Attachment: Theory, Research and Clinical Applications*. New York: Guilford Press.

Bridgeland, M. (1971). *Pioneer Work with Maladjusted Children*. London: Staples Press.

Briggs, A. (2004). Reversing a spiral of deprivation: Working to ameliorate the relationship of staff and boys in a residential home. *Journal of Social Work Practice, 18* (1): 33–48.

Britton, R. (1981). Re-enactment as an unwitting professional response to family dynamics. In: S. Box, B. Copley, J. Magagna, & E. Moustaki (Eds.), *Psychotherapy with Families: An Analytic Approach* (pp. 48–58). London: Routledge & Kegan Paul. Also in: M. Bower (Ed.), *Psychoanalytic Theory for Social Work Practice: Thinking under Fire* (pp. 165–174). London: Routledge, 2005.

Britton, R. (1989). The missing link. In: R. Britton, M. Feldman, & E. O'Shaughnessy, *The Oedipus Complex Today: Clinical Implications* (pp. 83–103). London: Karnac.

Brodzinsky, D. (2005). Reconceptualising openness in adoption: Implications for theory, research and practice. In: D. Brodzinsky & J. Palacios (Eds.), *Psychological Issues in Adoption: Research and Practice* (pp. 145–166). Westport, CT: Praeger.

Broucek, F. (1982). Shame and its relationship to early narcissistic developments. *International Journal of Psychoanalysis, 63*: 369–378.

Burnell, A. (2003) (with Archer, C.). Setting up the loom: Attachment theory revisited. In: C. Archer & A. Burnell (Eds.), *Trauma, Attachment and Family Permanence*. London: Jessica Kingsley.

Burnham, J. (1986). *Family Therapy: First Steps Towards a Systemic Approach*. London: Tavistock Publications.

Cafcass (2012). *Cafcass Care Demand*. Croydon. Available at: https://www.cafcass.gov.uk/media/6393/August%202012%20care%20demand%20update.pdf

Cameron, R. J., & Maginn, C. (2009). *Achieving Positive Outcomes for Children in Care*. London: Sage.

Canham, H. (2003). "Feelings into Words": Evocations of childhood in the poems of Seamus Heaney. In: H. Canham & C. Satyamurti (Eds.), *Acquainted with the Night: Psychoanalysis and the Poetic Imagination*. Tavistock Clinic Series. London: Karnac.

Care Leavers' Foundation (2012). *Access All Areas—A Developmental Perspective*. Bala, Wales. Available at: www.thecareleaversfoundation.org/sitedata/files/AAA_Developmental_and_Rese.pdf

Carlisle, Lord (2012). *The Edlington Case: A Review*. London: HMSO.

Carr, A. (2012). *Family Therapy: Concepts, Process and Practice*. Chichester: Wiley.

Case, C. (2008). The Mermaid: Moving towards reality after trauma. In: D. Hindle & G. Shulman (Eds.), *The Emotional Experience of Adoption: A Psychoanalytic Perspective* (pp. 121–136). London: Routledge.

Clough, R., Bullock, R., & Ward, A. (2006). *What Works in Residential Care: A Review of Research Evidence and the Practical Implications*. London: National Children's Bureau. Available at: www.ncb.org.uk/ncercc

Cozolino, L. (2006). *The Neuroscience of Human Relationships*. New York: W. W. Norton.

Dallos, R., & Draper, R. (2010). *An Introduction to Family Therapy: Systemic Theory and Practice*. Milton Keynes: Open University Press.

Damasio, A. (1994). *Descartes' Error: Emotion, Reason, and the Human Brain*. New York: Avon Books.

DfE (2012). *Statistical First Release. Children Looked After in England (Including Adoption and Care Leavers) Year Ending 31 March 2012*. London: Department for Education. Available at: http://dera.ioe.ac.uk/15513/1/sfr20-2012.pdf

DfE (2014). *Statistical First Release. Children Looked After in England (Including Adoption and Care Leavers) Year Ending 31 March 2014*. London: Department of Education. Available at: https://www.gov.uk/government/uploads/system/uploads/attachment_data/file/359277/SFR36_2014_Text.pdf

DfE and Care Leavers' Foundation. (2012). *Charter for Care Leavers*. London: Department for Education; Bala, Wales: Care Leavers' Foundation. Available at: www.thecareleaversfoundation.org/sitedata/files/CharterforCareLeavers.pdf

DfES (2006). *Care Matters: Transforming the Lives of Children and Young People in Care*. Department for Education and Skills. London: HMSO.

DfES (2007). *Care Matters: Time for Change*. Department for Education and Skills. London: HMSO.

Diamond, J. (2003). Organic growth and the collective enterprise. *International Journal of Therapeutic Communities, 25* (3): 169–184.

Diamond, J. (2013). The Mulberry Bush School and UK therapeutic community practice for children and young people. *International Journal of Therapeutic Communities, 34* (4): 132–140.

Dockar-Drysdale, B. (1968). *Therapy in Child Care*. London: Longman.

Dockar-Drysdale, B. (1973). *Consultation in Child Care*. London: Longman.

Dockar-Drysdale, B. (1990). *The Provision of Primary Experience*. London: Free Association Books.

Downs, A. (2012). *The Velvet Rage*. Boston, MA: De Capo Press.

Doyle, N. (2013). *Fostering in England—2013. What's New in Legislation and Practice?* Paper presented at BAAF Conference, London, March.

Dozier, M. (2005). Challenges of foster care. *Attachment and Human Development, 7* (1): 27–30.

Dozier, M., Peloso, E., Lewis, E., Laurenceau, J., & Levin, S. (2008). Effects of an attachment-based intervention on the cortisol production of infants and toddlers in foster care. *Development and Psychopathology, 20*: 845–859.

Eliot, T. S. (1958). *Four Quartets*. London: Faber.

Erikson, E. (1950). *Childhood and Society*. New York: W. W. Norton.

Everts, S. (2012). The truth about pheromones. *Smithsonian Magazine*, March. [Washington, DC: Smithsonian Institute]

Farmer, E., & Pollock, S. (1998). *Sexually Abused and Abusing Children in Substitute Care*. Chichester: Wiley.

Fonagy, P. (2009). *Child Abuse: Neuroscience and Intervention*. Keynote speech at Conference at Anna Freud Centre, London.

Fosha, D. (2003). Dyadic regulation and experiential work with emotion and relatedness in trauma and disorganised attachment. In:

M. Solomon & D. Siegel (Eds.), *Healing Trauma: Attachment, Mind, Body and Brain.* New York: W. W. Norton.

Fraiberg, S., Adelson, E., & Shapiro, V. (1975). Ghosts in the nursery: A psychoanalytic approach to the problems of impaired infant–mother relationships. *Journal of the American Academy of Child and Adolescent Psychiatry, 14* (3): 387–421.

Freud, S. (1939). *Moses and Monotheism. Standard Edition, 23.*

Friijda, N. (1988). The laws of emotions. *American Psychologist, 43:* 349–358.

Gorell Barnes, G. (1998). *Family Therapy in Changing Times.* London: Macmillan.

Grotevant, H. (1997). Coming to terms with adoption: The construction of identity from adolescence to adulthood. *Adoption Quarterly 1* (1): 3–27.

Guidry, T. (2012). *I Am Adopted, I Am Shame* [Blog]. Available at: www.73adoptee.com/2012/04/i-am-adopted-i-am-shame

Hagerty, B., Lynch-Sauer, J., Patusky, L., Bouwsema, M., & Collier, P. (1992). Sense of belonging: A vital mental health concept. *Archives of Psychiatric Nursing, 6* (3): 172–177.

Hannon, C., Wood, C., & Bazalgette, L. (2010). *In Loco Parentis: To Deliver the Best for Looked After Children, the State Must Be a Confident Parent.* London: Demos.

Harris, R., & Lindsey, C. (2002). How professionals think about contact between children and their parents. *Clinical Child Psychology and Psychiatry, 7* (2): 147–161.

Hart, C. (2008). Affective association: An effective intervention countering fragmentation and dissociation. *Journal of Child Psychotherapy, 34* (2): 259–277.

Heim, C., Young, L. J., Newport, D. J., Mletzko, T., Miller, A. H., & Nemeroff, C. B. (2008). Lower CSF oxytocin concentrations in women with a history of childhood abuse. *Molecular Psychiatry, 14* (10): 954–958.

Henry, G. (1983). Difficulties about thinking and learning. In: M. Boston & R. Szur (Eds.), *Psychotherapy with Severely Deprived Children* (pp. 82–89). London: Karnac, 1990.

Hills, J. (2005). Holding the looked after child through reflecting dialogue. *Context, 78:* 18–23. [Warrington: AFT Publishing]

Hills, J. (2013). *Introduction to Systemic and Family Therapy: A User's Guide.* Basingstoke: Palgrave Macmillan.

Hinshelwood, G. (1999). Shame: The silent emotion. *Institute of Psycho-Sexual Medicine Journal, 22*: 9–12.

Howe, D., & Steele, M. (2004). Contact in cases in which children have been traumatically abused or neglected by their birth parents. In: E. Neil & D. Howe (Eds.), *Contact in Adoption and Permanent Foster Care: Research, Theory and Practice*. London: BAAF.

Hughes, D. (2003). Psychological interventions for the spectrum of attachment disorders and intrafamilial trauma. *Attachment & Human Development, 6* (3): 263–278.

Hughes, D. (2006). *Building the Bonds of Attachment*. New York: Jason Aronson.

Izard, C. (1991). *The Psychology of Emotions*. New York: Plenum Press.

James, C. (2013). *Dante. The Divine Comedy: A New Verse Translation*. London: Picador.

Kaufman, G. (1985). *Shame: The Power of Caring*. Rochester, VT: Schenkman.

Laing, R. D. (1969). *Intervention in Social Situations* [Pamphlet]. London: Association of Family Caseworkers. Reprinted in 2002 as: Situation, situation, situation: The context of mental illness. *Context, 60*. [Warrington: AFT Publishing]

Lee, A. C., He, J., & Ma, M. (2011). Olfactory marker protein is critical for functional maturation of olfactory sensory neurons and development of mother preference. *Journal of Neuroscience, 31*: 2974–2982.

Lord, J., & Borthwick, S. (2009). Planning placements for sibling groups. In: G. Schofield & J. Simmonds (Eds.), *The Child Placement Handbook*. London: BAAF.

Macaskill, C. (2002). *Safe Contact? Children in Permanent Placement and Contact with Their Birth Relatives*. Lyme Regis: Russell House.

Macfarlane, A. (1977). *The Psychology of Childbirth*. Cambridge, MA: Harvard University Press.

Main, M., & Goldwyn, R. (1998). *Adult Attachment Scoring and Classification Systems*. Berkeley, CA: University of California at Berkeley.

Main, M., & Hesse, E. (1990). Parents' unresolved traumatic experiences are related to infant disorganized status: Is frightened and/or frightening behaviour the linking mechanism? In M. Greenberg, D. Cichetti, & E. Cummings (Eds.), *Attachment in the Pre-School Years*. Chicago, IL: University of Chicago Press.

Marvin, R., Cooper, G., Hoffman, K., & Powell, B. (2002). The circle of security project: Attachment-based interventions with caregiver–

preschool child dyads. *Attachment and Human Development, 4* (1): 1–31.

Maslow, A. (1954). *Motivation and Personality.* New York: Harper.

Meltzer, D. (1974). Adhesive identification. In: *Sincerity and Other Works: Collected Papers of Donald* Meltzer (pp. 335–351), ed. A. Hahn. London: Karnac, 1994.

Minnis, H., Bryce, G., Phin, L., & Wilson, P. (2010). The "Spirit of New Orleans": Translating a model of intervention with maltreated children and their families for the Glasgow context. *Clinical Child Psychology and Psychiatry, 15* (4): 497–509.

Mollon, P. (2002). *Remembering Trauma: A Psychotherapist's Guide to Memory and Illusion.* London: Whurr.

Monroe, M. (2015). *Embracing the Grief of Adoption.* Empowered to connect. Available at: www.empoweredtoconnect.org/embracing-the-grief-of-adoption

Morgan, R., & Lindsay, M. (2012). *Young People's Views on Care and After-care.* Office of Children's Rights Director. London: Ofsted.

Murray, L., Tarren-Sweeney, M., & France, K. (2011). Foster carer perceptions of support and training in the context of high burden of care. *Child and Family Social Work, 16*: 149–158.

Neil, E. (2004). The "Contact after Adoption Study": Indirect contact and adoptive parents' communication about adoption. In: E. Neil & D. Howe (Eds.), *Contact in Adoption and Permanent Foster Care: Research, Theory and Practice.* London: BAAF.

Neil, E., & Howe, D. (2004a) Conclusions: A transactional model for thinking about contact. In: E. Neil & D. Howe (Eds.), *Contact in Adoption and Permanent Foster Care: Research, Theory and Practice.* London: BAAF.

Neil, E., & Howe, D. (Eds.) (2004b). *Contact in Adoption and Permanent Foster Care: Research, Theory and Practice.* London: BAAF.

Office of the Children's Commissioner (2012). *"I Thought I Was the Only One, the Only One in the World." The Office of the Children's Commissioner's Inquiry into Child Sexual Exploitation in Gangs and Groups* [Interim Report]. London. Available at: www.childrenscommissioner.gov.uk/content/publications/content_636

O'Shaughnessy, E. (1989). The invisible Oedipus complex. In: R. Britton, M. Feldman, & E. O'Shaughnessy, *The Oedipus Complex Today: Clinical Implications* (pp. 129–151). London: Karnac.

Owusu-Bempah, J., & Howitt, D. (1997). Socio-genealogical connectedness, attachment theory and childcare practice. *Child and Family Social Work, 2* (4): 199–207.

Pearce, S., & Pickard, H. (2013). How therapeutic communities work: Specific factors related to positive outcome. *Journal of Social Psychiatry, 59* (7): 636–645.

Perry, B. D., Pollard, R. A., Blakely, T. L., & Vigilante, D. (1995). Childhood trauma, the neurobiology of adaption, and the "use dependent" development of the brain: How "states" become "traits". *Infant Mental Health Journal, 16*: 271–289.

Rayner, E. (1992). John Bowlby's contribution: A brief survey. *Bulletin of the British Psychoanalytical Society*: 20–23.

Reeves, C. (2012a). Can the State ever be a "good enough parent"? In: C. Reeves (Ed.), *Broken Bounds: Contemporary Reflections on the Antisocial Tendency*. London: Karnac.

Reeves, C. (2012b). Editor's Introduction. In: C. Reeves (Ed.), *Broken Bounds: Contemporary Reflections on the Antisocial Tendency*. London: Karnac.

Reeves, R. (2002). A necessary conjunction: Dockar-Drysdale and Winnicott. *Journal of Child Psychotherapy, 28* (1): 3–27.

Riley, P. (1999). Leibniz's political and moral philosophy in the *Novissima Sinica. Journal of the History of Ideas, 60* (2): 217–239.

Rivett, M., & Street, E. (2009). *Family Therapy: 100 Key Points and Techniques*. Hove: Routledge.

Rostain, M. (2011). *The Son,* trans. A. Hunter. London: Tinder Press, 2013.

Rowling, J. K. (1997). *Harry Potter and the Philosopher's Stone*. London: Bloomsbury.

Ruesch, J., & Bateson, G. (1951). *Communication: The Social Matrix of Psychiatry*. New York: W. W. Norton.

Rushton, A., Dance, C., Quinton, D., & Mayes, D. (2001). *Siblings in Late Permanent Placements*. London: BAAF.

Rustin, M. (2006). Where do I belong? Dilemmas for children and adolescents who have been adopted or brought up in long-term foster care. In: J. Kenrick, C. Lindsey, & L. Tollemache (Eds.), *Creating New Families: Therapeutic Approaches to Fostering, Adoption, and Kinship Care*. London: Karnac.

Rustin, M. (2008). Multiple families in mind. In: D. Hindle & G. Shulman (Eds.), *The Emotional Experience of Adoption: A Psychoanalytic Perspective* (pp. 77–90). London: Routledge.

Ryburn, M. (1995). Adopted children's identity and information needs. *Children & Society, 9* (3): 41–64.

Salzberger-Wittenberg, I. (2013). *Experiencing Endings and Beginnings.* London: Karnac.

Schofield, G., & Beek, M. (2005). Providing a secure base: Parenting children in long-term foster care. *Attachment and Human Development, 7* (1): 3–26.

Schore, A. (1994). *Affect Regulation and the Origin of the Self.* Mahwah, NJ: Lawrence Erlbaum Associates.

Schore, A. (2003a). *Affect Dysregulation and Disorders of the Self.* New York: W. W. Norton.

Schore, A. (2003b). Early relational trauma, disorganised attachment, and the development of a predisposition to violence. In: M. Solomon & D. Siegel (Eds.), *Healing Trauma: Attachment, Mind, Body and Brain.* New York: W. W. Norton.

Seikkula, J., & Arnkil, T. E. (2006). *Dialogical Meetings in Social Networks.* London: Karnac.

Siegel, D. (1999). *The Developing Mind: How Relationships and the Brain Interact to Shape Who We Are.* New York: Guilford Press.

Skynner, R., & Cleese, J. (2011). *Life and How to Survive It.* London: Random House.

Solomon, M. (2003). Connection, disruption, repair: Treating the effects of attachment trauma on intimate relationships. In: M. Solomon & D. Siegel (Eds.), *Healing Trauma: Attachment, Mind, Body and Brain.* New York: W. W. Norton.

Sprince, J. (2002). Developing containment: Psychoanalytic consultancy to a therapeutic community for traumatised children. *Journal of Child Psychotherapy, 28*: 147–161.

Steele, M., Kaniuk, J., Hodges, J., Haworth, C., & Huss, S. (2003). *The Use of the Adult Attachment Interview: Implications for Assessment in Adoption and Foster Care.* London: BAAF.

Stein, M. (2012). *Corporate Parenting from Care to Adulthood: A Research Perspective.* Bala, Wales: Care Leavers' Foundation. Available at: www.thecareleaversfoundation.org/sitedata/files/AAA_Developmental_and_Rese.pdf

Stokoe, P. (2003). Group thinking. In: A. Ward, K. Kasinski, J. Pooley, & A. Worthington (Eds.), *Therapeutic Communities for Children and Young People.* London: Jessica Kingsley.

Strathearn, L., Fonagy, P., Amico, J., & Read Montague, P. (2009). Adult attachment predicts maternal brain and oxytocin response to infant cues. *Neuropsychopharmacology, 34*: 2655–2666.

Taylor, D. (Trans.) (1998). *Oedipus the King.* In: *Sophocles: Plays 1—The Theban Plays.* London: Methuen Drama.

Thorburn, J. (2004). Post-placement contact between birth parents and older children: The evidence from a longitudinal study of minority ethnic children. In: E. Neil & D. Howe (Eds.), *Contact in Adoption and Permanent Foster Care: Research, Theory and Practice.* London: BAAF.

Tomkins, S. (1963). *Affect, Imagery, Consciousness, Vol. 2: The Negative Affects.* New York: Springer.

Triseliotis, J. (1984). Identity and security in adoption and long-term fostering. *Early Child Development and Care, 15*: 149–170.

Triseliotis, J. (2000). Identity-formation and the adopted person revisited. In: A. Treacher & I. Katz (Eds.), *The Dynamics of Adoption.* London: Jessica Kingsley.

Vaughan, J. (2003). Rationale for the intensive programme. In: C. Archer & A. Burnell (Eds.), *Trauma, Attachment and Family Permanence.* London: Jessica Kingsley.

Verrier, N. (2009). *The Primal Wound: Understanding the Adopted Child.* London: BAAF.

Voice for the Child in Care (1998). *Shout to be Heard: Stories from Young People in Care.* London.

Waddell, M. (1998). *Inside Lives: Psychoanalysis and the Development of Personality.* London: Duckworth.

Ward, A. (2003). The core framework. In: A. Ward, K. Kasinski, J. Pooley, & A. Worthington (Eds.), *Therapeutic Communities for Children and Young People.* London: Jessica Kingsley.

Whitaker, C., & Napier, A. (1988). *The Family Crucible.* New York: Bantam.

Wilkinson, R., & Pickett, K. (2009). *The Spirit Level.* London: Penguin.

Wilson, K. (2006). Can foster carers help children resolve their emotional behavioural difficulties? *Clinical Child Psychology, 11* (4): 495–511.

Winnicott, D. W. (1949). The ordinary devoted mother and her baby [Introduction]. In: *The Child and the Family.* BBC Broadcast Talks by Dr. D. W. Winnicott. Available at: Planned Environment Therapy Trust, Archive and Study Centre. Ref: (G)PP/JLS. Digitised versions: 2012.116/01–04.

Winnicott, D. W. (1952). Anxiety associated with insecurity. In: *Through Paediatrics to Psychoanalysis*. London: Hogarth Press: 1958; reprinted London: Karnac: 1984.

Winnicott, D. W. (1956). The antisocial tendency. In: *Deprivation and Delinquency*, ed. C. Winnicott, R. Shepherd, & M. Davis. London: Tavistock Publications, 1984.

Winnicott, D. W. (1960a). Ego distortion in terms of true and false self. In: *The Maturational Processes and the Facilitating Environment*. London: Hogarth Press: 1965; reprinted London: Karnac, 1990.

Winnicott, D. W. (1960b). The theory of the parent–infant relationship. In: *The Maturational Processes and the Facilitating Environment*. London: Hogarth Press: 1965; reprinted London: Karnac, 1990

Winnicott, D. W. (1965). *The Maturational Processes and the Facilitating Environment*. London: Hogarth Press; reprinted London: Karnac, 1990.

Winnicott, D. W. (1970). Residential care as therapy. In: *Deprivation and Delinquency*, ed. C. Winnicott, R. Shepherd, & M. Davis. London: Tavistock Publications, 1984.

Winnicott, D. W. (1971). *Playing and Reality*. London: Tavistock Publications.

INDEX

Fonagy, P., 161
forever family, 101
Fosha, D., 86, 87
foster care, 17, 26, 54, 65, 67, 68, 101,
        125, 138, 159, 166, 175, 179,
        180, 181, 187, 188
foster carer(s) (*passim*):
    child's placement with, 2
    training and support needs of,
        182–183
fostered children, 38, 124, 175, 183,
        185, 190, 196
foster family(ies) (*passim*):
    and primary family, olfactory
        conflict between, 159–160
foster family placement, 82
fostering, long-term, 197
foster parent(s), xxiii, 8, 15, 22, 69, 70,
        79, 100, 124, 125, 175
foster placement(s), 25, 53, 63, 66, 136,
        166, 167, 192
    multiple, 133
    stable, xxiv
    unstable, xxii
fragilely integrated child, 79
Fraiberg, S., 199
France, K., 182
Freud, S., 3, 4, 159, 203, 210, 211
Friijda, N., 90
frozen child(ren), 76

genealogical bewilderment, 93, 96,
        103
genealogical connectedness, sense of,
        93, 96, 97, 103
"George" (clinical example), 195, 196
Goldwyn, R., 87
good-enough experience of reciprocal
        ownership, 12, 111
good-enough family(ies), 106,
        109–112, 123
good-enough parent, State as, 49
"good-enough" self experience,
        Winnicott on, 201
Gorell Barnes, G., 223
Gove, M., 65
Grotevant, H., 36
group living, 74, 78, 83
guardians, special, xxix
guardianship, special, xxv, 1

Guidry, T., 92
Guthrie, W., 202

Hagerty, B., 36
"Hamid" (clinical example), 181–182
Hamlet, 200
Hannon, C., 71
Harris, R., 37
Hart, C., 172
Haworth, C., 94
He, J., 160
Heim, C., 161
Henry, G., 135
hermeneutic discipline,
        psychotherapeutic work as,
        73
Hesse, E., 86
Hewitt, C., 197
Hills, J., xiv, 16, 199–223
Hinshelwood, G., 39
Hobbes, T., 209
Hodges, J., 94
Hoffman, K., 87
holding:
    emotional:
        attuned, 69
        residential care as, 72–79
    lack of, 65
    Winnicott's concept of, 58, 63
holding environment, 71, 74, 82
    as foundation for belonging, 71–
        72
    Winnicott's concept of, 71, 74
home:
    and belonging, 202–203
    and difference, 203
Howe, D., 40, 98, 100, 103
Howitt, D., 93
Hughes, D., 94, 101
Huss, S., 94

identification(s):
    adhesive, 14, 134, 138, 154
        Meltzer's concept of, 135
    and belonging, 134–136
    introjective, 14, 135, 136, 154
    intrusive, 14, 147, 154
    modes of, 135–136
    projective, 31, 32, 34, 35, 135, 136
    split, 218